"This groundbreaking book introduces a fresh perspective on asylum cooperation between states. Nikolas Feith Tan develops an innovative framework of transnational asylum that carefully balances the control interests of states and obligations under human rights and refugee law. By addressing short comings of existing approaches and emphasising genuine cooperation, the work paves the way for a more equitable and effective refugee protection regime. Meticulously researched and beautifully written, this book is a must read for scholars, policy makers, asylum advocates and practitioners."

Daniel Ghezelbash, *University of New South Wales, Australia*

"Highlighting the vital need for reinforced international protection to address refugee protection challenges, Nikolas Feith Tan's work provides important new insights and ideas around how States can work more effectively together, in ways which uphold and recognize the enduring relevance and applicability of the 1951 Convention. It represents a comprehensive and timely contribution to work and discussions on ensuring access to international protection for those who need it in today's dynamic and complex global context, and will be of great interest to academics, policy-makers, international organizations and others working in the field."

Madeline Garlick, *Chief, Protection Policy and Legal Advice, Division of International Protection, UNHCR*

TRANSNATIONAL ASYLUM

This book presents an original framework of transnational asylum to inform future cooperation between states on asylum processing and refugee protection.

The book provides scholarly guidance on how policies can be undertaken in a way that conforms with the rights of asylum seekers and refugees under international law, asking if transnational asylum offers a workable model for lawful international cooperation and responsibility-sharing. It engages with the practical and legal modalities needed to ensure respect for binding obligations in the context of the current trend of rejection of territorial asylum among some states. The book puts forward a blueprint for how existing policies of deterrence and externalisation can be retooled to share, rather than shift, responsibility for refugees.

This book will be of key interest to scholars, students, policymakers and practitioners interested and working in Human Rights, International Refugee Law and Refugee Studies.

Nikolas Feith Tan is Senior Lecturer at Melbourne Law School in Australia and former Senior Researcher at the Danish Institute for Human Rights. He is also Visiting Professor at the MOBILE Centre, University of Copenhagen, Denmark, and Senior Research Affiliate at the University of London's Refugee Law Initiative, UK.

Routledge Studies in Human Rights

The Routledge Studies in Human Rights series publishes high-quality and cross-disciplinary scholarship on topics of key importance in human rights today. In a world where human rights are both celebrated and contested, this series is committed to creating stronger links between disciplines and exploring new methodological and theoretical approaches in human rights research. Aimed towards both scholars and human rights professionals, the series strives to provide both critical analysis and policy-oriented research in an accessible form. The series welcomes work on specific human rights issues as well as on cross-cutting themes and institutional perspectives.

Series Editors: Mark Gibney, UNC Asheville, USA, Bonny Ibhawoh, McMaster University, Canada, and Rossanna Rocha Reis, University of São Paulo, Brazil.

Human Rights and Climate Change
The Law on Loss and Damage
Linnéa Nordlander

States, Human Rights and Distant Strangers
The Normative Justification of Extraterritorial Obligations in Human Rights Law
Angela Müller

Childism, Intersectionality and the Rights of the Child
The Myth of a Happy Childhood
Rebecca Adami

Transnational Asylum
Toward a Principled Framework
Nikolas Feith Tan

TRANSNATIONAL ASYLUM

Toward a Principled Framework

Nikolas Feith Tan

Routledge
Taylor & Francis Group
LONDON AND NEW YORK

Designed cover image: © Matt Cardy / Stringer via Getty Images

First published 2025
by Routledge
4 Park Square, Milton Park, Abingdon, Oxon OX14 4RN

and by Routledge
605 Third Avenue, New York, NY 10158

Routledge is an imprint of the Taylor & Francis Group, an informa business.

British Library Cataloguing-in-Publication Data
A catalogue record for this book is available from the British Library.

ISBN: 978-1-032-73219-0 (hbk)
ISBN: 978-1-032-73215-2 (pbk)
ISBN: 978-1-003-46314-6 (ebk)

DOI: 10.4324/9781003463146

Typeset in Sabon
by SPi Technologies India Pvt Ltd (Straive)

CONTENTS

ACKNOWLEDGEMENTS

This book is the product of ten years work in the field of international refugee law and policy. The origins of the book lie with my PhD thesis, undertaken at Aarhus University and the Danish Institute for Human Rights between 2015 and 2019. The final manuscript was developed across my years at the Danish Institute for Human Rights, UNHCR and, most recently, Melbourne Law School.

My heartfelt thanks to the many friends and colleagues who have supported, by one means or another, the development of this book. I wish to thank Professor Jens Vedsted-Hansen and Professor Thomas Gammeltoft-Hansen, who were the supervisors for the PhD thesis that formed the basis for this book. Both have been constant, supportive and positive influences on the book and it has been my privilege to have them as supervisors and colleagues. I also thank Professor James Hathaway who encouraged me to develop the concept of transnational asylum to drive the manuscript well beyond the original PhD dissertation on which it is based.

My warm thanks to the many international refugee law colleagues who engaged with this work – offering generous, critical and thoughtful feedback and advice along various stages of the manuscript. Thanks to Professor David Cantor, Professor Cathryn Costello, Professor Michelle Foster, Dr Daniel Ghezelbash, Dr Asher Hirsch, Dr Eleni Karageorgiou, Professor Susan Kneebone, Dr Riona Moodley, Dr Bríd Ní Ghráinne, Dr Maria O'Sullivan and Professor Thomas Spijkerboer. Many thanks to Dr Pauline de Olivier, who generously allowed me to draw on our joint work in Chapter 4.

I owe thanks to UNHCR colleagues who offered critical insights on some of the ideas in the book and encouraged me to pursue the policy-relevance of the work. I thank Dr Madeline Garlick, Anne-Birgitte Krum-Hansen, Alex

Mundt and Dr Kees Wouters for their expert insights. The views expressed in the book are my own and do not reflect those of the United Nations or UNHCR.

My thanks, too, to my editors at Routledge, Sophie Iddamalgoda and Andrew Taylor. Thank you for your guidance and patience throughout the process. My thanks to the anonymous reviewers who improved the manuscript in the final stages of development with their careful critiques. Any errors remain mine alone.

The current dynamic policy environment means the area of cooperation on asylum area is in flux. This book reflects law and practice as it stood, to the best of my knowledge, on 1 December 2024.

ABBREVIATIONS

ACA	*Asylum Cooperative Arrangement*
APA	*Asylum Partnership Agreement*
ACHR	*American Convention on Human Rights*
APD	*Asylum Procedures Directive*
ARSIWA	*Articles on the Responsibility of States for Internationally Wrongful Acts*
CAT	*Convention against Torture and Other Cruel, Inhuman or Degrading Treatment or Punishment*
CEDAW	*Convention on the Elimination of All Forms of Racial Discrimination against Women*
CJEU	*Court of Justice of the European Union*
CRC	*Convention on the Rights of the Child*
CPA	*Comprehensive Plan of Action*
ECHR	*European Convention for the Protection of Human Rights and Fundamental Freedoms*
ECtHR	*European Court of Human Rights*
ETM	*Emergency Transit Mechanism*
EU	*European Union*
EUAA	*EU Asylum Agency*
EXCOM	*Executive Committee of the High Commissioner's Programme*
FCA	*Federal Court of Australia*
FRA	*European Union Agency for Fundamental Rights*
FRY	*Federal Republic of Yugoslavia*
Frontex	*European Border and Coast Guard Agency*
GCR	*Global Compact on Refugees*
HCA	*High Court of Australia*

HRC	*United Nations Human Rights Committee*
ICCPR	*International Covenant on Civil and Political Rights*
ICJ	*International Court of Justice*
ILC	*International Law Commission*
IOM	*International Organization for Migration*
MoU	*Memorandum of Understanding*
MRT	*Moldavian Republic of Transdniestria*
NATO	*North Atlantic Treaty Organization*
NGO	*non-governmental organisation*
OAS	*Organization of American States*
PCA	*Permanent Court of Arbitration*
PJSC	*Supreme Court of Papua New Guinea*
PNG	*Papua New Guinea*
RSD	*refugee status determination*
RPC	*Regional Processing Centre*
TFEU	*Treaty on the Functioning of the European Union*
UK	*United Kingdom*
UN	*United Nations*
UNHCR	*United Nations High Commissioner for Refugees*
UNTS	*United Nations Treaty Series*

1

INTRODUCTION

When can two or more states share responsibility for asylum processing or refugee protection? That is the central question of this book. Cooperation on asylum seekers and refugees is on the rise as states in the Global North cooperate with Global South countries to control the movement of asylum seekers and refugees across borders. For most of the past 20 years, asylum seekers arriving by boat to Australia have been unable to access territorial asylum. Denmark, the first state to ratify the Refugee Convention,[1] has passed legislation to allow for the transfer of asylum seekers to a third country outside the European Union (EU). The United Kingdom (UK) entered into a bilateral agreement with Rwanda to transfer asylum seekers arriving without authorisation for both asylum processing and, ultimately, refugee protection in the central African country. In November 2023, Italy and Albania signed an agreement for the extraterritorial processing of people rescued in the Mediterranean. The United States of America (US) has created 'Safe Mobility Offices' in Colombia, Costa Rica, Ecuador and Guatemala to profile asylum seekers before they reach the US southern border.

The proliferation of proposals and arrangements of this nature highlights the need for serious engagement with the practical and legal modalities required to ensure respect for binding obligations in this context. Significant aspects of existing cooperative asylum arrangements have rightly been criticised for breaching or undermining principles of international human rights law and refugee protection.[2] This book proceeds on the basis that cooperation of this sort will continue and seeks to set out how such arrangements can provide minimum acceptable levels of protection for asylum seekers and refugees required by international law, learn from the policy mistakes of the past and explore

DOI: 10.4324/9781003463146-1

whether future arrangements have the potential to develop into a form of responsibility-sharing.

This book explores the use of *pre-entry* asylum procedures carried out by the authorities of traditional asylum countries in the Global North ('destination states') in third states ('partner states'). This form of extraterritorial asylum processing in a transit state or first country of asylum may have the potential to create safe and controlled access to protection, relieve pressure on external borders and share responsibility for refugees.[3]

The book presents the original framework of *transnational asylum*, defined as the internationally lawful provision of asylum processing or international protection by two or more states. Transnational asylum seeks to chart a middle way between the control interests of states, on the one hand, and respect for binding obligations of human rights and refugee law, on the other. In other words, how can existing cooperation arrangements and proposals be adapted to guarantee minimum levels of protection while keeping cooperation within states' interests?

In an era where migration control has rendered access to asylum dangerous, unauthorised and expensive, transnational asylum may have the potential to provide controlled access to protection, prevent loss of life on asylum-seeking routes, combat people smuggling and support asylum systems in Global South states. However, for transnational asylum arrangements to work, they must provide for rights and protection in accordance with the Refugee Convention and relevant human rights law obligations, not simply shift asylum responsibilities to states in the Global South, which already bear disproportionate responsibility for refugees. This requires destination states to accept they must provide more protection to share responsibility for refugees, not less. According to the United Nations High Commissioner for Refugees (UNHCR), 75 per cent of refugees were hosted in developing countries in 2023, down from 83 per cent before the Ukraine conflict.[4]

Beyond a set of international legal standards and lessons derived from previous practice, this book further interrogates whether transnational asylum has the potential to form the basis for regional responsibility-sharing. The various forms of transnational asylum analysed do not operate in isolation but should be deployed in combination with territorial asylum. In this sense, the book explores 'add-ons' to existing norms of territorial asylum. The book thus explores whether a workable, principled framework to inform *future* cooperation between states on asylum processing and refugee protection, including between the EU and third countries, can be envisaged.

Ultimately, this book sets out for policymakers precisely what is required for such third country arrangements to be rendered workable and internationally lawful. It also explains how transnational asylum has the potential, if implemented in good faith, to form the building blocks of a protection framework based on genuine international cooperation with full respect for binding obligations of international human rights and refugee law.

1.1 The end of the right to seek asylum in the Global North?

Today, the individual right to seek asylum, understood as a procedural right to claim international protection from state authorities, is at risk of being extinguished in a number of states.[5] The possible demise of the right to seek asylum is not as a result of outright rejection of the international refugee regime by governments but rather a gradual but powerful hollowing out of its key principles.[6] In many cases, destination states do not explicitly *refoule* refugees but rather prevent access to their territories or transfer asylum seekers to other jurisdictions to avoid honouring obligations otherwise owed.

As a result, the tension between governments' desire for border and migration control and the individual right to seek asylum is increasingly resolved with state control overriding an individual's right to seek asylum. The combined effect of unilateral approaches – including visa regulations, carrier sanctions, border walls and boat turnbacks – and cooperative policies telegraph the end of the right to seek asylum in at least some developed states.[7]

The right to seek asylum in Australia is currently extinguished for those arriving by boat and has been for most of the past two decades. In the US, the COVID-19 pandemic further weakened the institution of asylum, as Title 42 public health orders allowed for the summary expulsion of 1.6 million protection seekers in 2020 and 2021.[8] Some European states are exploring plans to externalise both asylum procedures and refugee protection to a third country. In Europe, summary returns in the form of pushbacks at internal and external borders are, in some contexts, systemic.[9]

Notwithstanding deterrence efforts, asylum seekers continue to cross international borders in search of protection. At the end of 2023, for example, there were 6.9 million asylum seekers globally, a figure that only takes into account those protection seekers formally registered.[10] At the normative level, however, states' almost complete disregard for the right to leave a country in combination with destination states' strategic avoidance of the non-refoulement obligation leaves the right to seek asylum substantially weakened.[11]

Increasingly, refugees join other migrants in 'mixed movement' flows that complicate the reception of new arrivals.[12] According to the European Commission, for example, 40 per cent of return decisions are effectively enforced, a rate that has remained consistent since 2013.[13] A key issue here for European states is that access to territory for migrants not in need of international protection, who are travelling alongside refugees in mixed movements, results in high numbers of migrants effectively unable to be returned. EU return policy is costly, complex and inefficient, leaving open the possibility, even likelihood, that rejected asylum seekers and other irregular migrants remain in Europe.[14] As a result, the perception that, irrespective of their need for international protection, once a person reaches European territory, their removal will be extremely difficult drives the development of measures to prevent arrival in the first place.[15]

Destination states are increasingly learning from one another's practice and refining their own approaches. A couple of dynamics can be observed here. First, in order to circumvent the reach of obligations extraterritorially, some destination states are entrusting increasing operational control to their partner states, recognising that exercising authority or control over asylum seekers and refugees brings the risk of legal responsibility.[16] This accounts for the rise in more indirect forms of cooperation, such as funding, equipment and training. In the Central Mediterranean, for example, EU support for the Libyan Coastguard resulted in 57,000 'pullbacks' to Libya in 2021 and 2022 alone.[17]

Second, and in some contrast, other destination states are taking up third country processing policies with full knowledge of previous approaches and the legal responsibilities that come with conducting asylum processing on another state's territory. Hence, the proliferation of third country proposals and the need for serious scholarly engagement with the practical and legal modalities required to ensure respect for binding obligations in this context. In November 2023, for example, Italy and Albania signed a bilateral agreement for the extraterritorial processing, in Albania, of people rescued on the Mediterranean Sea by Italian authorities.[18]

Partner states are also evaluating their role in cooperation. A number of prospective partner states are considering their involvement in such initiatives, while others have rapidly become key partners in the 'upstreaming' of migration control.[19] Other, more experienced partner states are likely to reconsider their involvement. For example, it seems unlikely that Papua New Guinea will agree to a third iteration of cooperation on asylum processing at Australia's behest, given the legal and reputational harm the country has experienced.

The current role of partner states in asylum cooperation presents a paradox. On the one hand, stronger countries with robust state institutions and respect for the rule of law are more likely to be suitable partners. On the other hand, the general reluctance of states in the Global South to cooperate with destination states in this area means weaker states are those likely to enter into cooperation. There is no simple answer to this dilemma. A shift away from the deterrence mindset on the part of destination states would assist in rehabilitating the prospect of third country processing and protection arrangements, while pre-entry processing arrangements would emphasise willingness on the part of destination states to share responsibility.

1.2 International cooperation, responsibility-sharing and responsibility-shifting

Cooperation between states is an underlying principle generally encouraged, and sometimes required, by international law. International cooperation refers to 'two or more states working together towards a common goal'[20] or the 'voluntary coordinated action of two or more states which takes place under a legal regime and serves a specific objective'.[21] International law promotes cooperation among states in dealing with 'issues of transnational importance'.[22] The United Nations Charter requires 'joint action' on the part of states to promote universal respect for and observance of human rights.[23]

However, the law of international cooperation *on refugees* is inchoate, with no binding provision included in the Refugee Convention. A soft law principle of international cooperation has developed based on the Convention's Preamble, which acknowledges that:

> the grant of asylum may place unduly heavy burdens on certain countries, and that a satisfactory solution of a problem of which the United Nations has recognised the international scope and nature cannot therefore be achieved without international cooperation.[24]

The Refugee Convention drafters included a plea for states to admit refugees and 'act in concert in a true spirit of international cooperation in order that these refugees may find asylum and the possibility of resettlement'.[25] In the absence of a binding duty to cooperate, however, responsibility for refugees is essentially territorial, with responsibility for protection generally falling on the state where the asylum seeker arrives.

Confusion around terminology further clouds the meaning and content of the principle of international cooperation in this area. According to Dowd and McAdam:

> Burden-sharing and responsibility-sharing can be understood as particular forms of international cooperation, or as objectives thereof, arising in the context of refugee protection. These concepts have not been clearly defined… States adopt a variety of interpretations as to what they entail in practice.[26]

Similarly, Betts, Costello and Zaun consider international cooperation to be broader than responsibility-sharing, defining it as 'all forms of coordinated and collaborative action undertaken by states', without necessarily benefitting refugees.[27] They define the narrower concept of responsibility-sharing as 'the contribution of states towards supporting refugees who are on the territory of another state through the redistribution of money or people'.[28]

As a result, while the concepts of burden-sharing and responsibility-sharing involve cooperation between states in relation to the protection of refugees, international cooperation is a broader principle encompassing other actions such as combatting human smuggling.[29] A UNHCR expert roundtable on the principle recommends that cooperation 'enhance refugee protection and prospects for durable solutions' and 'be in line with international refugee and human rights law'.[30]

Responsibility-sharing may take many forms, including the provision of financial assistance between states and the physical relocation of asylum seekers and refugees.[31] Noll, writing in 2000, referred to three forms of responsibility-sharing, encompassing physical responsibility-sharing (sharing people), financial responsibility-sharing (sharing money) and harmonising asylum policy (sharing policy).[32] Examples of responsibility-sharing range from small-scale, ad hoc agreements, such as the 1999 Kosovo Evacuation Plan, to regional or international programmes, such as the Comprehensive Plan of Action, which provided for the admission and resettlement of Indochinese refugees in the 1980s and 1990s.[33]

Defining those situations in which refugee protection is expanded is not straightforward. One term used by UNHCR in this context is 'protection space', defined as 'the extent to which a conducive environment exists for the internationally recognised rights of refugees to be respected and their needs to be met'.[34] Despite its common use, particularly in states that are not parties to the Refugee Convention, the term lacks a formal definition.[35] A more concrete method of assessing the contraction or expansion of protection in a transnational asylum arrangement is an approach that measures the total number of individuals afforded a fair and effective asylum procedure and international protection in the cooperating states in question.

Responsibility-sharing is thus used here as those forms of international cooperation that comply with international refugee and human rights law obligations *and* enhance refugee protection.[36] To emerge as a form of responsibility-sharing, a transnational asylum arrangement would thus need to expand protection of refugees in cooperating states.

1.3 Non-entrée, deterrence and externalisation

Since the 1980s, the dominant policy response to irregular migration – including asylum seekers and refugees – among destination states has been one of control and deterrence.[37] Destination states have enacted a range of policies aimed at preventing access to their territories with the dual objectives of avoiding responsibility for any immediate protection claims and deterring prospective asylum seekers from attempting to reach a destination state. This tendency has become so entrenched that scholars have referred to current policymaking as a 'deterrence paradigm'.[38]

Hathaway first coined the term 'non-entrée' in 1992 to encompass both territorial and extraterritorial deterrence measures, posing the question:

> Why is non-entrée effectively replacing non-refoulement as the cornerstone of contemporary international law regarding refugees? From the perspective of states, its appeal is that it permits states to exercise *control*

> over refugee movements without also assuming *responsibility* for their welfare, as admission to that state's community would imply.[39]

In 1996, Goodwin-Gill identified a range of devices employed to 'keep asylum seekers from the procedural door'.[40] In 1999, Noll and Vedsted-Hansen bifurcated the umbrella category of non-entrée into 'non-admission' and 'non-arrival' policies. Non-admission policies refer to restrictive criteria for protection applied *after* arrival on the territory, notably the use of the exclusion clause, safe third country rules and procedural barriers to accessing asylum procedures.[41] Non-arrival policies, on the other hand, refer to extraterritorial migration control whereby the asylum seeker is prevented from stepping foot on the territory of the acting state, thus 'operating as barriers for asylum seekers to access a jurisdiction where they could seek protection'.[42] Most recently, Shachar has conceptualised the 'shifting border' as the restrictions on access that take place across the entire travel continuum.[43]

Existing scholarly work discusses a range of unilateral policies, which include boat turnbacks,[44] visa controls,[45] carrier sanctions,[46] the establishment of so-called 'international zones' within state borders,[47] excision of territory for the purposes of migration,[48] interdiction on the high seas[49] and information campaigns.[50] A number of more established forms of deterrence have been tested in national and international courts, leading in some cases to their abandonment.[51]

Over time, deterrence policies have evolved to include cooperation with third states, often countries of origin and transit in the Global South.[52] This form of 'international deterrence', defined as policies undertaken extraterritorially by a destination state in cooperation with a partner state to prevent asylum in the former, has become a part of states' 'toolbox' to prevent the arrival of irregular migrants.[53]

These approaches raise questions of jurisdiction under human rights and refugee law. Through extraterritorial cooperation with a partner state, destination states often seek to avoid jurisdiction over asylum seekers and refugees, or at least cloud the question of jurisdiction. International cooperation of this type thus complicates the dominant principle of territorial jurisdiction. While many states now acknowledge the existence of extraterritorial jurisdiction in certain limited circumstances, there remains a widespread belief among policymakers that extraterritorial actions are less likely to reach the threshold required to enliven obligations under human rights and refugee law.[54] Moreover, there seems to be little consideration given to the question of whether jurisdiction could be shared between cooperating states. Notwithstanding recent human rights law jurisprudence on extraterritorial jurisdiction, there is scant case law dealing with shared responsibility in the context of asylum.[55] These complex questions of jurisdiction and state responsibility are not the primary focus of this book, but they are examined as an important legal backdrop to the transnational asylum framework.[56]

Finally, since its emergence in the early 2000s, the term 'externalisation' has developed into an umbrella concept encompassing migration control measures affecting refugees undertaken either unilaterally or multilaterally, either extraterritorially or with extraterritorial effects.[57] Crisp defines externalisation as 'measures taken by states in locations beyond their territorial borders to obstruct, deter or otherwise avert the arrival of refugees'.[58] In its 2021 Note on the 'Externalization' of International Protection, UNHCR defined the term as 'measures preventing asylum seekers from entering safe territory and claiming international protection, or transfers of asylum seekers and refugees to other countries without sufficient safeguards'.[59] Most recently, the Refugee Law Initiative Declaration on Externalisation and Asylum defined externalisation as 'the process of shifting functions that are normally undertaken by a state within its own territory so that they take place, in part or in whole, outside its territory'.[60]

The relationship between transnational asylum and the non-entrée, deterrence and externalisation approaches outlined above may be understood as overlapping but not co-extensive. In other words, some deterrence policies may contain a number of elements for effective transnational asylum practices. For example, EU financial support for Syrian refugees in Turkey under the Facility for Refugees in Turkey expands protections for refugees in Turkey. Papua New Guinea's removal of reservations to the Refugee Convention as part of its Regional Resettlement Agreement with Australia is a small but positive step for enhanced refugee protection.[61] More generally, the methods employed to prevent access to protection may be usefully adapted to provide controlled access to protection.[62]

1.4 Defining transnational asylum

Transnational asylum is a term for the *internationally lawful provision of asylum processing or international protection by two or more states*. Equally, it may be termed a form of 'rights-based externalisation'.[63] More precisely, transnational asylum encompasses the following elements:

- the *transfer* of an asylum seeker or refugee between a destination and a partner state;
- *close cooperation* between a destination and a partner state on asylum procedures or refugee protection;
- the provision of processing or protection in *compliance* with binding obligations of human rights and refugee law.

The term 'transnational' describes policies that include a dimension beyond the border as multiple states negotiate the processing and protection of asylum seekers and refugees. The term 'asylum' relates to both the right of asylum seekers to access a fair and effective procedure and the right of recognised refugees to receive protection in accordance with the Refugee Convention.[64]

Transnational asylum may offer a framework for controlled, cooperation-based protection. As Garvey put it:

> Today's challenge is not the Sisyphean task of establishing a fundamentally different international refugee law regime in today's fundamentally unreceptive political climate... Sovereignty ultimately does rule, and any prescription for management of contemporary mass migration that fails to account for the concerns of state power and control is doomed to failure.[65]

This book focuses on three potential forms of transnational asylum: pre-entry processing, third country processing and third country protection. *Pre-entry processing* involves processing in a partner state *before* arrival in the destination state.[66] This form of extraterritorial processing, whereby a destination state carries out asylum processing in a transit state or first country of asylum, has the potential to create safe and controlled access to protection. In 2018, for example, the European Commission considered the creation of 'disembarkation platforms', including the establishment of UNHCR-operated regional processing centres outside the EU for asylum seekers rescued at sea by third countries.[67] Safe Mobility Offices in the Americas further represent a form of pre-entry processing, involving profiling and referral to safe and legal pathways as an alternative to irregular journeys.[68]

Third country processing involves the *post-arrival* transfer of an asylum seeker from the territory or jurisdiction of a destination state to a partner state for the purposes of processing their asylum claim.[69] This form of extraterritorial processing has also been defined by several authors. Ghezelbash refers to the screening of asylum claims in any place beyond the borders of the destination state, including unilateral screenings at sea.[70] Other authors refer to 'offshore processing' to describe the transfer of asylum seekers from one state to another.[71]

Transnational asylum also encompasses *third country protection*, involving the transfer of a refugee from a destination state to a partner state for the purposes of receiving protection. In contrast to extraterritorial processing (used here to encompass both pre-entry processing and third country processing), third country protection entails the long-term integration of refugees in a partner state. There is some variation in the form of third country protection arrangements. Most clearly, arrangements for the protection of recognised refugees in a third state fall under this category.[72] Other transfer arrangements may in practice result in third country protection for asylum seekers who are found to be refugees. The EU–Turkey Statement, for example, resulted in the protection of refugees in Turkey.

A number of asylum policies involving multiple states are beyond the limits of the transnational asylum framework. The use of 'safe third country' and 'first country of asylum' concepts have rightfully been the subject of scholarly attention but are not considered herein and of themselves.[73] Safe third country concepts are only considered where they are part of policies involving the *close cooperation* of multiple states in asylum processing or protection.[74] Furthermore, in-country processing involving the transfer of individuals directly from their state of origin is not addressed here, as a person only qualifies for refugee status once outside their country of origin.[75]

1.5 Critiquing transnational asylum

There are a number of arguments that may be raised against the thesis of this book. First, one could argue that a cooperative framework drawn from deterrence practices searches for solutions where there are none. Where deterrence is the *raison d'être* of third country arrangements, one could reasonably argue that constructing a framework built on such a rationale can never be lawful, much less a form of responsibility-sharing. However, this view does not take into account the objectives of policymakers tasked with pursuing third country arrangements while meeting their governments' international obligations. Denmark, for example, has committed to a third country asylum policy in accordance with its international obligations.[76]

In some asylum states, this book will be less relevant. Countries deeply committed to the principle of territorial asylum, either through policy or as a matter of constitutional law, for example, will have no interest in third country processing or protection. On the other hand, a growing number of states are implementing or proposing extraterritorial asylum approaches. In the two states where I have the most experience, Australia and Denmark, third country processing has been the settled policy of successive governments.

I stress here that most current attempts at cooperation in this area are deeply problematic and often breach human rights and refugee law obligations. Clearly, to be internationally lawful, transnational asylum must avoid the violations of previous attempts and learn from their many flaws. Nevertheless, certain elements of existing policies may provide the opportunity to improve and develop an approach that can both meet the interests of destination states and comply with binding principles of human rights and refugee law. Moreover, states seeking to exert control over their borders may be interested in more protective forms of controlled access to protection before arrival, such as pre-entry processing.

Second, transnational asylum may be seen to promote third country processing or protection policies. To be clear, territorial asylum should remain the normal practice when a state encounters an asylum seeker. However, as states are already implementing or exploring cooperative arrangements, this book sets out to appraise, inform and improve such proposals and approaches, rather than dismissing them out of hand. Indeed, this book is an attempt to alert policymakers to the significant scope and complexity of human rights and refugee law obligations in such cooperative arrangements and to discourage the adoption of yet more approaches that are ineffective, unlawful and in bad faith.

There are, of course, risks to accepting the premise that such cooperation arrangements may be implemented lawfully and, potentially, even amount to responsibility-sharing. States may 'cherry pick' from scholarship, using this book selectively to legitimise new forms of deterrence. Equally, however, there is a risk that refugee law scholarship may lose relevance, failing to engage with the intention and practice of governments. In my view, scholarship has a role to play in responding directly to the evinced intentions of states.

Finally, a third critique of transnational asylum may be that it too readily accepts the current status quo of migration control, hard borders and deterrence in the Global North. Critical legal scholars have rightly highlighted the historical roots of these approaches as echoing or outright reproducing the immobility of colonial structures.[77] Still, other scholars have focused on the role of race in the international refugee regime, including with respect to borders and mobility.[78] In this sense, transnational asylum is an attempt at 'politics of the possible'[79] – providing a principled yet pragmatic framework within present-day legal and policy modalities.

1.6 Locating transnational asylum: existing reform proposals

A number of scholars have put forward proposals that include the processing of asylum claims or provision of protection in third states. In 1995, Einarsen set out a vision of 'international asylum', comprising the leasing of land by the United Nations from first countries of asylum to create temporary protected territories in situations of mass influx. The scheme proposed a second protocol to the Refugee Convention, with supervisory mechanisms to implement and advise on operationalising 'international territories of asylum'.[80] Such territories would be temporary in nature, with a focus on voluntary repatriation following the conclusion of the cause for flight. The proposal seems to have stalled over the issue of territorial leases and, presumably, the unwillingness of states to commit to a binding second protocol.

In 1997, Hathaway and Neve put forward a 'solution-oriented' temporary protection approach.[81] Their appraisal of the crisis in international refugee law resonates today:

> First, governments increasingly believe that a concerted commitment to refugee protection is tantamount to an abdication of their migration

> control responsibilities. They see refugee protection as little more than an uncontrolled 'back door' route to permanent immigration, in conflict with official efforts to tailor admissions on the basis of economic or other criteria. Second, neither the actual duty to admit refugees nor the real costs associated with their arrival are fairly apportioned among governments. There is a keen awareness that the states in which refugees arrive presently bear sole legal responsibility for what often amounts to indefinite protection.[82]

Hathaway and Neve conceptualised a separation between 'responsibility-sharing' with respect to people and 'burden-sharing' with respect to financial assistance. The model contains three essential elements. First, refugee protection should be temporary and geared towards repatriation, in keeping with the intention of the drafters of the Refugee Convention and to relieve destination states of the burden of granting de facto permanent protection to any refugee granted asylum.[83] Second, the implementation of this temporary protection model should be based on the principle of common but differentiated responsibility, by which states contribute to refugee protection 'in ways that correspond to their relative capacities and strengths'.[84] This element includes the possibility of extraterritorial processing, provided there are sufficient safeguards against refoulement. As Hathaway and Neve note, 'There is no impediment to a system under which claims to refugee status and protection are delivered by a state other than that in which asylum is first requested'.[85] Third, the implementation of this approach is based on regional 'interest-convergence groups' of states motivated to respond to refugee movements.[86]

Also in 1997, Schuck put forward a 'modest proposal' for responsibility-sharing, emphasising the burdens of mass influx on destination states.[87] Under the proposal, regional groupings of states would commit to 'proportional' burden-sharing arrangements, with protection 'quotas' allocated by an international organisation, such as UNHCR. A state would commit to either providing temporary protection or permanent resettlement to refugees. Once such a regional quota system was in place, states could 'trade their quotas by paying others to fulfil their obligations'.[88] Schuck acknowledges that this marketplace of protection runs the risk of lowering protection standards, but argues:

> ... that the paramount goal for refugee policy should be to maximise the number of individuals receiving basic protection against threats to their lives and freedoms. Maximising the quality of life enjoyed by those who receive that basic protection is highly desirable, of course, but it remains secondary to this primary purpose.[89]

In 2014, Schuck revived his market-based proposal, reiterating his 1997 call for a 'regionally based, consensual arrangement' combining the allocation of refugee quotas to destination states with the trading of these quotas among countries within the region.[90]

All these proposals share certain key elements. Refugee protection should generally be temporary, rather than permanent. State interests should be mobilised by the promise of certainty and predictability in exchange for a commitment to responsibility-sharing. The form of contribution to that responsibility-sharing is negotiable among states. In addition, the proposals share a utilitarian focus on 'basic protection' for the greatest number, in an effort to protect as many refugees as possible from the most serious forms of harm.

In response to the Hathaway and Neve and Schuck proposals, Anker, Fitzpatrick and Shacknove criticised the models for proposing a shift from individual to collective refugee status determination, establishing a marketplace of refugee protection that tends towards commodification of refugees, and giving in to the worst instincts of states. Thus, the project ran the risk of 'de-emphasising the existing protection responsibilities of states toward refugees under international law... and aggravating the failures of protection that the authors wish to cure'.[91] Anker, Fitzpatrick and Shacknove suggested that physically shifting refugee protection from developed to developing states would remove the imperative for developed states to financially support the proposals.[92] The critics of the proposals hoped that 'humane values will again prevail in Northern States'.[93]

State policies over the past 25 years have settled a number of these questions. Developed states have strengthened rather than relaxed non-entrée policies, with deterrence becoming the norm rather than the exception.[94] While destination states may comply with the *letter* of human rights and refugee law when dealing with asylum seekers on their territories, there has generally been little appetite for the *spirit* of the Refugee Convention or 'humane values' vis-à-vis access to asylum. Moreover, destination states have shown a willingness to expend significant financial resources in the pursuit of deterrence policies on the basis that preventing access to asylum is an issue of national security or will save costs associated with integration.

A number of reform proposals have emerged in recent years. Since 2016, Hathaway has put forward a revised vision for a 'global and managed system of refugee protection', building on the 1997 proposal.[95] The plan abandons the regional focus of the original proposal for a global approach while maintaining the other two pillars of temporary protection for duration of risk and common but differentiated responsibility. The proposal rests on a number of ambitious steps, encompassing deterritorialised access to the international protection system, the replacement of national asylum procedures with an international corps of asylum decision-makers, state quotas for the provision of refugee protection, freedom of movement for refugees as a remedy to current encampment policies, guaranteed funding for Global South states via a burden-sharing formula and a binding commitment to resettle 1.7 million refugees annually, in order to remedy present-day protracted refugee situations.[96] The plan would be implemented via a binding optional protocol to the Refugee Convention.

In 2017, Betts and Collier sought to reimagine the international response to the Syrian crisis, putting forward a 'workable system that can sustainably offer sanctuary to the world's refugees'.[97] The model proposes the creation of safe havens in first countries of asylum via Special Economic Zones with a focus on refugees' *economic participation*. The proposal further relies on the expansion of resettlement to provide a durable solution where no other solution emerges. The model is being tested through the Jordan Compact, which seeks to create employment opportunities for Syrian refugees in Jordan.

Also in 2017, Wall put forward a proposal for a Framework Convention on Refugee Responsibility-sharing to be implemented alongside the 1951 Refugee Convention and its 1967 Protocol.[98] With reference to the United Nations Framework Convention on Climate Change, Wall argues for the establishment of a parallel instrument for refugees to:

> record the nature of the problem at hand, set out the agreed principles that are to be used to guide action to combat it, and establish an appropriate institutional structure within which further action (often including further legal obligations) can be taken to find a solution.[99]

Under Wall's proposal, the framework instrument would stand alone from the 1951 Refugee Convention and 1967 Protocol (thus allowing non-state parties to sign on), provide an institutional structure to monitor the implementation of the convention and include a responsibility-sharing pledging mechanism.[100] While a framework convention would not extend to implementing binding commitments or specific targets on states, according to Wall, it would benefit the refugee regime by being:

> widely ratified, and thus able to serve as a forum for global efforts; principled; comprehensive; accountable; capable of linking issues so as to better serve the interests of States and refugees; and able to serve as a forum for the discussion and generation of new and innovative ideas.[101]

The proposal was not taken up, but some elements would seem to have been included in the Global Compact on Refugees, discussed below.

The 2018 Model International Mobility Convention (MIMC), developed by a commission of more than 40 academic and policy experts, provides a single framework with the rights of migrants and refugees in a single instrument, with provisions on refugee rights contained in Chapter VII.[102] The MIMC further introduces the concept of 'responsibility-shares', including resettlement quotas and financial contributions for refugees and forced migrations, to be allocated by state parties each year.[103] No state has yet signed on to the MIMC framework.

In 2019, Aleinikoff and Zamore put forward five principles of protection rather than a specific model for reform of the refugee regime. These principles are *safety* for refugees through rescue and access to territory, *rights* for refugees in the enjoyment of asylum, *solutions* for refugee situations, *mobility* of refugees through the reinvigoration of the Nansen passport regime and *voices* of refugees in advocacy and institutional circles.[104]

1.7 The Global Compact on Refugees

The Global Compact on Refugees (GCR), passed by the United Nations General Assembly in 2018, is a non-binding instrument for 'more equitable and predictable burden- and responsibility-sharing' for refugees. In 2016, senior UNHCR staff foreshadowed the eventual soft law form of the GCR, acknowledging that while responsibility-sharing would ideally be tackled through an additional Protocol to the Refugee Convention, incremental reform via non-binding commitments was more achievable and realistic in the short term.[105]

While the GCR is an explicitly non-binding instrument, paragraph 5 reiterates that the Compact is 'grounded in the international refugee protection regime, centred on the cardinal principle of non-refoulement, and at the core of which is the 1951 Convention and its 1967 Protocol', as well as various regional protection instruments.[106] Paragraph 7 of the GCR lists four main overall objectives: (i) ease pressures on host countries, (ii) enhance refugee self-reliance, (iii) expand access to third country solutions and (iv) support conditions in countries of origin for return in safety and dignity.

Academic responses to the GCR have been largely skeptical, critiquing the failure to address the fundamental question of access to asylum, with no part of the Compact dedicated to the legally complex and highly politicised issues of access to territory, asylum procedures or the legality of safe third country or externalisation arrangements. Chimni notes the failure of the Compact to call 'for the dismantling of the existing non-entrée regime established by developed nations',[107] while Costello notes in her response to the GCR that 'lack of legal access to asylum for refugees has been perhaps the single most prominent topic in refugee studies for the past three decades'.[108] By failing to address these current failings in the international protection regime, the GCR would seem to tacitly endorse their continuation.

Academic responses have equally focused on the absence of a substantive responsibility-sharing mechanism within the Compact. The GCR contains no definition of what amounts to responsibility-sharing and, as a result, Doyle describes the instrument as 'long on principles but short on specific commitments'.[109] As a result, according to Aleinikoff:

> States that now benefit from a system that essentially locks refugees into host States have recognised that they can better protect their own interests by doubling down on deterrence measures than by joining a plan for responsible distribution of the world's displaced.[110]

The operational deficiencies of the GCR have also been criticised. Hathaway calls the Compact a 'thin' solution, focused on a series of meetings with 'nothing that comes even close to dependably addressing the operational deficits of the refugee regime'.[111] Aleinikoff similarly critiques the Compact for failing to establish structures for joint operations or accountability.[112] Cantor points out that while fora such as the Global Refugee Forum and Support Platforms provide structure for action, 'the criteria for its own success are not yet fully established'.[113]

Finally, some responses – largely led by current or former UNHCR staff members – are more optimistic about the GCR's reform potential. Volker Türk referred to an 'acceptable level of happiness, as [the CGR]has broad and overwhelming support'.[114] Following the first Global Refugee Forum, in December 2019, Triggs and Wall concluded the Compact had 'the makings of a success' with reference to pledges made at the Forum.[115]

1.8 Scope and definitions

This book focuses on the policies of Australia, the EU and its member states and the US as well as selected partner states. These three regions make up key destination states with a long history of receiving and integrating refugees.[116] These states are all parties to the Refugee Convention and core human rights treaties relevant to the protection of asylum seekers and refugees, including The Convention against Torture and Other Cruel, Inhuman or Degrading Treatment or Punishment (CAT)[117] and the International Covenant on Civil and Political Rights (ICCPR).[118]

This book draws on three legal frameworks in analysing international cooperation, namely international human rights law, international refugee law and the general international law doctrine of state responsibility. The book views human rights law and refugee law as complementary based on their common history, similar humanitarian aims and integrated uses.[119] The book thus analyses relevant obligations contained in the Refugee Convention and its 1967 Protocol[120] the ICCPR, CAT and the European Convention for the Protection of Human Rights and Fundamental Freedoms (ECHR).[121] EU law is addressed where relevant, but does not attempt an in-depth analysis of the EU law dimensions of transnational asylum, given the book's broad, inter-regional scope.

This book uses the term 'asylum seeker' to describe a person whose claim for protection has yet to be formally assessed and 'refugee' to describe a person who has been recognised as requiring international protection. This is a useful distinction to show the status of an individual vis-à-vis the receiving state, although refugee status is declaratory, not constitutive.[122] International protection encompasses both refugee protection, which flows from recognition under Article 1A(2) of the Refugee Convention, and complementary protection, flowing from human rights law obligations.[123]

The book employs the term 'unauthorised migrants' to denote people seeking to cross international borders without authorisation.[124] Unauthorised migration encompasses 'mixed' movements whereby refugees and other migrants not in need of international protection use the same routes. However, this study confines itself to the obligations owed to asylum seekers and refugees.

The terms 'Global North' and 'Global South' refer to countries with significant disparities in their levels of industrialisation and wealth. These are not absolute categories but indicate the relative power and resources of states involved in asylum cooperation and, in many cases, a discrepancy in the level of obligations owed to asylum seekers and refugees.

As noted above, 'destination states' refer to those traditional asylum states leading transnational asylum policies with the resources and political will to engage other states in cooperation. The book also refers to 'partner states', defined as Global South states – often countries of transit or first asylum– which cooperate with destination states on migration control and asylum. The term 'extraterritorial processing' is used to encompass both pre-entry processing and third country processing.

1.9 The road ahead

Chapter 2 introduces the transnational asylum framework. The chapter sets out key principles underpinning the concept: the necessity of maintaining territorial asylum in destination states, the general lack of refugee choice of country of protection, the need for a binding legal agreement governing transnational asylum approaches, the quality of the asylum procedure, the quality of international protection and the need for solutions for refugees.

Chapter 3 frames transnational asylum in terms of international law. The chapter addresses those situations in which the obligations of a destination state are triggered extraterritorially under human rights law treaties, the Refugee Convention and EU law. The chapter also addresses situations of shared jurisdiction and the role of territorial and extraterritorial jurisdiction in transnational asylum policies. Finally, the chapter sets out the law of shared state responsibility for breaches of primary obligations in the course of cooperative asylum policies.

Chapter 4 assesses proposals, practices and standards relating to pre-entry processing, defined as the full or preliminary pre-arrival processing of an asylum claim by the authorities of a destination country or region in a partner state. The chapter argues that pre-entry processing can serve as a mechanism to provide controlled access to protection in cooperation with regional countries providing temporary admission. The chapter thus examines historical proposals for and practice of pre-entry processing before setting out standards governing lawful implementation.

Chapter 5 considers third country processing, comprising the post-arrival transfer of an asylum seeker and processing of their claim for protection to a partner state from a destination state or region. The chapter first examines previous proposals for and practice of third country processing, tracing the rise and fall of the concept in various jurisdictions over the last 30 years. Second, the chapter explores scholarly responses to third country processing. Third, the chapter sets out standards for third country processing approaches, drawn from legal obligations with a focus on procedural, civil and political rights and policy lessons learned.

Chapter 6 addresses third country protection, involving the transfer of a refugee from a destination state to a partner state for the purposes of receiving protection. In contrast to extraterritorial processing, third country protection entails the integration of refugees in a partner state. The chapter provides standards to ensure respect for human rights and refugee law obligations in cooperation, with a focus on the integrative rights owed to refugees under the Refugee Convention.

Finally, Chapter 7 discusses how transnational asylum can amount to a form of responsibility-sharing before locating transnational asylum alongside those reform proposals presented above. The chapter illustrates how transnational asylum may function as a responsibility-sharing framework, discussing how such approaches could be operationalised at the regional level. Finally, the chapter draws some conclusions emerging from the book as a whole.

Notes

1 Convention Relating to the Status of Refugees (adopted on 28 July 1951, entered into force on 22 April 1954) 189 UNTS 137 (Refugee Convention).

2 See, for example, David Scott FitzGerald, *Refuge Beyond Reach: How Rich Democracies Repel Asylum Seekers* (Oxford University Press 2019); Thomas Gammeltoft-Hansen, *Access to Asylum: International Refugee Law and the Globalisation of Migration Control* (Cambridge University Press 2011); and Maarten den Heijer, *Europe and Extraterritorial Asylum* (Bloomsbury 2012).

3 Pauline Endres de Oliveira and Nikolas Feith Tan, 'External Processing: A Tool to Expand Protection or Further Restrict Territorial Asylum' (Migration Policy Institute, 2023); Riona Moodley, 'Rethinking "Regional Processing": Could the

Lessons Learned from the Comprehensive Plan of Action for Indochinese Refugees (CPA) Offer a Roadmap for International Cooperation in Response to "Regional" Refugee Situations?' (2022) UNSW Law Research Paper.

4 UNHCR, Global Trends: Forced Displacement in 2023 (2024) 2.

5 Daniel Ghezelbash, *Refuge Lost: Asylum Law in an Interdependent World* (Cambridge University Press 2018); Daniel Ghezelbash and Nikolas Feith Tan, 'The End of the Right to Seek Asylum? COVID-19 and the Future of Refugee Protection' (2020) 32 *International Journal of Refugee Law* 668; Andrew Ian Schoenholtz, Jaya Ramji-Nogales and Philip G Schrag, *The End of Asylum* (Georgetown University Press 2021).

6 Daniel Ghezelbash, 'Hyper-legalism and Obfuscation: How States Evade Their International Obligations Towards Refugees' (2020) 68 *American Journal of Comparative Law* 479.

7 Ghezelbash, *Refuge Lost: Asylum Law in an Interdependent World* 185–6.

8 United Nations Special Rapporteur on the rights of migrants, Human rights violations at international borders: trends, prevention and accountability A/HRC/50/31, 26 April 2022 para 41.

9 In 2021, for example, the Danish Refugee Council reported 12,000 pushbacks at EU borders. Danish Refugee Council, '12,000 pushbacks in 2021 reflects worrying normalisation of illegal practice' (16 December 2021) https://pro.drc.ngo/resources/news/12-000-pushbacks-in-2021-reflects-worrying-normalization-of-illegal-practice/ accessed 7 August 2024.

10 UNHCR, *Global Trends: Forced Displacement in 2023* 12.

11 Ghezelbash, 'Hyper-legalism and Obfuscation: How States Evade Their International Obligations Towards Refugees'.

12 Sharpe defines the term 'mixed migration' as 'complex migration phenomena, including irregular flows composed of people with varied and no international protection needs'. Marina Sharpe, 'Mixed Up: International Law and the Meaning(s) of "Mixed Migration"' (2018) 37 *Refugee Survey Quarterly* 116, 135.

13 European Commission, *A European Agenda on Migration* 2; European Commission, *Council EU Action Plan on return* COM(2015) 453 final, 9 September 2015; European Commission, *Communication on a more effective return policy in the European Union – a renewed action plan* COM(2017) 200 final, 2 March 2017 2.

14 Mixed Migration Platform, 'Rejected but remaining: Analysis of the protection challenges that confront rejected asylum seekers remaining in Europe' (Briefing Paper 5, May 2017).

15 The EU has emphasised the need for 'coherent, credible and effective policy with regard to the return of illegally staying third country nationals, which fully respects human rights and the dignity of the persons concerned as well as the principle of non-refoulement'. European Commission, *Communication on establishing a new Partnership Framework with third countries under the European Agenda on Migration* (2016) 2.

16 Nikolas Feith Tan and Thomas Gammeltoft-Hansen, 'A Topographical Approach to Accountability for Human Rights Violations in Migration Control' (2020) 21 *German Law Journal* 335.

17 ECRE, Med: Tragedy Continues as Routes Change and Situation in Libya Deteriorates Even Further (14 January 2022) https://ecre.org/med-tragedy-continues-as-routes-changes-and-situation-in-libya-deteriorates-even-further/ accessed 7 August 2024; IOM Libya, Maritime Update (3 January 2023) https://twitter.com/IOM_Libya/status/1610263422125461505 accessed 7 August 2024.

18 Protocol between the Government of the Republic of Italy and the Council of Ministers of the Republic of Albania for the Strengthening of Cooperation in Migration Matters, 2023.

19 Laura Lambert, 'Who is doing asylum in Niger?' *Anthropologie & Développement N° 51, 2020: Dossier–Perspectives Ouest-africaines Sur Les Politiques Migratoires Et Sécuritaires Européennes* (2020) 85.
20 Rebecca Dowd and Jane McAdam, 'International Cooperation and Responsibility-Sharing to Protect Refugees: What, Why and How' (2017) 66 *International and Comparative Law Quarterly* 863, 869.
21 Rüdiger Wolfrum, 'International law of cooperation' in Rudolf Bernhardt (ed), *Encyclopedia of Public International Law* (North-Holland 1995) 1242.
22 James C. Hathaway and R Alexander Neve, 'Making international refugee law relevant again: A proposal for collectivised and solution-oriented protection' (1997) 10 *Harvard Human Rights Journal* 170.
23 United Nations Charter arts 55 and 56. See also 1970 Declaration on Principles of International Law Concerning Friendly Relations and Co-operation Among States.
24 Refugee Convention preambular para 4. The 1967 Declaration on Territorial Asylum further provides in article 2(2): 'Where a State finds difficulty in granting or continuing to grant asylum, States individually or jointly or through the United Nations shall consider, in a spirit of international solidarity, appropriate measures to lighten the burden on that State'.
25 United Nations Conference of Plenipotentiaries on the Status of Refugees and Stateless Persons, Final Act of the United Nations Conference of Plenipotentiaries on the Status of Refugees and Stateless Persons, A/CONF.2/108/Rev.1 (25 July 1951) para IV(d).
26 Dowd and McAdam, 'International Cooperation and Responsibility-Sharing to Protect Refugees: What, Why and How' 869.
27 Alexander Betts, Cathryn Costello and Natascha Zaun, *A Fair Share: Refugees and Responsibility-sharing* (Delmi 2017) 20.
28 Alexander Betts, Cathryn Costello and Natascha Zaun, *A Fair Share: Refugees and Responsibility-sharing* 22.
29 Dowd and McAdam, 'International Cooperation and Responsibility-Sharing to Protect Refugees: What, Why and How' 871; Betts, Costello and Zaun, *A Fair Share: Refugees and Responsibility-sharing* 20; and UNHCR, *Expert Meeting on International Cooperation to Share Burdens and Responsibilities: Summary Conclusions* (Amman, Jordan, 27–28 June 2011) 2.
30 UNHCR, *Expert Meeting on International Cooperation to Share Burdens and Responsibilities: Summary Conclusions* 4.
31 UNHCR 2; Gregor Noll, 'Risky Games? A Theoretical Approach to Burden-Sharing in the Asylum Field' (2003) 16 *Journal of Refugee Studies* 236; Savitri Taylor, 'The Pacific Solution or a Pacific Nightmare: The Difference between Burden Shifting and Responsibility Sharing' (2005) 6 *Asian-Pacific Law & Policy Journal* 1; and Dowd and McAdam, 'International Cooperation and Responsibility-Sharing to Protect Refugees: What, Why and How'.
32 Noll, Gregor. *Negotiating asylum: the EU acquis, extraterritorial protection and the common market of deflection*. Brill, 2000.
33 Kirsten McConnachie, 'Refugee Protection and the Art of the Deal' (2017) 9 *Journal of Human Rights Practice* 190.
34 Jeff Crisp, 'Finding Space for Protection: An Inside Account of the Evolution of UNHCR's Urban Refugee Policy' (2017) 33 *Refuge* 87.
35 For a critical reading of the concept of protection space, see Martin Jones, 'Moving beyond protection space: developing a law of asylum in South-East Asia' in Susan Kneebone, Dallal Stevens and Loretta Baldassar (eds), *Refugee Protection and the Role of Law: Conflicting Identities* (Routledge 2014).

36 UNHCR, *Expert Meeting on International Cooperation to Share Burdens and Responsibilities: Summary Conclusions* 4.
37 James C. Hathaway, 'The emerging politics of non-entree' (1992) 91 *Refugees* 40.
38 Thomas Gammeltoft-Hansen and Nikolas Feith Tan, 'The End of the Deterrence Paradigm? Future Directions for Global Refugee Policy' (2017) 5 *Journal on Migration and Human Security* 28.
39 Hathaway, 'The emerging politics of non-entree' 41.
40 Guy S Goodwin-Gill, *The Refugee in International Law* (2nd edn, Oxford University Press 1996) 333.
41 Gregor Noll and Jens Vedsted-Hansen, 'Non-Communitarians: Refugee and Asylum Policies' in Philip Alston, Mara Bustelo and James Heenan (eds), *The EU and Human Rights* (Oxford: Oxford University Press 1999) 382; and Jens Vedsted-Hansen, 'Non-admission policies and the right to protection: refugees' choice versus states' exclusion' in Frances Nicholson and Patrick Twomey (eds), *Refugee Rights and Realities: Evolving International Concepts and Regimes* (Cambridge University Press 1999) 270–2.
42 Noll and Vedsted-Hansen, 'Non-Communitarians: Refugee and Asylum Policies' 382.
43 Ayelet Shachar, *The shifting border: Legal cartographies of migration and mobility* (Manchester University Press 2020).
44 Natalie Klein, 'Assessing Australia's Push Bank the Boats Policy Under International Law: Legality and Accountability for Maritime Interceptions of Irregular Migrants' (2014) 15 *Melbourne Journal of International Law* 414.
45 Eleanor Taylor Nicholson, 'Cutting Off the Flow: Extraterritorial Controls to Prevent Migration' (2011) Issue Brief, the Chief Justice Earl Warren Institute on Law and Social Policy, University of California, Berkeley Law School.
46 Antonio Cruz, *Shifting responsibility: carriers' liability in the member states of the European Union and North America* (Trentham Books and School of Oriental & African Studies 1995).
47 Leah Haus, 'Migration and international economic institutions' in AR Zolberg and PM Benda (eds), *Global Migrants, Global Refugees: Problems and Solutions* (New York, Berghahn Books 2001) 274–276.
48 Tara Magner, 'A less than Pacific' solution for asylum seekers in Australia' (2004) 16 *International Journal of Refugee Law* 53.
49 Stephen H Legomsky, 'Secondary Refugee Movements and the Return of Asylum Seekers to Third Countries: The Meaning of Effective Protection' (2003) 15 *International Journal of Refugee Law* 567.
50 Gammeltoft-Hansen and Tan, 'The End of the Deterrence Paradigm? Future Directions for Global Refugee Policy' 38.
51 *Amuur v France* App no 19776/92 (ECtHR, 10 June 1996); *Regina v Immigration Officer at Prague Airport and Another, Ex parte European Roma Rights Centre and Others* [2004] UKHL 55, House of Lords; *Plaintiff M70/2011 v Minister for Immigration and Citizenship; and Plaintiff M106 of 2011 v Minister for Immigration and Citizenship* [2011] HCA 32; and *Hirsi Jamaa and Others v Italy* App no 27765/09 (ECtHR, 23 February 2012).
52 Thomas Gammeltoft-Hansen and James C Hathaway, 'Non-Refoulement in a World of Cooperative Deterrence' (2014) 53 Columbia Journal of Transnational Law 235 and Gammeltoft-Hansen and Tan, 'The End of the Deterrence Paradigm? Future Directions for Global Refugee Policy'.
53 Nikolas Feith Tan, *International Cooperation on Refugees: Between Protection and Deterrence* (Aarhus University, 2018).
54 See for example *Sale v Haitian Centers Council* [1993] 509 US 155. In Australia's fifth periodic report under the ICCPR, the Australian government submitted:

'Australia accepts that there may be exceptional circumstances in which the rights and freedoms set out under the Covenant may be relevant beyond the territory of a State party (although notes that the jurisdictional scope of the Covenant is unsettled as a matter of international law). Although Australia believes that the obligations in the Covenant are essentially territorial in nature, Australia has taken into account the Committee's views in General Comment 31 on the circumstances in which the Covenant may be relevant extraterritorially'. Human Rights Committee, *Replies to the list of issues to be taken up in connection with the consideration of the 5th periodic report of the Government of Australia* (21 January 2009) 4.

55 An exceptional case is *MSS v Belgium and Greece* App no 30696/09 (ECtHR, 21 January 2011), in which both respondent states were held internationally responsible for the treatment of the applicant, an asylum seeker returned from Belgium to Greece.

56 See Chapter 3.

57 Nikolas Feith Tan, 'Conceptualising externalisation: still fit for purpose?' (2021) *Forced Migration Review* 8.

58 Jeff Crisp 'Externalization and the erosion of refugee protection' (University of Melbourne, 2019).

59 UNHCR Note on the 'Externalization' of International Protection, 28 May 2021.

60 Refugee Law Initiative Declaration on Externalisation and Asylum (2022) para 1. See also David Cantor and others, 'Externalisation, access to territorial asylum, and international law' (2022) 34 *International Journal of Refugee Law* 120.

61 Diana Glazebrook, 'Papua New Guinea's refugee track record and its obligations under the 2013 Regional Resettlement Arrangement with Australia' (SSGM discussion paper 2014/3, Australian National University 2014) 11.

62 Shachar, *The shifting border: Legal cartographies of migration and mobility*.

63 Jeff Crisp, What is Externalisation and Why is it a Threat to Refugees? *Chatham House*, 14 October 2020.

64 Roman Boed, 'The state of the right of asylum in international law' (1994) 5 *Duke Journal of Comparative and International Law* 1.

65 Jack I Garvey, 'The Future Legal Management of Mass Migration' (2018) 15 *International Lawyer* 121, 124. See also Karin Fathimath Afeef, *The Politics of Extraterritorial Processing: Offshore Asylum Policies in Europe and the Pacific*, 2006).

66 Also termed 'regional processing' by some authors. See Moodley, 'Rethinking "Regional Processing": Could the Lessons Learned from the Comprehensive Plan of Action for Indochinese Refugees (CPA) Offer a Roadmap for International Cooperation in Response to 'Regional'Refugee Situations?'.

67 European Council, Conclusions – 28 June 2018 http://www.consilium.europa.eu/media/35936/28-euco-final-conclusions-en.pdf accessed 7 August 2024.

68 US Department of Homeland Security, 'Fact Sheet: U.S. Government Announces Sweeping New Actions to Manage Regional Migration', 27 April 2023.

69 UNHCR, *Protection Policy Paper: Maritime interception operations and the processing of international protection claims: legal standards and policy considerations with respect to extraterritorial processing* (2010) 11.

70 Ghezelbash, *Refuge Lost: Asylum Law in an Interdependent World* 100–32.

71 Madeline Gleeson and Natasha Yacoub, 'Cruel, Costly and Ineffective: the Failure of Offshore Processing in Australia' (Kaldor Centre Policy Brief No. 11, 2021).

72 Memorandum of Understanding between the Government of the Kingdom of Cambodia and the Government of Australia, Relating to the Settlement of Refugees in Cambodia (26 September 2014).
73 Guy S Goodwin-Gill, 'Safe Country? Says Who?' (1992) 4 *International Journal of Refugee Law* 248; Kay Hailbronner, 'The Concept of "Safe Country" and Expeditious Asylum Procedures: A Western European Perspective' (1993) 5 *International Journal of Refugee Law* 31; and Cathryn Costello, 'The Asylum Procedures Directive and the proliferation of safe country practices: deterrence, deflection and the dismantling of international protection?' (2005) 7 *European Journal of Migration and Law* 35.
74 On the relationship between safe third country rules and 'protection elsewhere' policies, see Ghezelbash, 'Hyper-legalism and Obfuscation: How States Evade Their International Obligations Towards Refugees'.
75 For work on in-country processing, see Claire Higgins, 'In-country programs: the procedure and politics of an additional pathway to protection' in Satvinder Singh Juss (ed), *Research Handbook on International Refugee Law* (Edward Elgar Publishing 2019).
76 See Udlændinge- og Integrationsministeriet, Juridisk analyse af mulighederne for overførsel af asylansøgere til asylsagsbehandling i et tredjeland inden for rammerne af international ret (January 2021).
77 See, for example, Martin Lemberg-Pedersen, 'Manufacturing displacement. Externalization and postcoloniality in European migration control', *Global Affairs* 5(3) (2019) 247–271; Amy Nethery and Azadeh Dastyari, 'Refugee externalisation policies: What we have learnt and where are we going?' in Azadeh Dastyari, Amy Nethery and Asher Hirsch (eds), *Refugee Externalisation Policies: Responsibility, Legitimacy and Accountability* (Routledge 2022) 209–218; and Thomas Spijkerboer, 'Coloniality and case law on the Australian asylum offshoring scheme' (2023) 7 *International Journal of Migration and Border Studies* 132.
78 E Tendayi Achiume, 'Racial borders' (2021) 110 Georgetown Immigration Law Journal 445; E Tendayi Achiume, Race, 'Refugees, and International Law', in Cathryn Costello, Michelle Foster and Jane McAdam (eds), *The Oxford Handbook of International Refugee Law* (Oxford University Press 2021) 43–59; Thomas Spijkerboer, 'The Global Mobility Infrastructure: Reconceptualising the Externalisation of Migration Control' (2018) 20 *European Journal of Migration and Law* 452.
79 Cantor recently used this phrase with respect to the Global Compact on Refugees. David James Cantor, 'Fairness, Failure, and Future in the Refugee Regime' (2019) 30 *International Journal of Refugee Law* 627.
80 Terje Einarsen, 'Mass Flight: The Case for International Asylum' (1995) 7 *International Journal of Refugee Law* 551.
81 Hathaway and Neve, 'Making international refugee law relevant again: A proposal for collectivised and solution-oriented protection'.
82 Hathaway and Neve 117.
83 Hathaway and Neve 156–69. Temporary protection could thus 'regularly regenerate the asylum capacity of host states'. See also James C Hathaway, 'Why Refugee Law Still Matters' (2007) 8 *Melbourne Journal of International Law* 89.
84 Hathaway and Neve, 'Making international refugee law relevant again: A proposal for collectivised and solution-oriented protection' 211.
85 Hathaway and Neve 171.
86 Hathaway and Neve 188. Hathaway and Neve 'adopt the term "interest-convergence group" to identify the sub-global associations of states that ought reasonably to feel drawn together to create a mechanism of shared responsibility for refugee protection. The primary motivation for states to cooperate in

responding to the arrival of refugees will be the perceived cost of not responding. Cost, real or perceived, is therefore central to the model'.

87 Schuck thus states:

> I am convinced of the following three propositions. First, the emerging state responses to these burdens are seriously jeopardizing the viability of any meaningful regime of international human rights protection. Second, any realistic solution to this problem must somehow forestall these responses by easing these burdens in exchange for a set of obligations that states are more willing to accept and implement. Third, this can only be accomplished by distributing obligations more widely and fairly among states over time.
>
> Peter H Schuck, 'Refugee burden-sharing: A modest proposal' (1997) 22 *Yale Journal of International Law* 243, 246.

88 Schuck 248.

89 Schuck 295.

90 Peter H Schuck, "Refugee Burden-Sharing: A Modest Proposal Fifteen Years Later?" (John M. Olin Center for Studies in Law, Economics, and Public Policy, Research Paper No. 506, 2014).

91 Deborah Anker, Joan Fitzpatrick and Andrew Shacknove, 'Crisis and cure: A reply to Hathaway/Neve and Schuck' (1998) 11 *Harvard Human Rights Journal* 295, 296.

92 Anker, Fitzpatrick and Shacknove 300.

93 Anker, Fitzpatrick and Shacknove 298.

94 Gammeltoft-Hansen and Tan, 'The End of the Deterrence Paradigm? Future Directions for Global Refugee Policy'.

95 James C Hathaway, 'A global solution to a global refugee crisis' (*Open Democracy*, 29 February 2016) https://www.openglobalrights.org/global-solution-to-global-refugee-crisis/ accessed 5 March 2018; James C Hathaway, 'The Global Cop-Out on Refugees' (2019) 30 *International Journal of Refugee Law* 591.

96 Thus according to Hathaway: 'A focus on resettlement commitments would allow the developed world to protect refugees in an orderly, managed way, even as it would meet a critical gap in the current system, which leaves millions of refugees in permanent purgatory'. James C Hathaway, 'The Global Cop-Out on Refugees'.

97 Alexander Betts and Paul Collier, *Refuge: Refuge: Transforming a Broken Refugee System* (Penguin UK, 2017) 234.

98 Patrick Wall, 'A New Link in the Chain: Could a Framework Convention for Refugee Responsibility Sharing Fulfil the Promise of the 1967 Protocol?' (2017) 29 *International Journal of Refugee Law* 201.

99 Wall 218.

100 Wall 222–30.

101 Wall 235–6.

102 The Model International Mobility Convention (2018); Michael W Doyle, 'The Model International Mobility Convention' (2017) 56 *Columbia Journal of Transnational Law* 219.

103 The Model International Mobility Convention art 211.

104 Alexander T. Aleinikoff and Leah Zamore, *The Arc of Protection: Reforming the International Refugee Regime* (Stanford University Press, 2019).

105 Volker Türk and Madeline Garlick, 'From Burdens and Responsibilities to Opportunities: The Comprehensive Refugee Response Framework and a Global Compact on Refugees' (2016) 28 *International Journal of Refugee Law* 656.

106 Global Compact on Refugees para 3.

107 BS Chimni, 'Global Compact on Refugees: One Step Forward, Two Steps Back' (2019) 30 *International Journal of Refugee Law* 630.

108 Cathryn Costello, 'Refugees and (Other) Migrants: Will the Global Compacts Ensure Safe Flight and Onward Mobility for Refugees?' (2019) 30 *International Journal of Refugee Law* 634.
109 Michael W Doyle, 'Responsibility Sharing: From Principle to Policy' (2018) 30 *International Journal of Refugee Law* 30(4) 618–622.
110 T Alexander Aleinikoff, 'The Unfinished Work of the Global Compact on Refugees' (2018) 30 *International Journal of Refugee Law* 611.
111 James C Hathaway, 'The Global Cop-Out on Refugees'.
112 Aleinikoff, 'The Unfinished Work of the Global Compact on Refugees'.
113 David James Cantor, 'Fairness, Failure, and Future in the Refugee Regime'.
114 Volker Türk, 'The Promise and Potential of the Global Compact on Refugees' (2019) 30 *International Journal of Refugee Law* 575.
115 Gillian D Triggs and Patrick CJ Wall, "'The Makings of a Success': The Global Compact on Refugees and the Inaugural Global Refugee Forum' (2020) 32 *International Journal of Refugee Law* 283.
116 For a study incorporating Canada, see FitzGerald, *Refuge Beyond Reach: How Rich Democracies Repel Asylum Seekers*.
117 Opened for signature 10 December 1984, 1486 UNTS 85 (entered into force 26 June 1987).
118 Adopted 16 December 1966, entered into force 23 March 1976, 999 UNTS 171.
119 Jane McAdam, *Complementary Protection in International Refugee Law* (Oxford University Press 2007) 8; James C. Hathaway, *The Rights of Refugees under International Law* (Cambridge University Press 2005) 10; Kees Wouters, *International Legal Standards for the Protection from Refoulement* (Intersentia 2009) 526; and Jason M Pobjoy, *The Child in International Refugee Law* (Cambridge University Press 2017) 35.
120 Protocol Relating to the Status of Refugees (adopted 31 January 1967, entered into force 4 October 1967) 606 UNTS 267.
121 As amended by Protocols Nos. 11 and 14, 4 November 1950, ETS 5.
122 Accordingly, 'A person is a refugee within the meaning of the 1951 Convention as soon as he fulfils the criteria contained in the definition... Recognition of his refugee status does not therefore make him a refugee but declares him to be one'. UNHCR, *Handbook and Guidelines on Procedures and Criteria for Determining Refugee Status under the 1951 Convention and the 1967 Protocol Relating to the Status of Refugees*, HCR/1P/4/ENG/REV, December 2011 para 28.
123 James C Hathaway, *The Rights of Refugees under International Law* (Cambridge University Press 2005) 184 n 143; and Guy S Goodwin-Gill and Jane McAdam, *The Refugee in International Law* (Oxford University Press 2007) 51 and 244.
124 The term 'irregular migration' refers to 'entry into the territory of another country, without the prior consent of the national authorities or without an entry visa'. UNHCR EXCOM, Conclusion No 58 (XL), 'Problem of Refugees and Asylum-Seekers Who Move in an Irregular Manner from a Country in Which They Had Already Found Protection' (1989) para (a).

2

THE TRANSNATIONAL ASYLUM FRAMEWORK

2.1 Introduction

A primary purpose of the Refugee Convention is to 'assure refugees the widest possible exercise of their fundamental rights and freedoms'.[1] The Convention preamble further acknowledges that sharing responsibility for refugees between states is necessary, given that the grant of asylum can place an undue burden on some states. As a result, any framework for international cooperation on refugees must meet certain basic principles of international law and protection. According to McAdam:

> Any principled and sustainable response to displacement... must comply with the letter and spirit of international law (both substantive obligations and the duty to implement treaty obligations in good faith)... It should emphasize protection over deterrence (because people who need protection will seek it, however dangerous the journey might be). It should be founded on respect for human dignity, and the premise that every person should be able to live a safe and dignified life.[2]

In other words, asylum cooperation arrangements should provide genuine rights and protections and not amount to a system that shifts responsibility for protection from one state to another that is incapable of providing such protection.[3]

Transnational asylum is defined as the provision of asylum processing or international protection by two or more states. Conceptually, transnational asylum may be understood in two ways. First, transnational asylum is a *principled response* to existing deterrence policies. Transnational asylum

DOI: 10.4324/9781003463146-2

proceeds from the assumption that the 'deterrence paradigm' will endure as destination states continue to prevent asylum seekers from reaching their territories through cooperation with partner states.[4] Transnational asylum, therefore, provides a set of standards to inform future cooperation in accordance with international law. Any approach that does not meet the standards put forward here will thus fall outside the transnational asylum framework.

Second, transnational asylum may be considered the building blocks of a *protection framework* for responsibility-sharing. The key factor in enacting an effective transnational asylum policy is a shift from deterrent to protective intent on the part of cooperating states. Not only must cooperative approaches be rendered lawful, but transnational asylum should also share responsibility for refugees between destination and partner states.

The framework envisions the expansion of refugee protection through international cooperation between destination states – with considerable experience in processing asylum claims and protecting refugees – and partner states that may have limited asylum and protection systems. In the long-term, such cooperation can lead to protection for more refugees through the opening up of opportunities for protection in both destination and partner states. Through this framework, national asylum systems in partner states would be developed and supported while increased protection capacity in destination states may be filled by controlled access to protection via pre-entry processing and/or resettlement under a binding international agreement.

The transnational asylum framework fills a gap in the literature. In general, the terminology employed by refugee scholars in this area reflects a side-lining of the role of partner states. Terms such as 'protection elsewhere', 'externalisation' and 'offshoring' place destination states at the centre, notwithstanding the role of other states in carrying out cooperative asylum policies, thus reducing the role and responsibility of partner states in the implementation of such arrangements.[5]

Three potential forms of transnational asylum are considered in this book. First, and most promising, *pre-entry processing* involves the full or preliminary pre-arrival processing of an asylum claim by the authorities of a destination country or region in a partner state. A number of authors have considered the possibility of pre-entry processing. Garlick, writing in 2015, referred to 'external processing' as 'a wide variety of practices whereby a protection claim is examined to some extent before arrival in an asylum country'.[6] McAdam uses the term 'externalised asylum processing',[7] while Moodley refers to 'regional processing'.[8]

Third country processing involves the transfer of an asylum seeker from the territory or jurisdiction of one state to another for the purpose of processing their asylum claim.[9] Goodwin-Gill uses the term 'extraterritorial processing', defined as 'the processing of individuals outside the country in which they are looking for protection'.[10] Den Heijer describes approaches whereby 'asylum seekers are granted a temporary safe haven in a foreign location, allowing for their status to be determined and for a more durable solution to be arranged'.[11]

Transnational asylum also encompasses *third country protection*, involving the transfer of a refugee from the jurisdiction of a destination state to a partner state for the purposes of receiving international protection. Often such approaches are combined with third country processing arrangements, whereby both responsibility for the asylum procedure and subsequent international protection are delegated to a partner state.

The three forms of transnational asylum analysed in detail in this book are by no means exhaustive. For example, *in-country processing* involves protected entry procedures undertaken within a country of origin.[12]

2.2 Principles underpinning transnational asylum

A number of principles underpin the transnational asylum framework, and these are explored in detail in the following pages. These principles are drawn from binding international law obligations and international policy considerations. The principles are the need to maintain territorial asylum in destination states, the general lack of choice refugees have with regard to country of protection, the need for a binding legal agreement governing transnational asylum approaches, the quality of the asylum procedure, the quality of international protection and the need for durable solutions for refugees.

2.2.1 No replacement for territorial asylum

Transnational asylum arrangements must not replace territorial asylum in the destination state or region, for both legal and policy reasons. From an international law perspective, the principle of non-refoulement contained in both the Refugee Convention and international human rights law gives rise to a procedural obligation requiring that an asylum seeker within a state's jurisdiction receive an individual procedure to assess whether transferring them to a third state would breach the destination state's international obligations.[13] This obligation does not amount to an explicit right of admission on the part of the asylum seeker but, to comply with this obligation, states must conduct an individual, fair and efficient procedure to determine protection needs.[14] Hathaway argues that where there is a real risk of persecution on a relevant ground, Article 33(1) of the Refugee Convention 'amounts to a de facto duty to admit the refugee, since admission is normally the only means of avoiding the alternative, impermissible consequence of exposure to risk'.[15] Other scholars have concluded that while it is 'theoretically possible to provide such procedures extraterritorially, this is difficult, if not impossible'.[16]

As a result, any extraterritorial processing arrangement must not preclude the ability of an asylum seeker to apply for asylum in a destination state. However, there is no international legal requirement that such a procedure be lengthy or exhaustive; for example, where the asylum claim has already been fairly and effectively processed via a pre-entry processing mechanism.[17]

Moreover, in some cases, the principle of non-refoulement precludes the transfer of an asylum seeker to a third state. For example, the transfer of unaccompanied minors, seriously ill persons and nationals from the third state itself is highly unlikely to be internationally lawful.[18] In addition, further human rights obligations limit the ability of a destination state to transfer asylum seekers to a third country. Perhaps most notably, the right to family life requires that an asylum seeker with family members lawfully residing in the destination state are afforded family reunification there.[19] Furthermore, best interests of the child considerations under the Convention on the Rights of the Child (CRC) limit a destination state's ability to transfer children to a third state.[20]

Finally, principles of responsibility-sharing require that a destination state maintain access to territorial asylum. The possibility of receiving asylum seekers arriving spontaneously, as well as being a legal imperative, is important to maintain protection space in both destination and partner states. In sum, any transnational asylum arrangement requires the maintenance of national asylum procedures and protection in the destination state or region.

2.2.2 A refugee's right to choose?

Second, and related to territorial asylum, there is the question of whether a refugee has the right to choose their country of refuge. The question goes to the heart of the tension between the rights of the individual asylum seeker and the sovereign prerogatives of the state. As Vedsted-Hansen frames it:

> What commitments have states made under international law, vis-à-vis asylum seekers in general, and, hence, to what degree are states bound to accommodate the preference of the individual asylum seeker as to which country should offer protection, if and when the refugee status of the individual has been determined?[21]

As a matter of positive law, the Refugee Convention is silent on the question of an asylum seeker's right to choose, leaving a 'vacuum' in international law.[22] This silence has been interpreted in a variety of ways by both scholars and states.[23] Hathaway distinguishes between the individual prerogative to decide where to seek asylum and the state's ability to 'lawfully assign their protection responsibilities to another country, even without the refugee's consent'.[24] Other scholars have chosen to be agnostic on a definitive conclusion.[25] Mathew, for example, concludes:

> ... some states argue against giving asylum seekers any choice as to the country of asylum, while refugee advocates sometimes argue in favour of giving them an unfettered choice. An accurate reading of the law may lie somewhere between these extremes.[26]

At the level of soft law, UNHCR's Executive Committee (EXCOM) has put forward a compromise between individual choice and state sovereignty. In its Conclusion No. 15 of 1979, EXCOM stated that, in identifying the state responsible for assessing an asylum application, 'the intentions of the asylum seeker as regards the country in which he wishes to request asylum should as far as possible be taken into account'.[27] In its guidance, UNHCR states:

> There is no obligation for asylum seekers to seek asylum at the first effective opportunity, yet at the same time there is no unfettered right to choose one's country of asylum. The intentions of an asylum seeker, however, ought to be taken into account to the extent possible.[28]

However, as a matter of binding international law, there is *no general right to choose* one's country of asylum absent individual circumstances and, in practice, reaching the territory of a particular state does not guarantee the processing of an asylum seeker's claim there.[29] Recent state practice in this regard is telling, as destination states have crafted a wide range of mechanisms that place responsibility for the assessment of asylum claims at the feet of other states.

2.2.3 Creation of a binding international agreement

Transnational asylum arrangements should be based on international legal commitments entered into by cooperating states. The existence of such commitments provides an important framework of state obligations owed to asylum seekers and to each state, thereby clarifying questions of legal responsibility. A treaty binds the parties to the agreement and formalises commitments above the merely political.[30]

Entry into a treaty increases the likelihood of compliance, providing stronger guarantees for asylum seekers subject to transfer and greater certainty for cooperating states. In the Pacific, third country processing arrangements have been concluded under non-binding memorandums of understanding (MoUs) that do not create legally enforceable obligations in national courts.[31] The 'political volatility' of hastily concluded non-binding agreements poses risks for asylum seekers and states.[32] For example, under the MoU between

Australia and Papua New Guinea signed in 2013, the Papua New Guinean government undertook to locally integrate those asylum seekers transferred by Australia who were found to be refugees.[33] However, within weeks of the conclusion of the MoU, the government cast doubt on this provision of the agreement, insisting that Australia and New Zealand would need to assist in the settlement of refugees. Later, the Papua New Guinea prime minister stated that his government lacked the resources to resettle the refugees as required by the MoU.[34] As a result, only a few dozen refugees have been settled in the country, leaving hundreds of refugees without a durable solution.

International agreements allow for important parliamentary oversight and are more likely to better withstand judicial scrutiny. In the *M70* case, for example, the High Court of Australia invalidated a bilateral agreement between Australia and Malaysia, in part because of the lack of a legally binding commitment to uphold asylum and refugee law standards. Thus, the joint judgment found:

> where, as in the present case, it is agreed that Malaysia: first, does not recognise the status of refugee in its domestic law and does not undertake any activities related to the reception, registration, documentation and status determination of asylum seekers and refugees; second, is not party to the Refugees Convention or the Refugees Protocol; and, third, *has made no legally binding arrangement with Australia obliging it to accord the protections required by those instruments*; it was not open to the Minister to conclude that Malaysia provides the access or protections referred to in s 198A(3)(a)(i) to (iii) *[of the Australian Migration Act]*.[35]

The Danish and UK experiences have been instructive in this regard. On the one hand, the UK–Rwanda Asylum Partnership Agreement (APA), also referred to as Migration and Economic Development Partnership (MEDP), took the form of a non-binding MoU, with an express provision that its terms 'do not create or confer any right on any individual, nor shall compliance with this Arrangement be justiciable in any court of law by third-parties or individuals'.[36] This non-binding form was presumably chosen to secure a more rapid agreement and to avoid the creation of binding obligations between the UK and Rwanda and accompanying parliamentary oversight. The non-binding nature of the agreement left open the question of whether the agreement itself provides sufficient guarantees to uphold the substantive and procedural standards it contains.[37] Subsequently, the UK government sought to strengthen the guarantees contained in its MoU with Rwanda by crafting a treaty.[38]

The Danish plan, in contrast, has always foreseen the conclusion of a binding international agreement, with the relevant legal amendment to the Aliens Act making reference to an international agreement between Denmark and the third state, with the concrete instrument needing the approval of the Danish parliament before implementation.[39]

Importantly, however, a bilateral agreement will not shield the cooperating states from responsibility. Although the 2008 Treaty on Friendship, Partnership and Cooperation between Italy and Libya included a joint commitment to act in accordance with the principles of the Universal Declaration of Human Rights, the European Court of Human Rights (ECtHR) in *Hirsi* found Italy's presumption of compliance with international commitments, either on the basis of ratification of international treaties or obligations flowing from a bilateral treaty, was *insufficient* to guarantee the legality of international cooperation:

> 127. Confronted with the disturbing picture painted by the various international organisations, the respondent government argued that Libya was, at the material time, a 'safe' destination for migrants intercepted on the high seas. They based that belief on the presumption that Libya had complied with its international commitments as regards asylum and the protection of refugees, including the principle of non-refoulement. They claimed that the Italian–Libyan Friendship Treaty of 2008, in accordance with which clandestine migrants were returned to Libya, made specific reference to compliance with the provisions of international human rights law and other international conventions to which Libya was party.
>
> 128. In that regard, the Court observes that Libya's failure to comply with its international obligations was one of the facts denounced in the international reports on that country. In any event, the Court is bound to observe that the existence of domestic laws and the ratification of international treaties guaranteeing respect for fundamental rights are not in themselves sufficient to ensure adequate protection against the risk of ill-treatment where, as in the present case, reliable sources have reported practices resorted to or tolerated by the authorities which are manifestly contrary to the principles of the Convention (see *M.S.S.*, cited above, § 353, and, *mutatis mutandis*, *Saadi*, cited above, § 147).
>
> 129. Furthermore, the Court observes that Italy cannot evade its own responsibility by relying on its obligations arising out of bilateral agreements with Libya. Even if it were to be assumed that those agreements made express provision for the return to Libya of migrants intercepted on the high seas, the Contracting States' responsibility continues even after their having entered into treaty commitments subsequent to the entry into force of the Convention or its Protocols in respect of these States.

A bilateral treaty, therefore, is an important but *not sufficient* element of any transnational asylum arrangement. If states are serious about providing meaningful guarantees for asylum seekers, a binding international agreement is more likely to deliver results.

2.2.4 The quality of the asylum procedure

A further question arising from any transnational asylum policy is the quality of the asylum procedure carried out in the third country. As transnational asylum arrangement may involve pre-entry procedures or the transfer of an asylum seeker from a destination state with well-established asylum procedures to a partner state that may lack developed asylum procedures, this raises the question of the required standard of the asylum assessment. More specifically, which binding minimum standards exist on asylum processing?

The Refugee Convention is silent on this question, with 'no specific provisions...for the examination of asylum applications'.[40] Despite this, the Convention implicitly requires state parties to establish an asylum procedure, with a number of references to a 'determination' and 'regularised' status.[41] Therefore, according to Vedsted-Hansen:

> States have to establish an asylum procedure in order to fulfil their obligations under international law towards refugees, and hence refugee claimants seeking asylum as well. Since the asylum procedure is a tool necessary for States' fulfilment of their international protection obligations, domestic examination procedures are therefore bound to comply with certain minimum requirements so as to enable States to efficiently identify those persons to whom protection obligations are owed.[42]

Today, it is generally accepted that state parties carrying out asylum processing are obliged to carry out *fair and effective* procedures for determining refugee status. According to Thym and Hailbronner:

> General principles on a fair asylum procedure have been developed in the application of the Convention. They require state parties, in line with the principle of good faith, to institute 'fair and effective' procedures in order to determine who is entitled to the guarantees of the Convention.[43]

The meanings of the terms 'fair' and 'effective' need some fleshing out. Thym and Hailbronner state that

> fairness generally mandates a procedure providing for a reasonable chance to enforce a claim to protection. Applicants must be given an opportunity

> to present their claim by means of an application to asylum and to pursue it throughout the procedure.

In turn, effectiveness requires that asylum seekers' 'procedural rights and the legal status should allow them to enforce their claim within a reasonable period of time'.[44]

In Europe, the ECHR and EU law provide binding regional standards on the asylum procedure. The ECtHR has developed a number of principles through its Articles 3 and 13 jurisprudence, including the requirement that asylum applications be given 'rigorous scrutiny'.[45] Article 13 of the ECtHR, which provides the right to an effective remedy if an applicant has an arguable claim, applies in relation to the expulsion of asylum seekers. Article 13 has been interpreted as entailing an assessment of the individual facts and circumstances of the case.[46] In *Jabari v Turkey*, the Court stated:

> ... having regard to the fact that Article 3 enshrines one of the most fundamental values of a democratic society and prohibits in absolute terms torture or inhuman or degrading treatment or punishment, a rigorous scrutiny must necessarily be conducted of an individual's claim that his or her deportation to a third country will expose that individual to treatment prohibited by Article 3.[47]

Moreover, the right to an effective remedy includes a suspensive effect vis-à-vis domestic measures, such as deportation.[48]

A lack of a fair and effective asylum procedure in the third state will expose asylum seekers to a risk of indirect refoulement. In *AAA*, the UK Supreme Court examined the legality of the UK–Rwanda APA with explicit reference to Rwanda's national asylum system and broader judicial independence. The case concerned asylum seekers from Iran, Iraq, Sudan, Syria and Vietnam who had entered the UK irregularly and were slated for transfer to Rwanda. The Court found the UK–Rwanda APA unlawful due to a range of inadequacies in Rwanda's national asylum system that led to a 'real risk of ill-treatment by reason of refoulement' for transferred asylum seekers.[49]

EU asylum law imports detailed minimum standards on the asylum procedure.[50] The Asylum Procedures Directive (APD) sets out detailed, binding standards for member states in carrying out asylum determination on EU territory. Vedsted-Hansen notes:

> these principles and guarantees are in line with, and generally well beyond, the basic standards previously recommended by the UNHCR Executive Committee... the Directive has in many respects set high standards and formalised the core procedural rights for asylum applicants.[51]

The APD contains the right to access the asylum procedure; the right to remain in the state during processing; standards for state officers carrying out the procedure, including adequate training; procedural guarantees for asylum seekers, including the right to an interpreter, a personal interview, legal assistance and representation; and guarantees on the conditions of the asylum procedure, including the nature of the interview and a written decision.

Whether EU asylum law would apply in a policy of transnational asylum will depend on the modalities of the specific approach. On the one hand, the EU Charter on Fundamental Rights (EU Charter) is binding wherever EU law is applied, including extraterritorially. The application of the APD, on the other hand, is limited to the territory of the EU and does not extend extraterritorially.[52] According to Thym, third country processing would not trigger the application of EU asylum law on the basis of the distinction between the non-refoulement obligation and the asylum procedure itself.[53] Other authors insist that the EU asylum *acquis* would apply on the basis of EU competency under Article 78 of the Treaty of the Functioning of the European Union (TFEU) and the concept of 'portable responsibility' extending the effect of EU law extraterritorially.[54]

A number of soft law sources have driven the development of minimum standards on asylum procedures. In 1977, UNHCR's EXCOM put forward the following criteria as the basis for the national assessment of asylum claims:

i The competent official (e.g., immigration officer or border police officer) to whom the applicant addresses himself at the border or in the territory of a Contracting State, should have clear instructions for dealing with cases which might be within the purview of the relevant international instruments. He should be required to act in accordance with the principle of non-refoulement and to refer such cases to a higher authority.
ii The applicant should receive the necessary guidance as to the procedure to be followed.
iii There should be a clearly identified authority – wherever possible, a single central authority – with responsibility for examining requests for refugee status and taking a decision in the first instance.
iv The applicant should be given the necessary facilities, including the services of a competent interpreter, for submitting his case to the authorities concerned. Applicants should also be given the opportunity, of which they should be duly informed, to contact a representative of UNHCR.
v If the applicant is recognised as a refugee, he should be informed accordingly and issued with documentation certifying his refugee status.
vi If the applicant is not recognised, he should be given a reasonable time to appeal for a formal reconsideration of the decision, either to the same or to a different authority, whether administrative or judicial, according to the prevailing system.

vii The applicant should be permitted to remain in the country pending a decision on his initial request by the competent authority referred to in paragraph (iii) above, unless it has been established by that authority that his request is clearly abusive. He should also be permitted to remain in the country while an appeal to a higher administrative authority or to the courts is pending.[55]

In its 1983 conclusion on manifestly unfounded claims, EXCOM stated that all asylum seekers 'should be given a complete personal interview by a fully qualified official and, whenever possible, by an official of the authority competent to determine refugee status'. [56] Further, in response to an EXCOM request, UNHCR compiled a handbook on procedures and criteria for determining refugee status, providing a detailed framework for the determination of protection claims.

UNHCR itself has suggested further soft law standards in asylum procedures. Alongside its handbook, UNHCR's 2001 global consultations on international protection put forward 'core procedural standards necessary to preserve the integrity of the asylum regime as both fair and efficient'.[57] As part of this process, UNHCR identified examples of best practices recommended to form the basis of a proposed EXCOM Conclusion on Asylum Procedures (not yet forthcoming). These included:

g. At all stages of the procedure, including at the admissibility stage, asylum seekers should *receive guidance and advice on the procedure and have access to legal counsel*. Where free legal aid is available, asylum seekers should have access to it in case of need. They should also have access to qualified and impartial interpreters where necessary and the right to contact UNHCR and recognised NGOs working in cooperation with UNHCR. UNHCR's mandate requires that it have prompt and unhindered access to asylum seekers and refugees wherever they are.
h. The examination of applications for refugee status should in the first instance allow for a *personal interview*, if possible, before the decision-makers of the competent body, and should be based on a thorough assessment of the circumstances of each case. The asylum seeker should have the opportunity to present evidence concerning his/her personal circumstances and conditions in the country of origin. In manifestly well-founded cases, an interview may not always be necessary where a positive decision is expected.
i. The body responsible for examining and deciding on applications for refugee status in the first instance should be a *single, central specialised authority*. If an initial interview is made by a border official, there should be a provision that an applicant not be rejected or denied admission without reference to a central authority.

j. Decision-makers should have access to accurate, impartial, and up-to-date country of origin information from a variety of sources as a key decision-making tool. They should be trained in appropriate, cross-cultural interviewing skills, be familiar with the use of interpreters and have *requisite knowledge of refugee and asylum matters*.[58]

Under the Refugee Convention, therefore, states owe an obligation to provide a fair and effective procedure to asylum seekers in determining their protection needs. European law imports further minimum standards, notably the requirement of 'rigorous scrutiny' and an individual assessment under the ECHR. At the EU level, the APD adds a more detailed bundle of procedural guarantees for asylum seekers seeking protection from the authorities of a member state in the EU.

2.2.5 The quality of international protection

Finally, and fundamentally, transnational asylum approaches must provide protection to refugees. However, as with the *processing* of asylum seekers, international refugee law is silent on the question of where the *protection* of refugees must take place. According to Goodwin-Gill, 'States may be bound to the refugee definition and bound to observe the principle of non-refoulement, but they retain discretion as to whether to allow a refugee to settle locally'.[59] This normative gap raises the question: which binding minimum standards exist on the content of international protection?

Protection under the Refugee Convention affords an array of rights as the attachment of the refugee to the asylum state grows stronger. According to Goodwin-Gill, therefore:

> Given the further objective of a solution (assimilation or integration), the Convention concept of refugee status thus offers a point of departure in considering the appropriate standard of treatment of refugees within the territory of contracting states.... the Convention proposes, as a minimum standard, that refugees should receive at least that treatment which is accorded to non-citizens generally.[60]

More specifically, Articles 2–34 of the Refugee Convention contain rights that accrue according to the refugee's level of attachment to the asylum state.[61] There are five levels of attachment: within the state's jurisdiction, physically present, lawfully present, lawfully staying and, finally, where the refugee has durable residence. Rights accrue incrementally – a refugee is entitled to certain core rights by virtue of being under a state's jurisdiction, and these rights endure once that refugee is physically present in the state.

The structure of rights within the Refugee Convention is designed to allow for varying standards of treatment according to the asylum state's level of development. As a result, the standard of treatment owed to a refugee under the Refugee Convention is anchored to that accorded to other residents of the state. Depending on the right, refugees are afforded one of the following: the same treatment as is accorded to aliens generally, treatment at least as favourable as that accorded to nationals, the most favoured treatment accorded to nationals of a foreign country, and, finally, several absolute rights.

The Refugee Convention's structure of rights and standards of treatment allows for a wide variation in the quality of protection between states.[62] Unfortunately, there is very little case law on this important question. In *R v Secretary of State for the Home Department, ex parte Yogathas*, the UK House of Lords found that the transfer of two young Tamil men to Germany under the Dublin Regulation permitted a certain amount of variation in the application of the refugee definition under the Refugee Convention:

> the [Refugee] convention is directed to a very important but very simple and very practical end, preventing the return of applicants to places where they will or may suffer persecution. Legal niceties and refinements should not be allowed to obstruct that purpose. It can never, save in extreme circumstances, be appropriate to compare an applicant's living conditions in different countries if, in each of them, [they] will be safe from persecution or the risk of it.[63]

In the seminal case of *M70* the Australian High Court found that the third country must provide refugees with treatment at least as favourable as nationals with respect to employment, education and religious freedom, well beyond the scope of the non-refoulement obligation.

Thus, clearly human rights and refugee law require certain minimum levels of protection for refugees subject to transnational asylum policies, discussed in detail in Chapter 6.

2.2.6 The provision of durable solutions

Finally, transnational asylum approaches should provide durable solutions to refugees. There are three internationally accepted durable solutions: resettlement, local integration and voluntary repatriation.[64] In the context of transnational asylum, the provision of a durable solution to refugees is a paramount policy consideration, though not necessarily a binding obligation. Nevertheless, as destination states seek to shift away from the traditional approach of territorial asylum and protection, provision for durable solutions is key to effective policymaking.

Voluntary repatriation is the right to return to one's country of origin once the reason for flight has subsided. In general, a refugee should only return 'voluntarily and in conditions of security'.[65] In this context, voluntariness requires that a decision to return be 'fully informed and consensual, and not prompted by uncertainty and protracted detention'.[66] In the context of transnational asylum, the *voluntary* nature of repatriation assumes particular importance, as difficult and protracted conditions for asylum processing may lead refugees to return despite an extant risk of persecution.[67]

Local integration, in the context of transnational asylum, relates to the integration of a refugee in a partner state. A 'practical realisation of asylum', the drafters of the Refugee Convention considered local integration a primary solution to the plight of refugees.[68] Local integration need not be permanent, though it must last for the duration of the need for protection or until another durable solution is found.[69] Article 34 of the Refugee Convention calls for a conclusive form of long-term stay, requesting contracting states 'as far as possible to facilitate the assimilation and naturalisation of refugees'.

Finally, resettlement is the transfer of refugees from the asylum state to a state that has agreed to admit them and ultimately grant them permanent settlement.[70] Generally, resettlement involves the transfer of a refugee from a state with limited capacity to provide protection to a country with greater capacity. According to UNHCR, resettlement has three functions:

> First, it is a tool to provide international protection and meet the specific needs of individual refugees whose life, liberty, safety, health or other fundamental rights are at risk in the country where they have sought refuge. Second, it is a durable solution for larger numbers or groups of refugees, alongside the other durable solutions of voluntary repatriation and local integration. Third, it can be a tangible expression of international solidarity and a responsibility-sharing mechanism, allowing States to help share each other's burdens, and reduce problems impacting the country of first asylum.[71]

Durable solutions are not formally binding obligations (rooted as they are in the UNHCR Charter and not the Refugee Convention or customary international law), but they remain important policy priorities. A failure to provide durable solutions risks producing 'refugees in orbit' situations and will not solve the problem of irregular movement.

2.3 Conclusions

This chapter sets out the transnational asylum framework, defined as the provision of asylum processing or international protection by multiple states. Transnational asylum is not an ideal concept but rather a principled and pragmatic approach to how states could manage asylum seekers and refugees through a controlled protection framework. The chapter further set out international law and policy principles that underpin the framework: the need to maintain territorial asylum in destination states; the general lack of choice refugees have with regard to country of protection; the need for a binding legal agreement governing transnational asylum approaches; the quality of the asylum procedure; the quality of international protection and the need for durable solutions for refugees.

Notes

1 Preamble to the Convention Relating to the Status of Refugees (adopted 28 July 1951, entered into force 22 April 1954) 189 UNTS 137 (Refugee Convention).
2 Jane McAdam, 'The Enduring Relevance of the 1951 Refugee Convention' (2017) 29 *International Journal of Refugee Law* 1, 8.
3 'The Michigan Guidelines on Protection Elsewhere' (2006) 28 *Michigan Journal of International Law*.
4 Thomas Gammeltoft-Hansen and Nikolas Feith Tan, 'The End of the Deterrence Paradigm? Future Directions for Global Refugee Policy' (2017) 5 *Journal on Migration and Human Security* 28.
5 'The Michigan Guidelines on Protection Elsewhere'; and James C Hathaway and Michelle Foster, *The Law of Refugee Status* (Cambridge University Press 2014) 41.
6 Madeline Garlick, 'The Potential and Pitfalls of Extraterritorial Processing of Asylum Claims' (Migration Policy Institute, March 2015) http://www.migrationpolicy.org/news/potential-and-pitfalls-extraterritorial-processing-asylum-claims accessed 27 March 2024.
7 Jane McAdam, *Extraterritorial processing in Europe* (Kaldor Centre for International Refugee Law Policy Brief, 2015).
8 Riona Moodley, 'Rethinking "Regional Processing": Could the Lessons Learned from the Comprehensive Plan of Action for Indochinese Refugees (CPA) Offer a Roadmap for International Cooperation in Response to 'Regional' Refugee Situations?' (2022) UNSW Law Research Paper .
9 UNHCR, *Protection Policy Paper: Maritime interception operations and the processing of international protection claims: legal standards and policy considerations with respect to extraterritorial processing* (2011) 11.
10 Guy S Goodwin-Gill, 'The Extraterritorial Processing of Claims to Asylum or Protection: The Legal Responsibilities of States and International Organisations' (2007) 9 UTS Law Review 26.
11 Universal Declaration of Human Rights (adopted 10 December 1948 UNGA Res 217 A(III)).
12 On in-country processing more broadly, see Claire Higgins, 'In-country programs: the procedure and politics of an additional pathway to protection' in Satvinder Singh Juss (ed), *Research Handbook on International Refugee Law* (Edward Elgar Publishing 2019); and Claire Higgins, *Safe Journeys and Sound Policy: Expanding protected entry for refugees* (Andrew & Renata Kaldor Centre for International Refugee Law policy brief, 2019) 14.
13 See further Chapter 3.

14 Jens Vedsted-Hansen, 'The asylum procedures and the assessment of asylum requests' in Vincent Chetail and Céline Bauloz (eds), *Research Handbook on International Law and Migration* (Edward Elgar 2014); Álvaro Botero and Jens Vedsted-Hansen, 'Asylum Procedure', in Cathryn Costello, Michelle Foster and Jane McAdam (eds), *The Oxford Handbook of International Refugee Law* (Oxford University Press 2021) 597–606.
15 James C Hathaway, *The Rights of Refugees under International Law* (Cambridge University Press 2021) 339.
16 Asher Lazarus Hirsch and Nathan Bell, 'The Right to Have Rights as a Right to Enter: Addressing a Lacuna in the International Refugee Protection Regime' (2017) 18 Human Rights Review 417, 428.
17 See further Chapter 4.
18 See further Chapter 5.
19 Article 8 European Convention on Human Rights.
20 Article 3 Convention on the Rights of the Child.
21 Jens Vedsted-Hansen, 'Non-admission policies and the right to protection: refugees' choice versus states' exclusion' in Frances Nicholson and Patrick Twomey (eds), *Refugee Rights and Realities: Evolving International Concepts and Regimes* (Cambridge University Press 1999) 273.
22 Vedsted-Hansen 279.
23 Vedsted-Hansen 285–6; James C Hathaway, *The Law of Refugee Status* (Butterworths 1991) 48; and Hathaway and Foster, *The Law of Refugee Status* 30–2.
24 James C Hathaway, 'Why Refugee Law Still Matters' (2007) 8 *Melbourne Journal of International Law* 89, 96.
25 Vedsted-Hansen, 'Non-admission policies and the right to protection: refugees' choice versus states' exclusion' 287.
26 Penelope Mathew, 'Australian refugee protection in the wake of the Tampa' (2002) 96 *American Journal of International Law* 661, 688.
27 UNHCR EXCOM, Conclusion No 15 (XXX), 'Refugees without an Asylum Country' (16 October 1979) para (h)(iii).
28 UNHCR, *Summary Conclusions on the Concept of "Effective Protection" in the Context of Secondary Movements of Refugees and Asylum-Seekers* (Lisbon Expert Roundtable, 9–10 December 2002) para 11; UNHCR, *Guidance Note on bilateral and/or multilateral transfer arrangements of asylum-seekers* para 3(i). See also Hathaway and Foster, *The Law of Refugee Status* 30.
29 Hathaway, 'Why Refugee Law Still Matters', 101.
30 This position is supported by the Refugee Law Initiative Declaration on Asylum and Externalisation, which provides: 'International agreements concerning third country processing must take a form suitable for protecting transferees' rights and ideally be binding under international law'. Refugee Law Initiative Declaration on Externalisation and Asylum (2022) para 17.
31 Select Committee on the Recent allegations relating to conditions and circumstances at the Regional Processing Centre in Nauru, *Taking responsibility: conditions and circumstances at Australia's Regional Processing Centre in Nauru* (Parliament of Australia, 2015) 18.
32 Azadeh Dastyari and Maria O'Sullivan, 'Not for Export: The Failure of Australia's Extraterritorial Processing Regime in Papua New Guinea and the Decision of the PNG Supreme Court in Namah' (2016) 42 *Monash University Law Review* 308.
33 Memorandum of Understanding between the Government of the Independent State of Papua New Guinea and the Government of Australia, relating to the transfer to, and assessment and settlement in, Papua New Guinea of certain persons, and related issues (signed and entered into force 6 August 2013) art 13.

34 Peter O'Neill, 'Westpac Address at the National Press Club' (Speech delivered at the National Press Club, Canberra, 3 March 2016).
35 *Plaintiff M70/2011 v. Minister for Immigration and Citizenship; and Plaintiff M106 of 2011 v. Minister for Immigration and Citizenship*, [2011] HCA 32 (High Court of Australia, 31 August 2011) para 60 (emphasis added).
36 Memorandum of Understanding between the government of the United Kingdom of Great Britain and Northern Ireland and the government of the Republic of Rwanda for the provision of an asylum partnership arrangement, 13 April 2022 para 2.2.
37 Nikolas Feith Tan, 'Externalisation of asylum in Europe: Unpacking the UK-Rwanda Asylum Partnership Agreement' *EU Immigration and Asylum Law and Policy* (17 May 2022) https://eumigrationlawblog.eu/externalisation-of-asylum-in-europe-unpacking-the-uk-rwanda-asylum-partnership-agreement/ accessed 8 August 2024.
38 Agreement for the Provision of an Asylum Partnership to Strengthen Shared International Commitments on the Protection of Refugees and Migrants (5 December 2023).
39 L 226 Forslag til lov om andring af udlandingeloven og hjemrejseloven (Indforelse af mulighed for overforsel af asylansogere til asylsagsbehandling og eventuel efterfolgende beskyttelse i tredjelande), Lovforslag som vedtaget, 3 June 2021. See further Nikolas Feith Tan, 'Visions of the Realistic? Denmark's Legal Basis for Extraterritorial Asylum' (2022) 91 *Nordic Journal of International Law* 172.
40 Vedsted-Hansen, 'The asylum procedures and the assessment of asylum requests' 439. UNHCR's handbook similarly provides 'the Convention does not indicate what type of procedures are to be adopted for the determination of refugee status. It is therefore left to each contracting state to establish the procedure that it considers most appropriate, having regard to its particular constitutional and administrative structure'. UNHCR, *Handbook and Guidelines on Procedures and Criteria for Determining Refugee Status under the 1951 Convention and the 1967 Protocol Relating to the Status of Refugees* para 189.
41 Refugee Convention arts 9, 31(2).
42 Vedsted-Hansen, 'The asylum procedures and the assessment of asylum requests' 441.
43 Daniel Thym and Kay Hailbronner, 'Legal Framework for EU Asylum Policy' in Kay Hailbronner and Daniel Thym (eds), *EU Immigration and Asylum Law: Commentary* (2nd edn, C.H. Beck 2016) 1048.
44 Thym and Hailbronner 1049.
45 Vedsted-Hansen, 'The asylum procedures and the assessment of asylum requests' 446–7.
46 *Boyle and Rice v The United Kingdom* Appl nos 9659/82 and 9658/82 (ECtHR, 24 March 1988) para 55.
47 *Jabari v Turkey* Appl no 40035/98 (ECtHR, 11 July 2000) para 39.
48 Vedsted-Hansen, 'The asylum procedures and the assessment of asylum requests' 447–8.
49 R (on the application of AAA (Syria) and others) (Respondents/Cross Appellants) v Secretary of State for the Home Department [2023] UKSC 42 para 28.
50 Article 18 of the EU Charter guarantees the right to asylum in accordance with the 1951 Convention and Article 47 enshrines the right to an effective remedy.
51 Vedsted-Hansen, 'The asylum procedures and the assessment of asylum requests' 450.
52 Asylum Procedures Directive art 3(1) and (2). See further Hemme Battjes, *European Asylum Law and International Law* (Nijhoff 2006) 208–9.

53 Daniel Thym, 'Legal Framework for Entry and Border Controls' in Kay Hailbronner and Daniel Thym (eds), *EU Immigration and Asylum Law: Commentary* (2nd edn, C.H. Beck 2016).
54 Sergio Carrera and others, 'Offshoring Asylum and Migration in Australia, Spain, Tunisia and the US: Lessons learned and feasibility for the EU' (CEPS Research Report, September 2018) 50–51; Netherlands Advisory Committee on Migration Affairs, *External Processing: Conditions applying to the Processing of Asylum Applications outside the European Union* (Advisory Report No 32, 2010, 2010) 30–36.
55 UNHCR EXCOM, Conclusion No. 8 (XXVIII), 'Determination of Refugee Status' (12 October 1977) para(e); UNHCR, *Handbook and Guidelines on Procedures and Criteria for Determining Refugee Status under the 1951 Convention and the 1967 Protocol Relating to the Status of Refugees* paras 190–2.
56 UNHCR EXCOM, Conclusion No. 30 (XXXIV), 'The Problem of Manifestly Unfounded or Abusive Applications for Refugee Status or Asylum' (20 October 1983) para (i).
57 UNHCR, *Global Consultations on International Protection/Third Track: Asylum Processes (Fair and Efficient Asylum Procedures)* (31 May 2001) 6.
58 UNHCR 12–13 (emphasis added).
59 Guy S Goodwin-Gill, 'The International Law of Refugee Protection' in Fiddian-Qasmiyeh Elena and others (eds), *The Oxford Handbook of Refugee and Forced Migration Studies* (Oxford University Press 2014) 42.
60 Goodwin-Gill, 'The International Law of Refugee Protection' 42.
61 James C Hathaway, *The Rights of Refugees under International Law* (2 edn, Cambridge University Press 2021) 155–238.
62 Thomas Gammeltoft-Hansen, 'The extraterritorialisation of asylum and the advent of protection lite' (DIIS Working paper 2007/2, 2007).
63 *R v Secretary of State for the Home Department, ex parte Thangarasa; R v Secretary of State for the Home Department, ex parte Yogathas* 2002 UKHL 36 para 8 per Lord Bingham.
64 UNHCR EXCOM, 'Protection of Asylum Seekers in Situations of Large-scale Influx' (1981) para IV(3). See also Statute of the Office of the United Nations High Commissioner for Refugees, 14 December 1950, A/RES/428(V) art 1, which provides:

> The United Nations High Commissioner for Refugees, acting under the authority of the General Assembly, shall assume the function of providing international protection, under the auspices of the United Nations, to refugees who fall within the scope of the present Statute and of seeking permanent solutions for the problem of refugees by assisting Governments and, subject to the approval of the Governments concerned, private organizations to facilitate the *voluntary repatriation* of such refugees, or their *assimilation within new national communities.*
>
> *(emphasis added)*

65 Goodwin-Gill, 'The International Law of Refugee Protection' 40.
66 UNHCR, *UNHCR Mission to the Republic of Nauru* (2012) 10.
67 Paul Farrell and Ben Doherty, 'Syrian asylum seeker repatriated from Manus Island with Australian assistance' (*The Guardian*, 8 September 2015) https://www.theguardian.com/australia-news/2015/sep/08/syrian-asylum-seeker-repatriated-from-manus-island-with-australian-assistance accessed 30 October 2018.

68 Alice Edwards, 'Human rights, refugees, and the right 'to enjoy'asylum' (2005) 17 International Journal of Refugee Law 293, 307; Goodwin-Gill, 'The International Law of Refugee Protection' 42.

69 Alice Edwards 307; and James C. Hathaway and R Alexander Neve, 'Making international refugee law relevant again: A proposal for collectivised and solution-oriented protection' (1997) 10 *Harvard Human Rights Journal* 117.

70 UNHCR, *UNHCR Resettlement Handbook* (2011) 36.

71 UNHCR, *Global Consultations on International Protection/Third Track: Strengthening and Expanding Resettlement Today: Dilemmas, Challenges and Opportunities* (25 April 2002); and Maria O'Sullivan, 'The ethics of resettlement: Australia and the Asia–Pacific Region' (2016) 20 *The International Journal of Human Rights* 241, 243.

3

INTERNATIONAL LAW

3.1 Introduction

This chapter provides the legal backdrop to the transnational asylum framework, set out in the previous chapter and elaborated upon in subsequent chapters, and explains the international legal regimes within which states cooperating on asylum operate. The chapter proceeds in four sections. First, the chapter sets out the structure of rights under the Refugee Convention, crucial to understanding how responsibility may be shared for refugees between states. Second, the chapter addresses the applicability of international and regional human rights law to transnational asylum arrangements through an account of the law of jurisdiction, the threshold for the application of international law obligations in this area. These understandings of territorial jurisdiction, extraterritorial jurisdiction and shared jurisdiction are the building blocks of the transnational asylum framework. Third, the chapter briefly addresses the applicability of EU law to transnational asylum arrangements, given the specialised regional regime created under the Common European Asylum System (CEAS). Finally, the chapter sets out the law of state responsibility as applicable to states where cooperative asylum arrangements lead to breaches of international obligations.

3.2 The structure of rights under the Refugee Convention

3.2.1 Attachment to the asylum state

The Refugee Convention sets out a structure of rights to be afforded to refugees that accrue sequentially according to the refugee's attachment to the

DOI: 10.4324/9781003463146-3

asylum state. There are five cumulative levels of attachment, briefly explained below, where a refugee:

- is within a state's jurisdiction,
- is within a state's territory,
- has lawful presence,
- has lawful stay, or
- has durable residence.[1]

Where a refugee is merely *within the jurisdiction* (but not necessarily territory) of the destination state at the time of transfer, they are entitled to rights of non-discrimination (Article 3), property (Article 13), access to courts (Article 16), rationing (Article 20), the right to primary education (Article 22), freedom from fiscal charges (Article 29) and non-refoulement (Article 33). By way of example, asylum seekers transferred to a third country processing centre may be under destination state jurisdiction but not physically in that state, for example, where they are transferred from the high seas.

Where a refugee is *within the territory* of a destination state, they benefit from a further set of rights, notably rights to freedom of religion (Article 4), identity papers (Article 27), non-penalisation for illegal entry or presence (Article 31(1) and freedom of movement despite illegal entry or presence (Article 31(2)). For example, refugees who transit in a destination state before transfer to a third country protection arrangement will be owed rights flowing from their physical presence.[2]

As transnational asylum policies include the protection of refugees in third states, the obligations of both destination and partner states in providing rights to refugees with closer levels of attachment are crucial. *Lawful presence* applies to a refugee officially admitted to a state for a limited period of time, in the process of receiving documentation of refugee status from national authorities or receiving protection without adjudication of refugee status. A refugee lawfully present is entitled to self-employment (Article 18), freedom of movement (Article 26) and non-expulsion (Article 32).

Lawful stay, the fourth level of attachment, requires an ongoing 'settling down', in practical terms, but not an established residence in the asylum state.[3] With reference to the broad meaning of the French term résidant régulièrement, translated by the Conference of Plenipotentiaries as 'lawfully staying in the territory', Weis concludes:

> It results from the *travaux préparatoires* that any refugee who, with the authorisation of the authorities, is in the territory of a Contracting State otherwise than purely temporarily, is to be considered as 'lawfully staying' *('résidant régulièrement').*[4]

At this point, a refugee benefits from freedom of association (Article 15), the right to employment (Article 17), the right to practice a profession (Article 19), access to public housing and welfare (Articles 21 and 23), protection of labour and social security legislation (Article 24) and entitlement to travel documentation (Article 28).[5]

Finally, a number of final *durable residence* rights adhere to the Refugee Convention.[6] Article 34, for example, promotes naturalisation in fairly weak terms, requiring signatory states to 'consider' granting citizenship to refugees lawfully present.

3.2.2 Standards of treatment

The structure of rights afforded by the Refugee Convention allows for varying standards of treatment according to a state's level of development. Depending on their rights, refugees are afforded one of the following standards of treatment:

- same treatment as is accorded to aliens generally,[7]
- treatment at least as favourable as that accorded to nationals,[8]
- the most favoured treatment accorded to nationals of a foreign country,[9] and
- several absolute rights.[10]

As a result, the *standard of treatment* owed to a refugee under the Refugee Convention is anchored to that standard accorded to other residents of the state. In this way, the Refugee Convention ties the standard of treatment to the conditions in the asylum state rather than any fixed threshold.

A key question in transnational asylum arrangements is whether a destination state can transfer a refugee to a partner state where the standard of protection is significantly lower. As Vedsted-Hansen notes in relation to the first country of asylum concept, 'in order to be considered an adequate country of first asylum, the relevant state has to provide refugee protection of a *quality*, and at a *level*, in conformity with the protection scheme laid down in the Convention'.[11] Similarly, the Michigan Guidelines on Protection Elsewhere provide that a transferred refugee must benefit from the rights contained in the Refugee Convention as a matter of practice.[12]

As this book is inherently concerned with situations in which states cooperate in relation to asylum seekers and refugees, a key question is whether Refugee Convention rights adhere to refugees when they are transferred from one state to another. The transfer of an asylum seeker or refugee from one state to another does not absolve the transferring state of its international responsibility. Thus, in *TI v United Kingdom*, the ECtHR stated:

> Where States establish international organisations, or *mutatis mutandis* international agreements, to pursue cooperation in certain fields of activities,

> there may be implications for the protection of fundamental rights. It would be incompatible with the purpose and object of the [ECHR] if Contracting States were thereby absolved from their responsibility under the [ECHR] in relation to the field of activity covered by such attribution.[13]

The ECtHR has further held that states cannot avoid responsibility for asylum seekers based on a bilateral agreement.[14]

As a result, while responsibility endures despite the existence of a bilateral agreement, there is no international law requirement that the quality of protection in a partner state be equivalent to the destination state.

3.2.3 Rights owed at point of transfer

A further question is which Refugee Convention rights a destination state is obliged to ensure respect for in the partner country at the point of transfer. There are three possible positions when responding to this question. First, governments tend to claim that non-refoulement is the *only* relevant obligation when transferring a refugee to a third country.[15] While there is no doubt that destination states owe non-refoulement obligations under both the Refugee Convention and human rights law, governments tend to downplay further obligations at the point of transfer.[16]

As a matter of practice, transfer cases are routinely argued under the various strands of the non-refoulement obligation found in refugee and human rights law, rather than broader rights contained in the Refugee Convention.[17] One notable exception in the European context is the right to family and private life contained in Article 8 ECHR, which has been raised in deportation cases of persons who have resided for some duration in the destination state.[18]

Second, some scholars have argued that a destination state owes asylum seekers the 'acquired rights' to which they are already entitled under the Refugee Convention within a state's jurisdiction and territory.[19] This position is supported by the Michigan Guidelines on Protection Elsewhere, which provide:

> A refugee is entitled not simply to protection against refoulement, but more generally to benefit from the civil and socioeconomic rights set by Arts. 2–34 of the Convention. As such, *any refugee transferred must benefit in the receiving state from all Convention rights to which he or she is entitled at the time of transfer.*[20]

Under this line of argument, refugees who transit in a destination state before transfer to a transnational arrangement should be owed rights flowing from being within state jurisdiction or being physically present.

The third interpretation holds that the destination state is bound to respect all rights contained in the Refugee Convention.[21] Under this view, international law requires destination states to respect the principle of non-refoulement *and* those rights set out in Articles 2–34 of the Refugee Convention when transferring a refugee to a third state. If the Refugee Convention is designed to provide a maximal set of protections to refugees, then to transfer someone obliges a state to ensure that the full set of rights are, in fact, available.[22]

There is some support in the literature for this position. A 2002 expert roundtable on the question noted that, alongside non-refoulement, the destination state should ensure that a refugee transferred would not face a real risk of being 'deprived of his or her liberty in the third state without due process'.[23] Legomsky suggests a 'complicity principle' prohibiting the transfer of a refugee to a third country with the knowledge that the receiving state will 'do anything to that person that the sending state would not have been permitted to do itself'.[24] Thus, according to Foster:

> If it were possible to circumvent the considerable range of obligations imposed on state parties by simply transferring a refugee to another state, this would defeat the raison d'être of the Convention. Accordingly, a good faith application of Convention obligations requires that, in order to transfer a refugee to another state in accordance with the Refugee Convention, a state is under an obligation to ensure that the refugee will enjoy the rights to which [they are] entitled under the Convention scheme.[25]

UNHCR guidance argues for the full range of Convention rights in situations of third country protection, including:

> the recognised refugee is to be protected from refoulement, in any manner whatsoever; and otherwise enjoy the rights under the 1951 Refugee Convention in full and without discrimination, in law and in practice. In particular, the arrangement would provide for lawful stay, access to employment and/or self-employment opportunities, education for children, freedom of movement including the right to choose one's place of residence, and the right to travel outside the territory.[26]

The Michigan Guidelines on Protection Elsewhere similarly require that the full range of Convention rights be available in the partner state:

> The 1951 Convention and 1967 Protocol relating to the Status of Refugees ('Convention') neither expressly authorise nor prohibit reliance on protection elsewhere policies. As such, protection elsewhere policies are

> compatible with the Convention so long as they ensure that refugees defined by Art. 1 enjoy the rights set by Arts. 2–34 of the Convention.[27]

The 2022 Refugee Law Initiative Declaration on Externalisation and Asylum reaches a similar conclusion.

> Where third country arrangements extend to the provision of international protection by the receiving State, transferred asylum seekers must receive ongoing protection against refoulement in the receiving State. If the transferring State is a party to the Refugee Convention, then the full set of international law guarantees contained therein must be respected in law and practice in the receiving State, even if the receiving State is not a party to the Convention.[28]

As a result, the destination state should ensure that respect for all rights contained in the Refugee Convention is present in the partner state.

At a minimum, I argue that a number of 'core rights' essential for the realisation of protection in any asylum state contained in the Refugee Convention must be available in the third country. That is to say, non-discrimination (Article 3), freedom of religion (Article 4), the right to education (Article 22), the right to work (Article 17), access to housing (Article 21), freedom of movement (Article 26), access to courts of law (article 16) and the right to identity documents (Article 28). This view is drawn from the approach of the High Court of Australia in the *M70* case, finding that there were obligations owed well beyond non-refoulement, including treatment at least as favourable as nationals with respect to employment, education and religious freedom.[29] In the exceptional circumstances where a partner state has not acceded to the Refugee Convention, equivalent rights must in law and practice allow refugees to receive protection in accordance with the Refugee Convention regime.[30]

3.3 The law of jurisdiction

As a matter of human rights and refugee law, jurisdiction forms the crucial threshold requirement for the application of obligations to the conduct of a state, from which an assessment of direct international responsibility for violations can flow. In *Al-Skeini*, the ECtHR explained:

> 'Jurisdiction' under Article 1 is a *threshold criterion*. The exercise of jurisdiction is a *necessary condition* for a Contracting State to be able to be held responsible for acts or omissions imputable to it which give rise to an allegation of the infringement of rights and freedoms set forth in the Convention.[31]

A finding of jurisdiction denotes factual or legal power over an individual or territory that reaches the threshold of engaging a state's international obligations.[32] Where jurisdiction is not triggered, a state owes no legal obligations towards asylum seekers and refugees subject to transnational asylum polices.[33] In some cases, the question of jurisdiction will be straightforward where, for example, a partner state exercises territorial jurisdiction over asylum seekers and refugees. In other cases, the issue of jurisdiction will be complex, involving a detailed assessment of whether the conduct of a destination state is sufficient to trigger extraterritorial jurisdiction.

In other words, the application of human rights treaties is demarcated by the term 'jurisdiction'.[34] A finding of jurisdiction relies on a particular level of authority or control over persons or territory.[35] A finding of jurisdiction does not establish a breach of an international obligation but rather gives rise to an investigation of whether a breach has occurred, from which flows the international responsibility of that state.[36]

Human rights law jurisdiction deals with the vertical relationship between the state and the individual rather than the horizontal relationship between states. This relationship is enlivened by effective control and continues until the point it expires.[37] In this sense, human rights law jurisdiction is 'primarily about delineating as appropriately as possible the pool of persons to which a state ought to secure human rights'.[38] Jurisdiction is primarily territorial and presumed throughout a state's territory. However, jurisdiction can occur extraterritorially on the basis of a number of exceptions where a state exercises control beyond its borders, at times giving rise to situations of shared jurisdiction.[39]

3.3.1 Territorial jurisdiction

Territoriality, in almost all cases, triggers the human rights law jurisdiction of a state.[40] This basic premise is important to this book as, in many cases, transnational asylum policies take place on the territory of a partner state. In general, the territorial state has jurisdiction over asylum seekers and refugees.[41] There is a very narrow set of circumstances in which jurisdiction is divorced from territoriality.

First, jurisdiction may be displaced under a territorial lease, 'a treaty or other bilateral instrument that establishes sovereign rights for one state on the territory of another'. The US's use of Guantanamo Bay raises questions about Cuba's territorial jurisdiction. Under a 1903 lease agreement, the US exercises 'complete control and jurisdiction' over the area, while Cuba retains 'ultimate sovereignty'.[42] The lease agreement affords *complete* jurisdiction to the US, and the Cuban Supreme Court held in 1934 that Guantanamo Bay legally amounts to a foreign territory beyond Cuban jurisdiction.[43] In general, the use of territorial leases in this field is limited, and, in any case, any contemporary agreement ceding complete jurisdiction between states is unlikely.[44]

Second, situations of military occupation, war or rebellion may call into question the jurisdiction of the territorial state. In *Ilaşcu and Others v Moldova and Russia*, for example, the ECtHR considered the application of residents of the Moldavian Republic of Transdniestria (MRT), a separatist region in Moldova supported by the Russian government. The court found that while jurisdiction is presumed throughout a state's territory:

> .... this presumption may be limited in exceptional circumstances, particularly where a State is prevented from exercising its authority in part of its territory. That may be as a result of military occupation by the armed forces of another State which effectively controls the territory concerned, acts of war or rebellion, or the acts of a foreign State supporting the installation of a separatist State within the territory of the State concerned.[45]

The court went on to hold that although the Moldovan government lacked effective control over the area, Moldova retained jurisdiction over the MRT with regard to its positive obligations under the ECHR.[46] *Ilaşcu* demonstrates that there is a high bar for the displacement of the presumption of territorial jurisdiction.[47]

3.3.2 Extraterritorial jurisdiction

The following provides an account of five bases or models of extraterritorial jurisdiction drawn from treaty body jurisprudence and the literature, with an indication of their likely application to situations of transnational asylum.[48] These five more-or-less recognised models, upon which a finding of extraterritorial jurisdiction may be based, are subject to normative evolution in this area. New models of jurisdiction may be added, or, more probably, emerging jurisprudence will expand or contract the scope of different bases for jurisdiction. The models comprise effective control over territory, authority or control over persons, the public powers approach, the functional approach and the effects doctrine.

3.3.2.1 The spatial model: effective control over territory

Effective control over a defined territory is a well-established basis for extraterritorial jurisdiction under human rights law. Wilde defines this 'spatial model' in the following terms:

> Extraterritorial jurisdiction understood spatially conceives obligations as flowing from the mere fact of territorial control – if the state controls

territory, the state is responsible for what happens in it. Whether or not the state has title over the territory, and/or its presence there is or is not lawful, is irrelevant.[49]

The Human Rights Committee's General Comment No 31 refers to control over persons rather than over territory.[50] However, in *Legal Consequences of the Construction of a Wall in the Occupied Palestinian Territory* (*Wall case*), the International Court of Justice (ICJ) found the ICCPR to be 'applicable in respect of acts done by a state in the exercise of its jurisdiction outside its own territory'.[51] There is thus solid ground for the proposition that a state will be bound by its obligations under the ICCPR where it exercises effective control over an area extraterritorially.

In its general comment on Article 2, the Committee Against Torture confirmed that the Convention Against Torture and Other Cruel, Inhuman or Degrading Treatment (CAT) applies in a broad set of situations where a state party exercises 'directly or indirectly, in whole or in part, de jure or de facto effective control'.[52] In its 2006 Conclusions and Recommendations to the US, the committee restated that '"territory under the state party's jurisdiction" applies to all persons under the effective control of its authorities, of whichever type, wherever located in the world'.[53]

Under the ECHR, extraterritorial jurisdiction may be established where a Council of Europe state has *de jure* or *de facto* control over territory in another state. *Loizidou v Turkey* concerned the land rights of a Cypriot national prevented from returning to her property in Northern Cyprus under the control of Turkish troops. The ECtHR found that Turkey, which had militarily intervened in Cyprus, exercised effective control over the area where the applicant's land lay, thus triggering jurisdiction under the ECHR.[54] The spatial model of jurisdiction was further developed in *Cyprus v Turkey*, which also dealt with Turkey's occupation in Northern Cyprus. The court concretely extended effective control over the territory to include the administration of that area, not merely the acts of military forces.[55]

In *Bankovic and Others v Belgium and Others*, the ECtHR employed a general international law test of extraterritorial jurisdiction to find that aerial bombardment did not reach the threshold of effective control over territory.[56] In *Issa and Others v Turkey*, the Court returned to its approach to extraterritorial jurisdiction developed in the Cyprus cases, finding that Turkey lacked the requisite level of 'overall control' to import jurisdiction under the ECHR.[57]

The ECtHR has also used a 'decisive influence' standard in determining whether control over territory reaches the threshold to trigger jurisdiction. Thus far, this test has only been used in situations of military occupation or secession, but the court has noted that other factors, including economic and political support, may be relevant.[58] In *Ilaşcu*, the Court held that Russia exercised extraterritorial jurisdiction over the Transdniestria region on the following grounds:

> the 'MRT', set up in 1991–1992 with the support of the Russian Federation, vested with organs of power and its own administration, remains under the effective authority, or *at the very least under the decisive influence*, of the Russian Federation, and in any event that it survives by virtue of the military, economic, financial and political support given to it by the Russian Federation.[59]

The Court thus appeared to lower the test from effective control to a standard of 'decisive influence' in finding that Russia exercised jurisdiction in the MRT.

However, the decisive influence test should not be understood as replacing the effective control standard. Rather, decisive influence is a question of *attribution* for the purposes of jurisdiction, establishing whether the actions of the authority acting extraterritorially can be considered the conduct of the state. In subsequent cases, the ECtHR has found that a state's decisive influence over extraterritorial authorities indicates its effective control over that particular territory. In *Catan and Others v Moldova and Russia*, also concerning the MRT, the court walked back the decisive influence standard, finding a 'strong indication that Russia exercised effective control *and* decisive influence over the "MRT" administration'.[60]

In the 2015 case of *Chiragov and Others v Armenia*, which concerned Armenia's role in the Nagorno–Karabakh conflict, six refugee applicants claimed Armenia exercised effective control over the Azerbaijani district of Lachin from which they fled. The Court, in finding that Armenia exercised decisive influence over the Nagorno–Karabakh Republic (NKR) authorities in the disputed region, thus held:

> ...the Republic of Armenia, from the early days of the Nagorno–Karabakh conflict, has had a significant and decisive influence over the 'NKR', that the two entities are highly integrated in virtually all important matters and that this situation persists to this day. In other words, the 'NKR' and its administration survives by virtue of the military, political, financial and other support given to it by Armenia which, consequently, exercises effective control over Nagorno–Karabakh and the surrounding territories, including the district of Lachin. The matters complained of therefore come within the jurisdiction of Armenia for the purposes of Article 1 of the Convention.[61]

The leading recent case on extraterritorial jurisdiction, *Al-Skeini*, does not refer to the decisive influence standard. [62] Other authors have sought to rely on decisive influence in the context of cooperative asylum policies; however, this test cannot be relied upon in isolation from the more stringent effective control standard.[63]

In sum, control over territory as a basis for extraterritorial jurisdiction requires that a state party to the ICCPR, CAT or ECHR have effective control over a defined territory. The key question is factual – whether the state exercises control lawfully or unlawfully is irrelevant.[64]

The spatial model of extraterritorial jurisdiction appears to be of limited significance to transnational asylum policies. While a situation akin to the US territorial lease over Guantanamo Bay would clearly amount to the requisite level of control over a territory, it is less certain that control over other asylum processing centres would reach the required threshold to trigger jurisdiction. It remains an open question whether Australia's role in the running of the Regional Processing Centres (RPCs) in Nauru and Papua New Guinea, for example, amounts to effective control over *territory*. One may argue that Australian involvement in instigating, funding, contracting staff and advising staff reaches the threshold of effective control over the defined area of the Nauru and Manus Island RPCs. However, a destination state merely instigating or financing a centre does not amount to an exercise of jurisdiction as the law currently stands, though it may still result in derived responsibility for aiding or assisting in the case of breach of an international obligation.[65] As discussed below, establishing extraterritorial jurisdiction in this context is more straightforward on the basis of authority or control over persons.

3.3.2.2 The personal model: authority or control over persons

The most relevant basis for establishing extraterritorial jurisdiction is authority or control over an individual. This model has clear significance for transnational asylum policies, particularly in the context of extraterritorial processing, as destination states may exercise physical control over individuals seeking asylum.[66]

The Human Rights Committee has confirmed that authority or control over asylum seekers or refugees forms the basis for extraterritorial jurisdiction. A number of scholars have identified the Human Rights Committee decision in *Lopez Burgos* as an early example of the personal model of jurisdiction under the ICCPR. Uruguay's arrest and detention of one of its citizens in Buenos Aires brought the author (Sergio Lopez Burgos) within the authority and control of Uruguay.[67]

The Committee Against Torture has also confirmed that extraterritorial jurisdiction includes situations where a state party exercises, directly or indirectly, *de facto* or *de jure* control over persons in detention.[68] In *JHA v Spain*, which concerned an individual complaint relating to the maritime interception and subsequent detention by Spanish authorities of asylum seekers and migrants in Mauritania under a bilateral agreement, the committee stated:

> the State party maintained control over the persons on board the *Marine I* from the time the vessel was rescued and throughout the identification and repatriation process that took place at Nouadhibou. In particular, the State party exercised, by virtue of a diplomatic agreement concluded with Mauritania, constant *de facto* control over the alleged victims during their detention in Nouadhibou.[69]

The Committee thus found that Spain's jurisdiction was triggered from the moment of towing *Marine I* until the release from detention of the vessel's passengers, extending Spanish jurisdiction from international waters into Mauritanian territory.

A particularly relevant element of the Committee's decision is its consideration of the Spain–Mauritania bilateral agreement. The Committee indicated that the existence of the agreement increased the level of control over the passengers of *Marine I*. The basis of this reasoning is not explicit: on the one hand, the Committee may be asserting Spain's *de facto* control over the passengers was guaranteed by the agreement; on the other hand, the committee may be suggesting that the agreement gave Spain *de jure* authority to effect control over the individuals.[70]

The ECtHR has developed three strands of jurisprudence on authority or control over persons as a basis for extraterritorial jurisdiction, discussed separately below: the acts of diplomatic and consular agents, aircraft and vessels flying under the flag of the state, and the use of force or other physical power or control by state agents acting abroad.

First, the acts of diplomatic and consular agents may amount to authority and control over individuals, such as to trigger jurisdiction. This basis is drawn directly from general international law, which carves out sovereign entitlements for diplomatic and consular relations between states.[71] Thus, the court has consistently recognised:

> instances of the extraterritorial exercise of jurisdiction by a State include cases involving the activities of its diplomatic or consular agents abroad and on board aircraft and ships registered in, or flying the flag of, that State. In these specific situations, customary international law and treaty provisions have clearly recognised and defined the extraterritorial exercise of jurisdiction by the relevant State.[72]

In the 1965 case of *X. v Germany*, the European Commission on Human Rights dismissed as manifestly unfounded the application of a German citizen expelled from Morocco with, he claimed, the connivance of German consular officials. However, the Court did recognise:

> Whereas, in certain respects, the nationals of a Contracting State are within its 'jurisdiction' even when domiciled or resident abroad; whereas, in particular, the diplomatic and consular representatives of their country of origin perform certain duties with regard to them which may, in certain circumstances, make that country liable in respect of the Convention.[73]

In *WM v Denmark*, the commission considered the application of an East German national who entered the Danish embassy in Berlin seeking negotiations with Deutsche Demokratische Republik (DDR) authorities to leave the country. The Danish ambassador called the DDR police, who subsequently arrested and detained the applicant. The commission found that the conduct of the Danish ambassador amounted to 'an exercise of authority over the applicant to an extent sufficient to bring him within the jurisdiction of the Danish authorities'.[74]

In the 2004 UK Court of Appeal case of *'B' and Others v Secretary of State for the Foreign & Commonwealth Office*, the applicants were minor asylum seekers who escaped detention in Western Australia and sought asylum in the British consulate in Melbourne. The Court of Appeal did not question whether the conduct of the British consular staff could trigger jurisdiction, but rather whether it had in the concrete case. With direct reference to *WM v Denmark*, the Court of Appeal found:

> We are content to assume (without reaching a positive conclusion on the point) that while in the Consulate the applicants were sufficiently within the authority of the consular staff to be subject to the jurisdiction of the United Kingdom for the purpose of Article 1 (of the ECHR).[75]

Such decisions should be understood with reference to the concept of jurisdiction under general international law, as well as human rights law notions of authority and control over persons. On the basis of this caselaw, diplomatic staff may exercise jurisdiction over asylum seekers and refugees in a state's embassies and consulates.

Second, jurisdiction extends However, as discussed below, this does not mean that the act of applying for a visa triggers ECHR jurisdiction. to aircraft and vessels flying under the flag of the state. In *Xhavara v Italy and Albania*, the ECtHR found that Italy's ECHR obligations were enlivened, notwithstanding the fact that the Italian agents did not board the applicants' vessel.[76]

Hirsi Jamaa and Others v Italy also concerned the maritime interdiction and return of asylum seekers and refugees by Italian naval forces to Libya under a bilateral treaty. The applicants, 11 Somalis and 13 Eritreans, were intercepted in a group of around 200 people on the high seas 36 nautical miles off Lampedusa, transferred to Italian ships, and returned to Tripoli.[77] The Italian government submitted that although the events had occurred on an Italian vessel, state authorities lacked 'absolute and exclusive control' over the applicants. The ECtHR rejected this argument, finding that flag ship jurisdiction under the law of the sea imported *de jure* control over the applicants:

> The Court observes that by virtue of the relevant provisions of the law of the sea, a vessel sailing on the high seas is subject to the exclusive jurisdiction of the State of the flag it is flying. This principle of international law has led the Court to recognise, in cases concerning acts carried out on board vessels flying a State's flag, in the same way as registered aircraft, cases of extra-territorial exercise of the jurisdiction of that State. Where there is control over another, this is *de jure* control exercised by the State in question over the individuals concerned.[78]

While the Court in *Medvedyev and Others v France* and *Xhavara* was not explicit in basing a finding of ECHR jurisdiction on flag state jurisdiction, both judgments can be read this way. In *Hirsi*, the court was clear in establishing the *de jure* responsibility of Italy by virtue of its use of flag state vessels, rather than solely because of *de facto* control over the applicants.

Third, the use of force or other physical power or control by state agents acting abroad can trigger jurisdiction in a range of situations, including military occupation, detention, abduction and maritime interdiction. In the context of *military occupation*, the Court in *Isaak v Turkey* considered the killing of a Cypriot who was beaten to death during a demonstration against Turkish occupation of Northern Cyprus in the United Nations buffer zone. Mr Isaak's widow brought the application against Turkey for a failure to investigate her husband's death. In its admissibility decision, the court found that Turkish–Cypriot policemen had taken part in the beating of Mr Isaak and thus found that he had been under the authority or effective control of Turkey through its agents.[79]

Issa concerned the application of Iraqi nationals whose relatives had allegedly been ill-treated and summarily executed by Turkish forces carrying out a six-week military operation in Iraq. The facts of this case, therefore, concerned not a full-fledged occupation, but rather a temporary operation in Iraqi territory by Turkish forces. The Court found Turkey lacked the requisite level of 'overall control' over the area of Iraq to import jurisdiction. However, the Court did state:

> a State may also be held accountable for violation of the Convention rights and freedoms of persons who are in the territory of another State but who are found to be under the former State's *authority and control through its agents operating* – whether lawfully or unlawfully – in the latter State.[80]

Further, the Court indicated that had Turkish forces taken the victims into custody before executing them, the applicant's relatives would have fallen under Turkey's jurisdiction based on the soldiers' authority and control over them.

Moreover, in *Pad and Others v Turkey* and *Solomou and Others v Turkey*, the *shooting* of individuals by Turkish forces amounted to the necessary authority and control giving rise to a finding of jurisdiction.[81] Milanovic, in a recent chapter on the ECtHR's practice on the personal model, concluded:

> The bottom-line of this approach is that whenever the military forces of a European state capture any individual, the Convention will apply by virtue of the personal conception of Article 1 jurisdiction as authority and control over individuals, no matter where that individual is located.[82]

Physical power and control need not include the use of force *per se*. In the context of detention, the Court in *Al-Saadoon and Mufdhi v the United Kingdom* considered the detention of Iraqi nationals by British soldiers, who claimed that their transfer to Iraqi authorities would expose them to a real risk of the death penalty, to be in violation of Article 2 of the ECHR. The court found that British forces had total and exclusive control over both the area and individuals detained, thus engaging the obligations of the UK under the Refugee Convention.[83] Moreover, in *Hassan v the United Kingdom*, the ECtHR found that 'the exercise of physical power and control over the person in question' is decisive for establishing jurisdiction.[84]

In *Öcalan v Turkey*, the Court found that extraterritorial *abduction* by state agents triggers jurisdiction. In an analogous factual situation to the Human Rights Committee communication of *Lopez*, Turkish agents arrested Mr Öcalan, the alleged leader of the Workers' Party of Kurdistan (PKK) movement, in Kenya, with the cooperation of local authorities. The court found that the direct physical control exerted over the applicant reached the threshold of jurisdiction, as the applicant was effectively under Turkish authority.[85]

Finally, in relation to *maritime interdiction, Medvedyev* and *Hirsi* confirm that authority or control over persons triggering jurisdiction extends to control of a vessel on the high seas. *Medvedyev* concerned the maritime interdiction by French armed commandos of a ship sailing under the Cambodian flag, the *Winner*. French agents boarded the ship and arrested and detained the crew on board under suspicion of drug smuggling. The Court found that this action enlivened France's jurisdiction as its agents:

> … exercised full and exclusive control over the *Winner* and its crew, at least *de facto*, from the time of its interception, in a continuous and uninterrupted manner until they were tried in France, the applicants were effectively within France's jurisdiction.[86]

In *Hirsi*, the court found that Italian authorities had *de facto* control over the applicants from the moment of interception until the moment of transfer, as:

> … the events took place entirely on board ships of the Italian armed forces, the crews of which were composed exclusively of Italian military personnel. In the Court's opinion, in the period between boarding the ships of the Italian armed forces and being handed over to the Libyan authorities, the applicants were under the continuous and exclusive *de jure* and *de facto* control of the Italian authorities. Speculation as to the nature and purpose of the intervention of the Italian ships on the high seas would not lead the Court to any other conclusion.[87]

The personal model of jurisdiction is of particular importance to transnational asylum policies, which often involve a level of physical control over asylum seekers and refugees.

Clearly, the degree of authority or control over an individual required to trigger jurisdiction varies from case to case. The above jurisprudence demonstrates that *interception* operations involving direct contact with an individual reach the threshold of jurisdiction. Direct forms of interception, such as seizing, boarding, turning back a vessel, detention on a vessel or transferring asylum seekers over to third countries, will trigger jurisdiction.[88] Less direct forms of interdiction, such as warning, blockading, re-routing or ordering a change of course, may lack the direct personal control required to reach the threshold of jurisdiction; however, this may shift as new jurisprudence emerges.[89]

Third country processing involving the detention of asylum seekers will engage the jurisdiction of destination states where state agents are directly involved in exerting authority or control over an individual, such as detaining, guarding or using force.[90] More uncertain are situations where state agents do not exercise direct control, such as the provision of funding, training and equipment to the partner state or the engagement of private contractors to administer detention. Such situations at the outer limits of current conceptions of jurisdiction are addressed under the functional model below.

3.3.2.3 The hybrid model: exercise of public powers

The public power model is a hybrid of the spatial and personal models explored above. The approach was introduced by the ECtHR in *Al-Skeini*, a case concerning the killing of six Iraqi nationals in military operations conducted by British soldiers in Basra following the 2003 invasion of Iraq. The Court, emphasising the exceptional nature of the case, found that the UK had 'assumed authority and responsibility' for that region of the country on the following basis:

> the Court has recognised the exercise of extraterritorial jurisdiction by a Contracting State when, through the consent, invitation or acquiescence of the Government, it exercises all or some of the public powers normally to be exercised by that Government. Thus, where, in accordance with custom, treaty or other agreement, authorities of the Contracting State carry out executive or judicial functions on the territory of another State, the Contracting State may be responsible for breaches of the Convention thereby incurred, as long as the acts in question are attributable to it rather than to the territorial State.[91]

Following *Al-Skeini*, three criteria must be met to trigger jurisdiction on this basis. Firstly, the destination state must exercise public powers normally carried out by the territorial government. The ECtHR in *Al-Skeini* did not define public powers, referring only to 'executive or judicial functions', but as migration control is a 'core law enforcement task and exclusive sovereign prerogative', it clearly falls under the public powers category.[92] This first criterion lowers the threshold required of the spatial model, requiring that the acting state exercise 'elements of governmental authority' on the territory of another state, clearly a lesser standard than effective control.[93] In *Al-Skeini*, the UK and US had assumed responsibility for security in Iraq, a public power normally exercised by the territorial government.

Secondly, cooperation must take place 'in accordance with custom, treaty or other agreement', requiring the existence of a formal agreement for the purposes of migration control between the parties. This criterion requires a certain level of *entitlement* on the part of the destination state, acknowledging the general international law basis of the approach. Importantly, however, this authorisation to act on partner state territory need not be regulated by a binding compact; the term 'other agreement' clearly encompasses non-binding agreements commonly employed in the course of transnational asylum.[94] Nevertheless, the requirement that there exists an international agreement rules out certain forms of cooperation falling under the public powers model. Clearly, any exercise of powers without the 'consent, invitation or acquiescence' of the territorial state is ruled out.[95] Moreover, ad hoc cooperation arrangements lacking a formal agreement will necessarily fall outside of the public powers approach.

Third, and perhaps most importantly, following *Al-Skeini*, the public powers approach requires that the conduct in violation of an international obligation be attributable to the destination state and *not* the partner state. Attribution, discussed at length in the following chapter, refers to the designation of conduct to a state for the purposes of international responsibility.[96] This exclusive approach to attribution imports a high bar, requiring either that the conduct of the destination state be clearly more decisive than the conduct of the partner state or that the conduct of the partner state be attributable to the destination state.[97]

In *Al-Skeini*, British soldiers exercised 'authority and control' over the individuals killed only in the context of the UK's exercise of public powers in Southern Iraq. Once it is established, a state is exercising public powers extraterritorially, and the standard to establish authority and control is effectively lowered. The Court thus found:

> ... the United Kingdom (together with the United States) assumed in Iraq the exercise of some of the public powers normally to be exercised by a sovereign government. In particular, the United Kingdom assumed authority and responsibility for the maintenance of security in south-east Iraq. In these exceptional circumstances, the Court considers that the United Kingdom, through its soldiers engaged in security operations in Basra during the period in question, exercised authority and control over individuals killed in the course of such security operations, so as to establish a jurisdictional link between the deceased and the United Kingdom for the purposes of Article 1 of the Convention.[98]

In the 2014 case of *Jaloud v The Netherlands*, the Court appeared to alter the public powers approach slightly. *Jaloud* concerned the death of an Iraqi national at a Dutch checkpoint in south-eastern Iraq in 2004. The Court found that the Netherlands exercised jurisdiction despite not formally acting as an 'occupying power' in Iraq under United Nations Security Council Resolution 1483.[99] Jurisdiction was triggered on the basis of a combination of the Netherlands mandate to restore conditions of stability and security as part of the stabilisation force in Iraq and its purpose of asserting authority and control over persons passing through the checkpoint.[100] Having found that the Netherlands exercised jurisdiction over Mr Jaloud at the time of his death, the Court went on to find that the Dutch authorities failed to carry out an adequate investigation into the applicant's death, as required by Article 2 of the ECHR.[101]

The sovereign nature of the tasks of migration control and asylum processing renders the public powers basis of some relevance to transnational asylum policies. Indeed, some authors have voiced strong support for the public power approach as an extra avenue to challenge deterrence policies.[102] However, the ECtHR's emphasis on the 'exceptional circumstances' of *Al-Skeini* and the apparent requirement that conduct be attributable *exclusively* to the destination state make the public powers approach problematic in practice. As a result, there is likely only a very narrow set of circumstances in which destination state jurisdiction will be triggered based on the public powers model.

3.3.2.4 The functional model

A further basis for extraterritorial jurisdiction has been termed the *functional* model. Unlike jurisdiction on the basis of control over persons or territory, the functional model conceives of 'authority or control' as equating to *power* over an individual, whether that power be physically manifest or otherwise. A functional model of jurisdiction may resolve those cases in a grey zone where the question of jurisdiction is not straightforward.[103] Clearly, any such functional model will be of vital importance to situations of transnational asylum as, in some cases, destination states attempt to avoid enlivening obligations.

Gammeltoft-Hansen first put forward the concept of a functional approach to extraterritorial human rights jurisdiction, arguing:

> What matters is not a generalised test of personal or geographic control, but rather the specific power or authority assumed by the state acting extraterritorially in a given capacity… jurisdiction in this sense flows from the *de facto* relationship established between the state and the individual through the act itself, or the potential of acting.[104]

In short, therefore, 'power entails obligations',[105] where there is a 'direct and immediate link' between the conduct of the state and the individual.[106] In *Al-Skeini*, the concurring opinion of Judge Bonello argued for a functional approach where:

> Jurisdiction means no less and no more than 'authority over' and 'control of'. In relation to Convention obligations, jurisdiction is neither territorial nor extraterritorial: it ought to be functional.[107]

The functional approach may be used to address 'hard' cases that fall outside the scope of existing legal bases. The personal model generally requires physical power and control over the person in question, while a functional model may encompass situations where a state holds authority or control over a person that falls short of physical or coercive control. As Taylor argues in relation to the limits of the personal model, 'it seems highly unlikely that an individual would be regarded as being subject to the effective control of a state unless an agent of that state is exercising some kind of coercive power over that person'.[108]

A functional approach has been employed in a number of contexts by courts and tribunals willing to extend the normative scope of the law of jurisdiction to hold states responsible for extraterritorial conduct. First, where a state exercises a high level of *incidental power* over an individual, jurisdiction may be triggered. In *Brothers to the Rescue*, the Inter-American Commission on Human Rights found Cuba held jurisdiction over victims in two civilian aeroplanes shot down by Cuban authorities in international airspace.[109] In contrast, the ECtHR in *Bankovic* rejected the assertion that North Atlantic Treaty Organization (NATO) member states exercised extraterritorial jurisdiction when carrying out airstrikes in the Federal Republic of Yugoslavia. In *Bankovic*, therefore, the power to kill was insufficient to trigger jurisdiction.[110] However, the ECtHR has taken a decidedly functionalist turn since *Bankovic*, with a number of judgments finding jurisdiction on the basis of more or less incidental events.[111] The key point here is that when a state acting extraterritorially wields the power to violate the most basic rights of an individual in a concrete situation, jurisdiction is triggered.

Second, the functional approach focuses on the *particular relationship* between the state and the individual. In *Al-Skeini*, for example, the power of the UK forces to 'safeguard the rights of individuals' gave rise to jurisdiction.[112] The Human Rights Committee in its jurisprudence has placed emphasis on the relationship of power exercised by the state over an individual, notably in *Lopez Burgos*, discussed above.[113] The nature of the relationship between state and individual may vary; however, a common thread here is the power of the state to directly impact an individual's rights. In its recent general comment on the right to life, the Human Rights Committee suggested a test of 'impact' for the application of the right to life obligation, where a person's life is affected in a 'direct and reasonably foreseeable manner' extraterritorially.[114]

Third, an *accumulation* of factors can amount to the exercise of authority or control. The Human Rights Committee and Committee Against Torture have recently put forward a cumulative approach in which a number of individual elements combined to trigger jurisdiction. In 2014, the Committee Against Torture found Australia held jurisdiction over asylum seekers detained at the Manus Island RPC.

> All persons who are under the effective control of the State party, because inter alia they were transferred by the State party to centres run with its financial aid and with the involvement of private contractors of its choice, enjoy the same protection from torture and ill-treatment under the Convention .[115]
>
> *(Articles 2, 3 and 16)*

In 2017, the Human Rights Committee similarly held:

> the Committee recalls the 'power or effective control' standard for jurisdiction laid out in its general comment 31 and considers that the significant levels of control and influence exercised by the State party over the operation of the offshore regional processing centres, including over its establishment, funding and service provided therein, amount to such effective control.[116]

Both committees appear to conclude that Australian jurisdiction is established by virtue of its multifaceted *power* over the individuals offshore. The committees do not state whether all these elements are required or whether one would be sufficient to trigger jurisdiction. While the precise scope of the level of control required remains unclear, these findings are a clear shift towards a functional model of extraterritorial jurisdiction based on cumulative factors falling short of direct physical control.

In these three situations, then, a functional approach may establish the requisite level of control or authority, either independent of or in combination with the other, more established bases. The fundamental question here centres on whether the state exercises a sufficient degree of *power* over an individual to reach the 'authority or control' standard. While the terms 'power', 'authority' and 'control' are similar, they are not synonymous. 'Authority' in this context connotes a *de jure* right to wield influence over a person, while 'control' relates to the *de facto* situation of physical custody over an individual. The term 'power', employed from time to time by treaty bodies in this context,[117] offers a holistic parameter by which to assess both the capacity of the state to impact an individual's rights and the nature of the relationship between the state and the individual.

Not all extraterritorial conduct affecting an individual brings that person within the jurisdiction of a destination state. For example, pre-departure screenings carried out by immigration liaison officers in partner states have a clear impact on the rights of asylum seekers and refugees denied embarkation. However, current authority holds that such screenings do not enliven the jurisdiction of destination states.[118] Furthermore, the power to grant a visa at an embassy has been found not to enliven the obligations of the state. In *MN and Others v. Belgium*, testing whether a Syrian family's humanitarian visa application at the Belgian embassy in Beirut triggered the state's human rights law obligations, the ECtHR held that the process of applying for a visa in person did not bring the applicants within ECHR jurisdiction, declaring the case inadmissible.[119] The Grand Chamber held that the relationship between the applicants and the Belgian state was not such as to bring the family within Belgium's ECHR jurisdiction. The Court went on to confirm that neither the physical presence of asylum seekers in an embassy or consulate nor the handling of a visa application by national authorities trigger

ECHR jurisdiction, in and of themselves. With respect to their presence at the embassy, the Court found:

> at no time did the diplomatic agents exercise de facto control over the applicants. The latter freely chose to present themselves at the Belgian Embassy in Beirut, and to submit their visa applications there – as indeed they could have chosen to approach any other embassy; they had then been free to leave the premises of the Belgian Embassy without any hindrance.[120]
>
> *(para 118)*

In the similar case of *X and X v Belgium*, the Court of Justice of the European Union (CJEU) considered whether a Syrian family's application for a humanitarian visa submitted to the Belgian embassy in Beirut triggered Belgium's non-refoulement obligations under the EU Charter. The court found that the issuing of humanitarian visas falls outside the scope of EU law and is a question for national authorities.[121]

A clear problem with the functional approach is that its outer limits are inchoate. An insistence upon too low a threshold of power, authority or control may lead to states avoiding contact with asylum seekers and refugees altogether. For example, a state agent interviewing a refugee for resettlement or a visa is in a position of power with respect to that person. Yet a finding that such an interview amounts to an exercise of jurisdiction would likely deter states from offering resettlement places or humanitarian visas in the first place.[122]

In sum, a functional approach based on power over persons requires further elaboration and development. Previous jurisprudence has focused on direct, physical control exercised by the state, while the possibility of non-physical authority has been overlooked. The concept of power is useful here as it encompasses a range of scenarios where a state has the capacity to directly impact the rights of an individual. Power clearly extends to *incidental exercises* of authority and control, such as the ability to kill an individual. Similarly, a number of *relationships* between state and individual, such as nationality, are encompassed by the concept. Finally, and perhaps most crucially, the concept of power considers the situation holistically, weighing all the elements of influence wielded by the state over an individual in a given case. This *cumulative* approach may prove crucial to the development of extraterritorial jurisdiction in situations of transnational asylum and other areas of transnational cooperation.

3.3.2.5 The effects model

Finally, jurisdiction may be triggered via the extraterritorial effects doctrine, an approach stemming from general international law prohibiting the use of one state's territory to the detriment of another state.[123] While the extraterritorial effects doctrine is relatively well established in other branches of international law, notably environment law and financial law, there has been relatively little consideration given to the approach in the context of human rights law.[124] Given the 'infancy' of the doctrine in human rights jurisprudence, the precise scope of its application needs clarification, but in general terms, a state's jurisdiction is enlivened where domestic conduct directly causes effects in another state in breach of its obligations.[125] In contrast to the other models for extraterritorial jurisdiction discussed above, the effects doctrine does not require the presence of state agents exercising control over territory or authority or control over persons.

Hitherto, the effects doctrine has primarily been applied in three areas: cross-border environment harms, domestic economic subsidies affecting the interests of other states and transnational surveillance.[126] Perhaps the classic conception of the effects doctrine is the cross-border river pollution leading to the *Trail Smelter Arbitration*, in which a Canadian company released sulphur into the Columbia river flowing into the US.[127] In the context of human rights law, the ECtHR in *Andreou v Turkey* considered the shooting of the applicant by Turkish military forces from Turkish-controlled Northern Cyprus into a United Nations buffer zone. In its admissibility decision, the court invoked the effects doctrine, finding:

> in exceptional circumstances, the acts of Contracting States which produce effects outside their territory and over which they exercise no control or authority may amount to the exercise by them of jurisdiction within the meaning of Article 1 of the Convention. ... even though the applicant sustained her injuries in territory over which Turkey exercised no control, the opening of fire on the crowd from close range, which was the direct and immediate cause of those injuries, was such that the applicant must be regarded as "within [the] jurisdiction" of Turkey.[128]

Kessing has suggested that the 'direct and immediate' standard set out by the Court in *Andreou* could be met in extraterritorial drone operations carrying out targeted killings.[129] Gammeltoft-Hansen has suggested:

> extraterritorial effects jurisdiction may come about as a result of actions taking place within a state's own territory, leading to human rights violations on the territory of another state. In contrast to bases for extraterritorial jurisdiction involving effective control over individuals or territory, there is thus no requirement that the responsible state itself acts extraterritorially.[130]

More ambitiously, Altwicker has proposed a new 'effective control over situation' standard drawing on the effects doctrine. Under this proposal, where a state exercises effective control over a situation extraterritorially, it will owe human rights law obligations to individuals whose rights are directly interfered with as a result.[131]

Applied to transnational asylum, the effects doctrine may have the potential to enliven obligations for more passive forms of cooperation, notably destination state funding or equipping of partner state authorities. The key question of the doctrine, however, is the direct and immediate standard referred to in *Andreou*. While direct causation for cross-border harms between neighbouring states is often relatively easy to establish, much of the cooperation in the context of transnational asylum may be considered too remote to trigger effects jurisdiction. In sum, therefore, the effects model has the potential to impact transnational asylum approaches but needs further judicial development.

3.3.3 Shared jurisdiction

Historically, jurisdiction was considered an exclusive test, an 'all or nothing proposition' dictating that only one state could be internationally responsible for a particular area or group of individuals.[132] However, the possibility of two or more states holding concurrent or *shared jurisdiction* over territory or individuals is now recognised in the literature and jurisprudence. This development is a key plank of this study, concerned as it is with the responsibility of multiple states involved in cooperation. In this context, shared jurisdiction may arise where a partner state exercises territorial jurisdiction and a destination state exercises jurisdiction extraterritorially over, for example, an asylum processing centre. Moreover, two states may share jurisdiction when conducting joint operations on the high seas.

Jurisprudence recognises, explicitly or implicitly, situations of shared jurisdiction. In *Ilaşcu*, the ECtHR confirmed that Moldova retained jurisdiction over the MRT, although the government lacked effective control over the secessionist area, and Russia simultaneously exercised extraterritorial jurisdiction.[133] Similarly, in *Öcalan*, Turkey was found to exercise jurisdiction over the applicant notwithstanding Kenya's presumed territorial jurisdiction.[134] More recently, in a string of cases dealing with the rendition of persons from European countries to US interrogation sites, the Court has acknowledged the shared jurisdiction of the territorial European state and the extraterritorial conduct of the US.[135] In *JHA v Spain*, Mauritania retained territorial jurisdiction but allowed Spain to exercise control over migrants detained under a bilateral agreement.[136] In *Namah v Pato*, the Papua New Guinean Supreme Court addressed both the national and Australian governments in ruling the detention of asylum seekers at the Manus Island RPC unconstitutional, implying the shared jurisdiction of both states.[137]

At the systemic level, shared human rights law jurisdiction fits neatly with an integrative approach to general international law, where situations of shared jurisdiction are commonplace. In fact, most accepted categories of extraterritorial jurisdiction countenance situations of shared jurisdiction.[138] For example, the nationality principle allows a state to assert jurisdiction over its nationals on the territory of another state for the purposes of criminal prosecution, creating a situation of joint or competing jurisdiction.[139]

Finally, there is broad scholarly support for the existence of shared jurisdiction.[140] Gammeltoft-Hansen notes that the 'proliferation of auxiliary legal bases for jurisdiction makes coexisting and competing jurisdictional claims unavoidable'.[141] Similarly, Klug and Howe suggest that extraterritorial jurisdiction 'must be regarded as concurrent to *de jure* territorial jurisdiction'.[142]

However, a number of qualifications to the concept of shared jurisdiction are noteworthy. First, extraterritorial jurisdiction does not necessarily import the full catalogue of obligations under a human rights treaty. Such a standard would require that a state party be capable of securing *all* rights under the given instrument whenever jurisdiction is triggered.[143] Instead, the obligations owed to an individual in a given situation may be *modulated* in accordance with the degree of authority and control exercised by the state in a given situation. This position is borne out in the jurisprudence. In its advisory opinion on *Legal Consequences of the Construction of a Wall in the Occupied Palestinian Territory* (*Wall advisory opinion*), the ICJ found that Israel owed obligations extraterritorially only to the extent to which competence had been transferred to Palestinian authorities.[144] Neither the Human Rights Committee nor the Committee Against Torture have suggested that jurisdiction imports an obligation to protect the totality of rights. Moreover, the jurisprudence of both treaty bodies strongly suggests that the applicability of obligations may be adapted in light of the degree of authority and control exercised and the concrete situation. For example, the Human Rights Committee has found that an applicant seeking the issue of a passport has been found to be within the jurisdiction of state authorities for that particular purpose.[145]

The ECtHR in *Bankovic* applied an all-or-nothing approach to jurisdiction, finding that Refugee Convention rights cannot be 'divided and tailored'. However, the Court in both *Al-Skeini* and *Hirsi* found that extraterritorial jurisdiction requires a state to secure only those rights relevant to the situation of the individual.[146] This modulated approach to obligations is an important ancillary principle in situations of transnational asylum, as it increases the number of scenarios in which shared jurisdiction will be in play.

Second, in many current third country arrangements, there exists an *asymmetry* of obligations whereby the partner state owes fewer obligations to asylum seekers and refugees than the destination state. The most obvious disparity in obligations occurs where the partner state is not a party to the

Refugee Convention.[147] In other cases, the territorial state may not be a party to the CAT, ICCPR or ECHR. However, very rarely are partner states not party to any of these core instruments. Irrespective of whether the partner state is a party to the Refugee Convention or other human rights instruments, there may be no national asylum system to access the rights contained in these instruments.

Third, as noted above, in exceptional cases the territorial state will be unable to exercise jurisdiction, leaving *exclusive jurisdiction* to the state acting extraterritorially. In general, however, where a state carries out deterrence policies on the territory of a third state, the territorial state's jurisdiction will also be triggered.

3.3.4 Jurisdiction in transnational asylum

Questions of territorial, extraterritorial and shared jurisdiction are pivotal to the legality of any transnational asylum arrangement. With respect to territorial jurisdiction, the jurisdiction of the hosting state will be presumed to exist even where that state exercises no control over an extraterritorial processing facility, subject only to a very narrow set of circumstances in which jurisdiction will not be found.

With respect to extraterritorial jurisdiction, I have conceptualised five possible bases: control over territory, authority or control over persons, the exercise of public powers, an emerging functional approach based on power over an individual and the effects model.

The spatial model of extraterritorial jurisdiction on the basis of control over territory is most relevant to situations of military occupation and control over an area by armed forces.[148] This model may be applicable to situations where a destination state is involved in operating a processing centre on the territory of a partner state. However, effective control over territory is a high threshold, and it is uncertain that control over an asylum processing centre would trigger jurisdiction.

The personal model of jurisdiction holds particular relevance for transnational asylum policies, particularly in the context of third country processing. Jurisdiction is triggered where the acting state exercises physical power and control over an individual, though the degree of power, authority or control required to trigger jurisdiction will depend on the circumstances.[149] Direct forms of control are likely to amount to jurisdiction, while indirect or 'contactless' policies are less likely to trigger the obligations of the destination state.

The public powers model is a hybrid of the spatial and personal models, where a state exercises public powers normally exercised by the territorial government under an agreement and holds 'authority and control' over the individual claiming a violation of their rights. As transnational asylum involves destination states carrying out immigration functions of territorial states, this basis of jurisdiction may be in play in situations of interdiction and third country processing. However, the requirement that any violations be exclusively attributable to the state acting extraterritorially makes this possibility remote.

The functional model encompasses a range of scenarios where a state has the *power* to directly impact the rights of an individual. While yet to establish a robust normative footing, the caselaw suggests this basis for jurisdiction extends to *incidental exercises* of authority and control, such as the ability to kill an individual. Similarly, particular *relationships* between state and individual are encompassed by the concept (e.g., nationality). Lastly, a *cumulative* approach considering multiple contributions of a state to a violation may prove crucial to the development of extraterritorial jurisdiction in situations of transnational asylum and other areas of international cooperation.

Finally, the effects model has the potential to impact transnational asylum approaches. On face value, the effects doctrine may enliven obligations for more passive forms of cooperation, notably destination state funding or equipping of partner state authorities; however, the approach needs elaboration and application in the field of migration control to better define its scope.

3.4 The applicability of European Union law

Where a transnational asylum arrangement involves the EU through its agencies, notably the EU Asylum Agency (EUAA) or Frontex, or one of its member states, the applicability of EU law to any such cooperation is an additional legal question. The EU Charter is not territorially bound and thus applies wherever EU agencies operate (in the case of Frontex or the EUAA) or wherever EU law is applied (in the case of member states).[150] EU Charter obligations thus track EUAA and Frontex activities in third countries, on the basis of the concept of 'portable responsibility'.[151] Where the EU Charter applies, EU agencies and EU member states are, *inter alia*, extraterritorially bound to respect the principle of non-refoulement (Articles 4 and 19(2)) and the right to an effective remedy (Article 47).

On this basis, some authors argue that EU asylum law would apply extraterritorially, on the basis of EU competency under Article 78 of the Treaty of the Functioning of the European Union (TFEU) and the concept of 'portable responsibility' extending the effect of EU law extraterritorially.[152] Other authors suggest that third country processing or protection would not trigger the application of EU asylum law on the basis of the distinction between non-refoulement and the asylum procedure itself.[153]

Key elements of the EU asylum *acquis*, including the Asylum Procedures Directive (APD) and Reception Conditions Directive, are territorially bound. Article 3(1) of the APD provides:

> This Directive shall apply to all applications for international protection *made in the territory*, including at the border, in the territorial waters or in the transit zones of the Member States.[154]

Article 3(1) of the Reception Conditions Directive provides:

> This Directive shall apply to all third-country nationals and stateless persons who make an application for international protection *on the territory*, including at the border, in the territorial waters or in the transit zones of a Member State.[155]

It is clear from the *rationae loci* of both instruments that they apply only once a person has reached EU territory.[156] As a result, these instruments would seem *only to apply within the EU's territorial boundaries* and would not be enlivened through the extraterritorial processing of asylum claims by an EU member state.[157] In contrast, the Qualification Directive, like the Refugee Convention, contains no territorial delimitation and would seem to apply extraterritorially, providing uniform rules relating to who qualifies for international protection even when applied in a third country. [158]

EU member states may attempt to carve out 'extraterritorial zones' within their territories to circumvent the application of the EU asylum law. Given the plain wording of the APD, or Reception Conditions Directive, however, these would ultimately be likely to fail legal tests.[159] The territorial nature of the EU asylum *acquis* leads us to the conclusion that where a member state carries out pre-entry processing or third country processing outside EU territory, the standards and safeguards set out in the EU asylum *acquis* will not bind that state, with the exception of the Qualification Directive. Of course, where an EU member state exercises jurisdiction over asylum seekers at such a facility, the ECHR would apply.

Nevertheless, EU member states bound by these instruments are required to allow asylum seekers to file a protection claim and remain on EU territory until a final decision is reached. Thus, EU member states are generally precluded from transferring a person already present to a third state outside the EU, unless certain exceptions apply. The designation of a partner state as a *safe third country* can relieve EU member states of the obligation to process an asylum claim within the territory. Article 38 of the APD allows for the return of an asylum seeker to a particular country on the basis that they can access a fair and efficient asylum procedure and receive international protection in accordance with the Refugee Convention there. Article 38 further requires that EU member states set down national rules limiting the operation of the safe third country concept to those situations where there is a *connection between the asylum seeker and the third country* and it would be reasonable for that person to go to that country. While this connection requirement is not reflected in general international law, its current implications for EU member states are clear: asylum seekers can only be transferred under the safe third country concept where there exists a sufficient connection between the individual and the third state.

Finally, presently Article 35 of the APD provides for the possibility to transfer an asylum seeker to a third country where they have already received international protection under the *first country of asylum* concept. The first country of asylum concept allows for the return of a person to a country where they have already been recognised as a refugee or otherwise enjoy international protection. Article 35 requires that the individual:

(a) has been recognised in that country as a refugee and he or she can still avail himself/herself of that protection, or
(b) otherwise enjoys sufficient protection in that country, including benefiting from the principle of non-refoulement, provided that he or she will be readmitted to that country.[160]

Article 35 thus requires either formal recognition of the individual as a refugee in compliance with the standards set out in the Refugee Convention or for the individual to 'otherwise enjoy sufficient protection' treatment by the third state that meets the minimum human rights standards contained in the ECHR and the EU Charter.[161]

3.5 The law of state responsibility

Following the previous analysis of jurisdiction as the threshold for triggering obligations, this chapter proceeds on the basis that attempted transnational asylum policies may, in some cases, breach human rights and refugee law obligations. This section thus employs the doctrine of state responsibility to understand and allocate international responsibility for breach of those obligations.

The law of state responsibility provides a general framework of rules governing responsibility for breaches of primary rules of international law.[162] The doctrine operates as a residual system of 'secondary rules' that *lies behind* the 'primary rules' provided by specialised branches of law.[163] The law of state responsibility is not concerned with the content of primary rules nor whether a violation has occurred, but rather which state – or states – bear responsibility for the breach.[164]

3.5.1 Shared responsibility

Shared responsibility under international law has been described as 'indistinct',[165] 'undeveloped' [166] and even 'disturbingly immature'.[167] Recent scholarly work and, to a lesser extent, jurisprudence have begun the work of filling in the gaps, exploring the growing number of situations involving multiple actors contributing to breaches of international obligations.[168] Cooperative asylum arrangements clearly call for an analysis of shared responsibility as they can involve two states contributing to breaches of obligations owed to asylum seekers and refugees. As the commentaries to the Articles on the Responsibility of States for Internationally Wrongful Acts (ARSIWA) point out:

> ... internationally wrongful conduct often results from the collaboration of several States rather than of one State acting alone. This may involve independent conduct by several States, each playing its own role in carrying out an internationally wrongful act. Or it may be that a number of States act through a common organ to commit a wrongful act. Internationally wrongful conduct can also arise out of situations where a State acts on behalf of another State in carrying out the conduct in question.[169]

Shared responsibility is a descriptive rather than legal term with no accepted definition. Nollkaemper and Jacobs define shared responsibility as comprising four elements: the presence of multiple actors, their contribution to a single harmful outcome, a lack of responsibility based on causation, and responsibility being allocated separately rather than collectively.[170] The separate, rather than collective, allocation of responsibility is counterintuitive given the term 'shared' responsibility but the fundamental point here is that the allocation of responsibility to one state *does not exclude* the responsibility of other contributing states.[171]

Nollkaemper defines shared responsibility as situations where 'a multiplicity of actors contributes to a single harmful outcome, and legal responsibility for this harmful outcome is distributed among more than one of the contributing actors'.[172] Den Heijer, writing about shared responsibility before the ECtHR, uses the term to describe 'all situations that deal with the allocation of responsibility... where multiple entities have contributed to an injury arising from an internationally wrongful act'.[173]

Within human rights law, scholarship in the past decade has addressed shared responsibility before the UN treaty bodies[174] and the ECtHR[175] and argued for a relational account focused on cooperation between actors.[176] Within the discrete field of international refugee law, shared responsibility has been considered in work analysing the principle of non-refoulement,[177] the role of Frontex in carrying out border control,[178] Italy–Libya cooperation on the Mediterranean,[179] Australia–Indonesia migration control cooperation,[180] third country asylum processing[181] and the Australia–Cambodia third country protection agreement.[182]

In a similar vein to the above definitions, shared responsibility is used here to refer to *a situation where multiple states contribute to a breach of an obligation they owe to asylum seekers or refugees*. More specifically, three forms of shared responsibility are considered in this study:

1. *concurrent responsibility*, where two states exercise jurisdiction over asylum seekers and refugees;
2. *joint responsibility*, where two states acting in concert exercise jurisdiction over asylum seekers and refugees;
3. *derived responsibility*, where one state aids and assists another state in carrying out an internationally wrongful act.

These three models of shared responsibility are discussed at length below.

3.5.1.1 Concurrent responsibility

The most likely way to establish responsibility in transnational asylum involves parallel findings of responsibility for conduct resulting in the same harm.[183] The term *concurrent* responsibility refers to multiple states causing harm in situations where 'each individual contribution in itself is sufficient to cause the harm, and the law considers each individual contribution as wrongful'.[184] Concurrent responsibility allows for separate findings of liability on the part of each state where the cooperative conduct satisfies the tests of attribution and breach on the part of *both* states.

Concurrent responsibility requires that both states exercise *jurisdiction* over the harmed individual.[185] For example, one can readily conceive a situation where a partner state exercises territorial jurisdiction over persons intercepted at sea, while the destination state simultaneously exercises extraterritorial jurisdiction. Where the destination state does not exercise jurisdiction, that state cannot be held directly responsible for subsequent breaches.

Cooperative conduct in concurrent responsibility must breach an international obligation of *both* states. Where both states are party to a particular treaty, such as the Refugee Convention or ICCPR, the breach requirement will be relatively straightforward as both states are bound by the same obligation. However, these obligations need not be identical. In situations where the cooperating states do not share the same treaty obligations, two possible solutions are available. First, the obligation may be drawn from a treaty to which the partner state is party. For example, a partner state may not be party to the CAT or ECHR but may nonetheless be bound by the prohibition against arbitrary detention by virtue of its ratification of the ICCPR. Second, in the absence of a relevant treaty obligation the obligation may be drawn from customary law.[186]

3.5.1.2 Joint responsibility

Joint responsibility involves the direct responsibility of two or more states for the same internationally wrongful act during a *concerted* course of cooperation. The emphasis here is on the *relationship* between the acting states, requiring consensual co-authorship of an internationally wrongful act. Article 47 of ARSIWA thus provides:

> Where several States are responsible for the same internationally wrongful act, the responsibility of each State may be invoked in relation to that act.

In practice, the distinction between concurrent and joint responsibility will be one of degree, as this study is already concerned with situations of interstate cooperation. However, joint responsibility only applies in situations where multiple states carry out the *same* internationally wrongful act. While the International Law Commission (ILC) commentaries refrain from defining this requirement in the abstract,[187] d'Argent usefully distinguishes between two situations of cooperative conduct to delimit the scope of joint responsibility. The 'A-type' situation is multiple state conduct resulting in several internationally wrongful acts. For example, one state transfers an asylum seeker to another state, where they are tortured. The first state's conduct is in violation of the principle of non-refoulement, while the second state's conduct breaches the prohibition against torture. In the 'B-type' situation, multiple states are responsible for the same internationally wrongful act where, for example, the common organ of two states pollutes a boundary river it is charged with managing.[188] Joint responsibility is confined to this latter, the 'B-type' scenario.

The ILC commentaries note three situations in which joint responsibility may apply. First, when multiple states cooperate via a *common organ*, the acts of the organ are attributable to each contributing state. Second, where two or more states undertake a *joint venture*, by 'carrying out together an internationally wrongful act in circumstances where they may be regarded as acting jointly in respect of the entire operation'. Third, joint responsibility may arise when one state *directs and controls* another in carrying out the same internationally wrongful act, drawing on Article 17 of ARSIWA.[189] The former two are of particular interest to the object of this study and are explored below.

The existence of a common organ is the clearest indicator of a situation of joint responsibility, as the harmful conduct of the organ will form the internationally wrongful act of contributing states. In its 1978 Report, the ILC concluded that the harmful conduct of a common organ is a case of 'parallel attribution of a single course of conduct to several States'.[190] Further, the *Case concerning certain phosphate lands in Nauru* (*Nauru* case) and the

Eurotunnel Arbitration case confirm that the conduct of a common organ will be attributable to each contributing state.[191]

The ICJ in the *Nauru* case centred on responsibility for the excessive mining of phosphate reserves on the island by the Administrative Authority established under the United Nations Trusteeships mandate. Australia, the UK and New Zealand were jointly designated as trustees, and the court found that the Administrative Authority lacked any international legal personality independent from the contributing states.[192] It follows from the *Nauru* case that any common organ cannot have a separate legal personality for its conduct to be jointly attributable to the constituting states.[193]

The Permanent Court of Arbitration (PCA) in the *Eurotunnel Arbitration* case considered the claim of damages from the Eurotunnel company due to the failures of the Intergovernmental Commission (IGC), a common organ initiated by France and the UK to supervise the Channel Tunnel between the two countries. Eurotunnel claimed that the IGC, through its constituting states, failed to adequately address the persistent problem of irregular migrants attempting to cross the channel from Calais, France, to reach the UK. The company claimed damages for the disruption of transport operations, damage to property and impact on staff morale caused by unauthorised migration. The PCA, in finding that each respondent state was responsible for the conduct of the ICG, stated:

> Of more significance is the IGC itself, which is "established to supervise, *in the name and on behalf of the two Governments*… The IGC is a joint organ of the two States, whose decisions require the assent of both Principals. If a breach of the Concession Agreement resulted from action taken by the IGC both States would be responsible accordingly.[194]

The European Commission on Human Rights case of *Hess v United Kingdom* concerned the solitary detention of Rudolph Hess by a common organ of the Allied powers, the military prison in Berlin–Spandau.[195] Although the facility was managed by four governors, each appointed by one of the four allied powers, the case was brought against the UK alone.[196] Somewhat confusingly, the commission found that the UK exercised joint *responsibility* over the prison, but ruled the complaint inadmissible on the basis that the UK lacked *jurisdiction* over the facility for the purposes of Article 1 of the ECHR. The commission thus found:

> … the joint authority cannot be divided into four separate jurisdictions and that therefore the United Kingdom's participation in the exercise of the joint authority and consequently in the administration and supervision of Spandau Prison is not a matter "within the jurisdiction" of the United Kingdom.[197]

It is likely this 1975 complaint would be decided differently today. Subsequent jurisprudence has developed the possibility of shared jurisdiction under the ECHR, whereby two states exercise control over an individual or territory simultaneously.[198]

In relation to transnational asylum, the establishment of a common organ for the purposes of migration control or asylum processing may conceivably bring cooperation within the scope of joint responsibility. In the Pacific, joint committees were envisaged in the bilateral MoUs between Australia and Nauru and Australia and Papua New Guinea. The Joint Advisory Committee for Nauru, for example, is described as:

> ... bilateral governance committee between the Republic of Nauru and the Commonwealth of Australia established under the terms of the Memorandum of Understanding to oversee the implementation and operation of regional processing arrangements in Nauru.[199]

An equivalent joint committee was envisaged in the MoU between Australia and Papua New Guinea but was never put into operation.[200] Moreover, Italy and Libya have reportedly set up a 'joint operations room' to coordinate cooperation on the prevention of people smuggling across the Central Mediterranean route.[201]

The question of when a cooperative body can be described as a common organ is left open by the ARSIWA.[202] D'Argent argues that the high threshold suggested by the commentaries requiring that states act jointly 'in respect of the entire operation' limits the application of Article 47 to a very narrow set of circumstances 'usually not present in regular situations of co-perpetration'.[203] It seems that the existence of a common organ giving rise to joint responsibility is indeed a very specialised circumstance, requiring a highly organised body created and managed by cooperating states for some substantial duration.

In the absence of a common organ, the difference between cooperation resulting in concurrent responsibility, on the one hand, and joint responsibility, on the other, will not always be clear. The distinction appears to lie in the *intensity* of cooperation between the two states. Joint responsibility requires a high level of concerted conduct between states that is attributable to each state. Thus, according to the commentaries to the ARSIWA:

> ... the situation can arise where *a single course of conduct* is at the same time attributable to several States and is internationally wrongful for each of them. It is to such cases that Article 47 is addressed.[204]

As den Heijer notes, joint responsibility requires multiple states to 'truly act in concert'.[205] In the *Oil Platforms Case*, Judge Simma, in his separate opinion, referred to the requirements of Article 47 in considering the role of Iran and Iraq in the laying of landmines and subsequent deleterious effects on commerce in the region.

> Article 47 would apply only if both Iran and Iraq were responsible for a given action – for instance, if Iran had carried out an attack against a ship engaged in treaty-protected commerce, *jointly planning and co-ordinating* the operation with Iraq.[206]

In *Saddam Hussein v Albania and twenty other states*, the Strasbourg Court found that cooperation between states fell below the level required to amount to joint responsibility. Saddam Hussein alleged that all Council of Europe members who took part in the 2003 invasion of Iraq were internationally responsible for his ill treatment following his handing over to Iraqi authorities by US forces. While the ECtHR struck out the application at the admissibility phase, on the basis that none of the respondent states exercised control over the territory where his treatment took place, the Court also noted that there was no evidence of international responsibility on the part of any of the respondent states. The Court emphasised that the application failed to detail links between the conduct of the US in arresting, detaining and handing over the applicant and the role of the respondent European states.[207]

In sum, joint responsibility arising from a joint venture requires intensive and concerted cooperation with respect to a particular policy or practice leading to the same internationally wrongful act.

3.5.1.3 Derived responsibility

Finally, state responsibility for wrongful acts in the course of an attempted transnational asylum arrangement may be shared on the basis of derived responsibility.[208] Within the ARSIWA, derived responsibility arises in Chapter 4, which concerns the international responsibility of a state in connection to the acts of another, 'principal' state. Derived responsibility is an indirect form of responsibility, in the sense it does not require attribution of a wrongful act on the part of the 'assisting' state.[209] Moreover, derived responsibility does not necessarily require jurisdiction over the victims of the wrongful act, thus opening up a finding of responsibility without the essential precondition for direct responsibility.

Derived responsibility falls under the umbrella of shared responsibility as it involves multiple states contributing to a wrongful act and being held internationally responsible for that conduct.[210] In contrast to concurrent and joint responsibility, derived responsibility arises where one state's involvement in the commission of a wrongful act of *another* state attracts international responsibility.[211] Of the three forms of derived responsibility under the ARSIWA, only aid and assistance under Article 16 are relevant to this study.[212]

Crucially, the ICJ has declared Article 16 reflects a customary rule of international law.[213] Article 16 provides:

A State which aids or assists another State in the commission of an internationally wrongful act by the latter is internationally responsible for doing so if:

a that State does so with knowledge of the circumstances of the internationally wrongful act, and
b the act would be internationally wrongful if committed by that State.

Article 16 contains three elements: *aid or assistance* from one state to another in carrying out a wrongful act; *knowledge* of the circumstances of the wrongful act and *common obligations* on behalf of both cooperating states with respect to the wrongful act.

Before analysing these three elements in depth, it is worth noting the increasing scholarly attention derived responsibility has received in relation to migration control and asylum policy. In 2003, Legomsky applied a 'complicity principle', including with reference to Article 16 of ARSIWA, to safe third country practices.[214] More recently, den Heijer has considered European aid or assistance in the context of extraterritorial migration control.[215] Giuffré argued for Italy's derived responsibility vis-à-vis cooperation with Libya in carrying out extraterritorial border controls, finding that 'the conditions posed by Article 16 ILC Articles appear to be fully met'.[216] Gammeltoft-Hansen and Hathaway applied Article 16 to situations of cooperative deterrence more generally, concluding that 'States that believe that the more diffuse forms of non-entrée involving no exercise of jurisdiction are thus necessarily immune from legal liability are thus proceeding with false confidence'.[217] Markard, in her article on the right to leave, suggested that EU member states could be 'complicit in internationally wrongful departure prevention by third countries'.[218] Similarly, Moreno-Lax and Giuffré raise the possibility of derived responsibility on the part of the EU and its member states in cooperating with Turkey and Libya on preventing departures.[219]

3.5.1.3.1 Aid or assistance

The first element of derived responsibility is the nature of the aid or assistance provided to the principal state by the assisting state. The phrase 'aids or assists' is left undefined by the ILC Commentaries, leaving its interpretation wide open.[220] Thus, 'there is no requirement that the aid or assistance should have been essential to the performance of the internationally wrongful act; it is sufficient if it *contributed significantly* to that act'.[221] Den Heijer suggests assistance must be that 'which enables another state, or which makes it materially easier for another state, to commit an international offence'.[222] The commentaries provide a number of examples of conduct that may amount to aid and assistance for the purposes of Article 16: the use of a state's territory to carry out a military attack, helping a state to avoid United Nations Security Council sanctions or the provision of 'material aid to a state that uses the aid to commit human rights violations'.[223]

Article 16 also includes a *nexus* requirement between the assistance given and the wrongful act, which requires that the aid and assistance be directly related to the wrongful act. During the development of the ARSIWA, one member of the ILC located complicity between direct and indirect participation in a wrongful act in the following terms:

> participation must be active and direct. It must not be too direct, however, for the participant then became a co-author of the offence, and that went beyond complicity. If, on the other hand, participation were too indirect, there might be no real complicity.[224]

Therefore, according to Nolte and Aust, there must be a particular nexus between assistance and the primary wrongdoing, as 'it is implausible that Article 16 should cover "aid or assistance" which is only remotely or "indirectly" related to an internationally wrongful act'.[225] Nonetheless, derived responsibility is not so direct as to come under the scope of joint responsibility. Joint responsibility requires that the conduct in breach of an obligation be attributable and wrongful on the part of both states. In contrast, derived responsibility requires no attribution of the principal wrongful act to the assisting state, and the giving of aid or assistance may be perfectly lawful.[226]

In relation to transnational asylum, the funding, equipping and training of partner states by destination states may well fall under the rather broad concept of aid and assistance. According to Markard in respect of the right to leave:

> If a third country prevents departure in violation of international norms, the provision of patrol boats for ship riders, the supply of equipment, training and funding for such operations and sharing information on the position of departing boats would clearly be contributing to the violation or significantly facilitating this violation.[227]

Clearly, a broad set of cooperation will meet the aid and assistance element of Article 16. However, the knowledge requirement, discussed below, imports a far stricter test.

3.5.1.3.2 Knowledge of the circumstances of the wrongful act

While Article 16 only refers to 'knowledge' of the circumstances of the wrongful act on the part of the assisting state, the ILC Commentaries clarify that aid or assistance must be given 'with a view to' the commission of the wrongful act. The phrase 'with a view to' appears to introduce a higher standard of *intention* on the part of the assisting state. According to the ILC Commentaries:

> A State is not responsible for aid or assistance under Article 16 unless the relevant State organ *intended*, by the aid or assistance given, to facilitate the occurrence of the wrongful conduct and the internationally wrongful conduct is actually committed by the aided or assisted State.[228]

Elsewhere, the commentaries use terms synonymous with intention, such as 'deliberately' and 'intended to', suggesting that Article 16 requires a level of knowledge approaching wrongful intent.[229] In relation to derived responsibility for aiding and assisting in human rights violations, the commentaries note:

> Where the allegation is that the assistance of a State has facilitated human rights abuses by another State, the particular circumstances of each case must be carefully examined to determine whether the aiding State by its aid was *aware of and intended to* facilitate the commission of the internationally wrongful conduct.[230]

What is striking here is the contrast between the text of Article 16, requiring knowledge on the part of the assisting state, and the Commentaries, which seem to require intent.[231] This disjoint reflects the diverging views of the ILC in drafting Article 16. As Aust explains, the question of intent in aid and assistance divided the Commission into two camps. One group considered that a standard of intent would 'nullify the scope of the article. No state would admit that it was helping another state to commit a wrongful act'.[232] The other group argued that a requirement of intent would solve the issue of the rule being otherwise overly broad.[233] Without a clear resolution, the final elucidation was left to the Commentaries.[234]

In the *Genocide Case*, the ICJ considered, by analogy, the question of intent under Article 16, stating that, at a minimum, the assisting state must be aware of the intent of the 'principal state'. The Court used Article 16 indirectly to consider the role of Serbia and Montenegro in assisting Republika Srpska, a non-state actor, in the commission of genocide.[235] Thus, the Court found:

> there is no doubt that the conduct of an organ or a person furnishing aid or assistance to a perpetrator of the crime of genocide cannot be treated as complicity in genocide unless at the least that organ or person acted knowingly, that is to say, in particular, was aware of the specific intent (*dolus specialis*) of the principal perpetrator.[236]

The finding of the ICJ suggests that the minimum knowledge standard in situations of aid and assistance is *knowledge of the intent of the principal state*. This seems to present a middle ground between knowledge of the circumstances of the wrongful act and clear intent. However, whether the ICJ's views are of general application is unclear, as the Court only considered the intent question by way of analogy and the case concerned the crime of genocide, which has a special intent element, *dolus specialis*.[237]

Various scholars have weighed in on the issue of knowledge and intent in Article 16. Graefrath, for example, argued that a strict intent requirement would make the rule 'unworkable' on the basis that:

> a requirement of intent would seriously narrow the scope of the norm because states will seldom act out of the specific motivation or desire to commit international wrongs, less still to violate human rights, but are more likely prepared to incur the occasional breach of certain obligations while being in the pursuit of some perceivably higher aim.[238]

Lanovoy also argues against a strict intent requirement on the basis that the general tenor of the ARSIWA does not include a 'fault' requirement. Thus, according to Lanovoy, reading in an intent standard to Article 16 would be 'at odds with the general framework of international responsibility of states'.[239] Relatedly, Palchetti suggests that the assisting state's conduct must be deliberate in nature, but not that the intention extends to sharing the ultimate aim of the principal state.[240] Jackson argues that knowing participation is sufficient, defined as 'something approaching practical certainty as to the circumstances of the principal wrongful act'.[241]

Moreno-Lax and Giuffré argue that an overly strict intent requirement would lead to no responsibility for conduct that falls short of an express desire to violate obligations, but nonetheless involves acceptance of the risk that wrongful acts will occur.[242] Gammeltoft-Hansen and Hathaway argue for a broader reading requiring 'constructive' knowledge on the part of the assisting state, with reference to the ECtHR decision in *Hirsi*.[243] However, that case concerned the primary rule of non-refoulement, which requires a considerably lower standard of knowledge than Article 16 ARSIWA.[244] In fact, the ECtHR has very rarely had recourse to Article 16. In *El-Masri v Former Yugoslav Republic of Macedonia*, an extraordinary rendition case, the Court heard the complaint of a German citizen detained by Macedonian authorities, handed over to US agents and flown to Afghanistan for interrogation.[245] The Court referred briefly to Article 16 in its deliberations but ultimately found Macedonia responsible for violations of the primary norms contained in Articles 3 and 5 of the ECHR.[246]

Nolte and Aust argue for a narrow interpretation of the intent requirement and point to three factors in support of this reading. First, interpretation should not discourage ordinary forms of international cooperation to encourage the 'stability and smooth running of the international system as a whole'.[247] However, transnational asylum cannot be described as ordinary cooperation in its current form. Second, the ARSIWA includes a further prohibition against aid and assistance in relation to situations in violation of *jus cogens* norms of international law. Article 41(2) proscribes aid and assistance after an internationally wrongful act breaching a *jus cogens* norm and assumes knowledge on the part of the assisting state, as 'it is hardly conceivable that a state would not have notice of the commission of a serious breach by another State'.[248] According to Nolte and Aust, this variation across three regimes lends itself to a narrow reading of Article 16, as embodying the general rule. Finally, according to Nolte and Aust, the several complicity rules drawn from primary obligations impose a lower standard on states in relation to the level of knowledge required than Article 16, with specific mention of the principle of non-refoulement. However, non-refoulement is a primary obligation that stands independent of any subsequent violation by another state. On these bases, Nolte and Aust argue that a 'systematic and functionalist' view of these three different regimes calls for a restrictive reading of Article 16 to complement the lower standards imposed by primary rules and peremptory norms.[249]

Thus, the required mental element of Article 16 appears to fall somewhere between knowledge of the circumstances of the internationally wrongful act and wrongful intent. Given the fuzziness of this definition, and the broad category of cooperation encompassed by transnational asylum, definitive conclusions are not possible in the abstract.

3.5.1.3.3 Common obligations of cooperating states

Finally, Article 16(b) imports an opposable obligations rule, requiring that the principal act be 'wrongful had it been committed by the assisting state itself'.[250] An obvious arising question is whether this element requires that the assisting and principal states have identical relevant primary obligations.[251] The answer must surely be in the negative, as the purpose of the rule is to ensure 'a state cannot do by another what it cannot do by itself'.[252] This position is confirmed by Crawford, who notes that Article 16(b) 'merely requires that the conduct in question would have been internationally wrongful if committed by the assisting state and says nothing about the identity of norms or sources'.[253]

Thus, as Gammeltoft-Hansen and Hathaway note, Article 16(b) allows for derived responsibility where the internationally wrongful act is unlawful to both the assisting and principal state on the basis of legal obligations drawn from different sources.[254] Moreover, as with general rules of attribution discussed above, conduct that breaches a customary rule will meet the opposable obligations requirement. For example, where a destination state owing treaty obligations against torture and inhuman and degrading treatment assists a partner state in carrying out such conduct, the partner state will be bound by the customary prohibition in the absence of any treaty obligations.[255]

3.5.2 State responsibility in transnational asylum

In situations of extraterritorial processing, questions of shared responsibility assume particular complexity. Under Article 4(1) ARSIWA, where two states cooperate in a third country processing arrangement involving both states' organs – such as immigration department agents – any wrongful act will normally be attributable to each state individually.

In exceptional situations, the conduct of a state organ may be attributable to another state under Article 6 of ARSIWA, as discussed in relation to funding, equipment and training above. In the Nauru and Papua New Guinea RPCs, Australian immigration officials were seconded to local immigration authorities in order to conduct refugee status determination (RSD) and, in the case of Nauru, to carry out merits review. Drawing on *X and Y*, one could argue that despite their secondment, the decisions of these agents are nevertheless attributable to Australia, particularly given Australia's clear interest in the operation of the RPCs. However, as distinct from the facts in *X and Y*, Australian officials were acting under Nauruan and Papua New Guinean law.

On the other hand, relying on *Drozd and Janousek*, one may maintain that the seconded officials were placed 'at the disposal of' Nauruan and Papua New Guinean state machinery and were not acting in their capacity as Australian agents. On this basis, their conduct would be attributable to the partner state and not the destination state. Thus, where agents from a destination state's immigration authorities are placed at the disposal of and under the exclusive direction and control of a partner state, the conduct of those agents is likely to be attributed to the partner state.

Questions of attribution are further raised where a destination state engages private actors to operate a processing site in cooperation with a partner state. Under Article 4(2) of ARSIWA, a private contractor may be a *de facto* state organ for the purposes of attribution where there exists a relationship of 'complete dependence' between the entity and the state. However, such a finding is unlikely. With reference to the three factors set out by ICJ jurisprudence, a contracting state does not create or organise a private company engaged to deliver services. For example, the Australian government did not create G4S or Broadspectrum for the purposes of delivering services at an RPC. Second, the provision of financial aid from the state to a private entity can indicate a relationship of dependence. The relationship between a state and a contractor certainly involves financial contributions but is unlikely to be decisive for the contractor's survival. While entering into a contract includes the provision of payment for services, multinational contractors are rarely entirely reliant on a single state for revenue, given their significant international operations.[256]

Finally, a private entity's strategic dependence on the state may lead to a finding of attribution. A private entity may be substantively dependent on the contracting government, which wields significant power in the terms and performance of the agreement, through reporting requirements and oversight.[257] However, the contractor is likely to have significant autonomy over the logistics of any asylum processing centre. Furthermore, all such contractors retain the autonomy to terminate their contractual agreement, which suggests a degree of independence incompatible with Article 4(2). Thus, the conduct of private contractors may be attributed to the contracting state in certain narrow circumstances. A private entity created for the purpose of carrying out third country processing, entirely dependent on the state for its survival and exclusively following its instructions, may well be characterised as a *de facto* state organ for the purposes of attribution.

Under Article 5 of ARSIWA, the conduct of private contractors may be attributed to the state where they are empowered by the law of that state to exercise governmental authority. The involvement of private contractors in third country processing is likely to amount to an exercise of governmental authority. Immigration control and asylum processing are traditionally the exclusive prerogative of the state and cannot be performed by private actors alone.[258] Both are intimately linked to sovereignty: immigration control concerns the state's capacity to regulate its borders, while asylum processing involves the state's procedure for affording international protection.

Doubt as to the meaning of 'empowered by the law' in Article 5 makes a clear finding problematic. On the one hand, one could argue that the contractual arrangements between a private entity and the state amount to a delegation of state powers to the private contractor. On the other hand, Article 5 may require the adoption of legislation or regulations specifically empowering the private contractor to carry out public functions at the third country processing site. While the terms of Article 5 clearly need further development, in my view the conduct of private contractors may well be attributable to a destination state on this basis. Given the clear governmental authority required to carry out third country processing and the public contracting of private entities to act as government proxies, there is a strong argument that the conduct of private contractors in operating a third country processing site will be attributable to a destination state.

Finally, under Article 8 of ARSIWA, the conduct of a private actor may be attributed to a state where it is acting under the direction or control of the state. The key question here is whether a contractual relationship between a destination state and a private actor can be characterised as one of direction or control in the sense of Article 8. Unlike a state-financed and controlled militia, such private actors have multiple sources of income and are able to terminate their contractual agreement with the state at any time. In sum, the factual relationship of direction or control between state and private actors is unlikely in this context, unless the relationship amounts to one of complete dependence.[259]

With respect to a breach, third country processing may fall into the category of concurrent or joint responsibility as the wrongful conduct may involve the breach of identical or distinct obligations. For example, where a jointly planned and operated third country processing centre exposes asylum seekers and refugees to arbitrary detention, the wrongful act will be attributable to both states. Equally, where transfer to a third country processing site amounts to *refoulement* in and of itself, states may be found responsible on an individual basis.

In sum, wrongful acts that occur in state-run pre-entry or third country processing centres will be attributable to both destination and partner states under Article 4(1) of ARSIWA, unless the conduct is solely imputed to the destination state in the narrow circumstances prescribed by Article 6. In third country processing arrangements involving private contractors, attribution is possible on the basis of a private actor functioning as a *de facto* state organ under Article 4(2), where a private actor is empowered by law to exercise governmental authority under Article 5, or where a private actor functions under the direction or control of the state under Article 8. Article 5 is the most likely avenue to attribution in relation to current practice. Finally, of course, where cooperation falls short of direct responsibility, a destination state may be held responsible on a derived basis.

Under Article 4(1) of ARSIWA, where two states cooperate in a third country protection arrangement involving state organs, any wrongful act will normally be attributable to each state individually. In general, only partner state agents are present in situations of third country protection, following the transfer of a refugee from destination state jurisdiction; however, where destination state agents accompany refugees transferred or, more likely, where private actors are engaged by the destination to state to act in a partner state, the analysis of attribution undertaken above in relation to third country processing is relevant.

Third country protection may fall into the category of concurrent or joint responsibility as the wrongful conduct may involve the breach of identical and distinct obligations. For example, where a jointly planned and implemented third country protection arrangement leads to breaches of obligations, wrongful acts may be attributable to both states. Equally, where transfer under a third country protection arrangement amounts to refoulement in and of itself, states may be found responsible on separate bases. Moreover, a scenario of derived responsibility is further possible, whereby a destination is held internationally responsible for aiding and assisting a partner state under Article 16.

3.6 Conclusions

This chapter sets the legal scene by framing transnational asylum in terms of international law. First, the chapter considered the structure of the Refugee Convention, which neither explicitly prohibits nor allows the transfer of asylum seekers and refugees between states. Beyond relatively narrow non-refoulement obligations, compliance with the integrative rights contained in Articles 2–34 of the Refugee Convention is fundamental to the merits of any transnational asylum arrangement.

Second, the chapter addressed the law of jurisdiction in detail as the decisive threshold for the application of human rights law obligations. With respect to extraterritorial jurisdiction, transnational asylum confirms the responsibility of destination states where they exercise authority or control over people or effective control over places in partner states. Shared jurisdiction is further vital for cooperation where two states simultaneously exercise jurisdiction, for example through joint asylum processing.

Third, the chapter addressed aspects of EU law relevant to transnational asylum. While the EU Charter applies wherever EU law is applied and governs the extraterritorial conduct of EU agencies, most of the EU asylum *acquis* is territorially bound, suggesting that an EU member state carrying out extraterritorial processing will not presently be bound by the EU asylum *acquis*, with the exception of the Qualification Directive.

Fourth, the chapter sets out applicable rules of state responsibility, on the basis that attempted transnational asylum policies may breach human rights and refugee law obligations. This final part of the chapter addressed situations of shared responsibility for the breach of obligations in the course of cooperative asylum policies, spanning concurrent, joint and derived responsibility.

Notes

1 For a full account, see James C Hathaway, *The Rights of Refugees under International Law* (2 edn, Cambridge University Press 2021) 173–311.

2 Refugees transferred from Nauru to Cambodia were first flown to Darwin before onwards passage to Phnom Penh. Monique Failla, 'Outsourcing obligations to developing nations: Australia's refugee resettlement agreement with Cambodia' (2016) 42 Monash University Law Review 638, 655–6.
3 Hathaway, *The Rights of Refugees under International Law* 175–86.
4 UNHCR, *The Refugee Convention, 1951: The Travaux Preparatoires Analysed, with a Commentary by Dr Paul Weis* (1995).
5 Hathaway, *The Rights of Refugees under International Law* 187.
6 Hathaway, *The Rights of Refugees under International Law* 190–2.
7 See, for example, art 7(1).
8 See, for example, art 4.
9 See, for example, arts 15 and 17.
10 See, for example, art 33.
11 Jens Vedsted-Hansen, 'The asylum procedures and the assessment of asylum requests' in Vincent Chetail and Céline Bauloz (eds), *Research Handbook on International Law and Migration* (Edward Elgar 2014) 269.
12 The Michigan Guidelines on Protection Elsewhere (2006) 28 Michigan Journal of International Law para 11.
13 *T.I. v The United Kingdom* App no 43844/98 (ECtHR, 7 March 2000) 15 (emphasis added).
14 *Hirsi Jamaa and Others v Italy* App no. 27765/09 (ECtHR, 23 February 2012) para 129.
15 *Plaintiff M70/2011 v. Minister for Immigration and Citizenship; and Plaintiff M106 of 2011 v. Minister for Immigration and Citizenship*, [2011] HCA 32 (High Court of Australia, 31 August 2011) para 220 per Keifel J. See further Michelle Foster, 'Responsibility Sharing or Shifting? "Safe" Third Countries and International Law' (2008) 25 Refuge 66.
16 Michelle Foster, 'The Implications of the Failed "Malaysian Solution": The Australian High Court and Refugee Responsibility Sharing at International Law' (2012) 13 Melbourne Journal of International Law 21–2.
17 *K.R.S. v the United Kingdom* App no 32733/08 (admissiability decision) (ECtHR, 2 December 2008); *MSS v Belgium and Greece* App no 30696/09 (ECtHR [GC], 21 January 2011); *Hirsi Jamaa and Others v Italy*; and *Warda Osman Jasin et al v Denmark* CCPR/C/114/D/2360/2014 (Human Rights Committee, 25 September 2015).
18 See, for example, *Üner v the Netherlands* App no 46410/99 (ECtHR, 18 October 2006); and *Maslov v Austria*, App no 1638/03 (ECtHR [GC], 23 June 2008).
19 The Michigan Guidelines on Protection Elsewhere para 8.
20 The Michigan Guidelines on Protection Elsewhere para 8 (emphasis added).
21 The Michigan Guidelines on Protection Elsewhere.
22 Foster, 'The Implications of the Failed "Malaysian Solution": The Australian High Court and Refugee Responsibility Sharing at International Law'.
23 UNHCR, *Summary conclusions on the concept of 'Effective Protection' in the context of secondary movements of refugees and asylum seekers (*Lisbon Expert Roundtable, 9–10 December 2002) para 15(b).
24 Stephen H Legomsky, 'Secondary Refugee Movements and the Return of Asylum Seekers to Third Countries: The Meaning of Effective Protection' (2003) 15 International Journal of Refugee Law 567, 620.
25 Michelle Foster, 'Protection Elsewhere: The Legal Implications of Requiring Refugees to Seek Protection in Another State' (2006) 28 Michigan Journal of International Law 223.

26 UNHCR, *Bilateral and/or Multilateral Arrangements for Processing Claims for International Protection and Finding Durable Solutions for Refugees* (2016) para 9(f)(i).

27 The Michigan Guidelines on Protection Elsewhere para 1.

28 Refugee Law Initiative Declaration on Externalisation and Asylum (2022) 34 International Journal of Refugee Law 114 (2022) para 24.

29 *Plaintiff M70/2011 v. Minister for Immigration and Citizenship; and Plaintiff M106 of 2011 v. Minister for Immigration and Citizenship*, [2011] HCA 32 (High Court of Australia 31 August 2011). See also The Michigan Guidelines on Protection Elsewhere and Foster, 'The Implications of the Failed "Malaysian Solution": The Australian High Court and Refugee Responsibility Sharing at International Law'.

30 UNHCR, *Legal considerations on the return of asylum-seekers and refugees from Greece to Turkey as part of the EU-Turkey Cooperation in Tackling the Migration Crisis under the safe third country and first country of asylum concept* (2016); Refugee Law Initiative Declaration on Externalisation and Asylum para 24.

31 *Al-Skeini and others v United Kingdom* App no 55721/07 (ECtHR, 7 July 2011) para 13 (emphasis added).

32 Marko Milanovic, 'From Compromise to Principle: Clarifying the Concept of State Jurisdiction in Human Rights Treaties' (2008) 8 Human Rights Law Review 411, 417.

33 An absence of jurisdiction does not rule out a finding of state responsibility. See International Law Commission, *Draft Articles on Responsibility of States for Internationally Wrongful Acts, with commentaries* (Yearbook of the International Law Commission, Volume II, 2001) arts 16, 17 and 18.

34 Hugh King, 'The Extraterritorial Human Rights Obligations of States' (2009) 9 Human Rights Law Review 521.

35 Milanovic, 'From Compromise to Principle: Clarifying the Concept of State Jurisdiction in Human Rights Treaties' 417; Samantha Besson, 'The Extraterritoriality of the European Convention on Human Rights: Why Human Rights Depend on Jurisdiction and What Jurisdiction Amounts to' (2012) 25 Leiden Journal of International Law 857, 860.

36 Aurel Sari, 'Untangling Extra-Territorial Jurisdiction from International Responsibility in Jaloud v. Netherlands: Old Problem, New Solutions?' (2015) 53 Military Law and the Law of War Review 287.

37 Besson, 'The Extraterritoriality of the European Convention on Human Rights: Why Human Rights Depend on Jurisdiction and What Jurisdiction Amounts to' 862–3. Besson argues: 'The relational nature of jurisdiction between a subject and the authority needs to be stressed, as it corresponds to the relational nature of human rights between a right-holder and a duty-bearer'.

38 Maarten den Heijer and Rick Lawson, 'Extraterritorial Human Rights and the Concept of "Jurisdiction"' in Malcolm Langford and others (eds), *Global Justice, State Duties: The Extraterritorial Scope of Economic, Social, and Cultural Rights in International Law* (Cambridge University Press 2013) 163.

39 *Al-Skeini v United Kingdom* para 131; *Ilaşcu and Others v Moldova and Russia* App no 48787/99 (ECtHR, 8 July 2004) para 312; *Hirsi Jamaa and Others v Italy* paras 71–2. See also Besson, 'The Extraterritoriality of the European Convention on Human Rights: Why Human Rights Depend on Jurisdiction and What Jurisdiction Amounts to' 876.

40 Territory comprises a state's land, territorial sea and airspace. ICCPR art 2(1); CAT art 2; ECHR art 1; and *Assanidze v Georgia* App no 71503/01 (ECtHR [GC], 8 April 2004) paras 139–41.

41 According to Wouters and den Heijer:

> Specifically, under human rights law, the presumption is generally recognised that States must be considered both competent and able to fulfil their human rights obligations throughout their territorial jurisdiction, implying that States may be under a positive duty to prevent human rights violations from occurring within their territories, even when other States are involved in the conduct giving rise to the violation'.
>
> Kees Wouters and Maarten Den Heijer, 'The Marine I Case: a Comment' (2010) 22 International Journal of Refugee Law 1, 11.

42 *Agreement Between the United States and Cuba for the Lease of Lands for Coaling and Naval stations*, 23 February 1903, US-Cuba Treaty Series no 418 art 3. See further Harold Hongju Koh, 'America's Offshore Refugee Camps' (1994) 29 University of Richmond Law Review 139; and Azadeh Dastyari, *United States Migrant Interdiction and the Detention of Refugees in Guantánamo Bay* (Cambridge University Press 2015).

43 *In re Guzman & Latamble* (1934) 7 Ann. Dig. (I.L.R.) 112. See further Michael J Strauss, 'Cuba and State Responsibility for Human Rights at Guantanamo Bay' (2012) 37 Southern Illinois University Law Journal 533.

44 For a proposal for territorial leasing in mass influx situations, see Terje Einarsen, 'Mass Flight: The Case for International Asylum' (1995) 7 International Journal of Refugee Law 551.

45 *Ilaşcu and Others v Moldova and Russia* para 312. See further *Loizidou v Turkey* App no 15318/89 (ECtHR, 18 December 2006) (references omitted).

46 The Court noted:

> where a Contracting State is prevented from exercising its authority over the whole of its territory by a constraining *de facto* situation, such as obtains when a separatist regime is set up, whether or not this is accompanied by military occupation by another State, it does not thereby cease to have jurisdiction within the meaning of Article 1 of the Convention over that part of its territory temporarily subject to a local authority sustained by rebel forces or by another State'.
>
> *Ilaşcu and Others v Moldova and Russia* para 333.

47 Of course, in situations of occupation or war, it is open to states to derogate from non-absolute obligations under human rights law instruments. In *Assanidze v Georgia* at para 142 the ECtHR noted:

> But for the presumption [of territorial jurisdiction], the applicability of the Convention could be selectively restricted to only parts of the territory of certain States Parties, thus rendering the notion of effective human rights protection underpinning the entire Convention meaningless'.

See further *Öcalan v Turkey* App no 46221/99 (ECtHR, 12 May 2005) para 93. In relation to the ICCPR, see *Mohammed Alzery v Sweden* Communication no 1416/2005 (Human Rights Committee, 10 November 2006) para 11.6.

48 For detailed accounts on extraterritorial jurisdiction in this context, see Maarten den Heijer, *Europe and Extraterritorial Asylum* Maarten (Bloomsbury, 2012); and Thomas Gammeltoft-Hansen, *Access to Asylum: International Refugee Law and the Globalisation of Migration Control* (Cambridge University Press, 2011).

49 Ralph Wilde, 'Triggering State Obligations Extraterritorially: The Spatial Test in Certain Human Rights Treaties' (2007) 40 Israel Law Review 503, 508.

50 Human Rights Committee, *General comment no. 31: The nature of the general legal obligation imposed on States Parties to the Covenant*, CCPR/C/21/Rev.1/Add.13, 26 May 2004 para 10.

51 *Legal Consequences of the Construction of a Wall in the Occupied Palestinian Territory* ICJ GL No 131 (2004) para 111.
52 Committee Against Torture, *General comment No. 2 on the implementation of article 2 by States parties* CAT/C/GC/2 (2007) para 16.
53 Committee Against Torture, *Conclusions and Recommendations, United States of America* CAT/C/USA/CO/2 (25 July 2006) para 15 (emphasis added).
54 According to the Court in Loizidou v Turkey at para 56:

'The responsibility of a Contracting Party may also arise when as a consequence of military action – whether lawful or unlawful – it exercises effective control of an area outside its national territory. The obligation to secure, in such an area, the rights and freedoms set out in the Convention derives from the fact of such control whether it be exercised directly, through its armed forces, or through a subordinate local administration'

(emphasis added)

See also Cyprus v Turkey App no 25781/94 (ECtHR, 10 May 2001).
55 *Cyprus v Turkey* para 77; Ralph Wilde, 'The extraterritorial application of international human rights law on civil and political rights' in S. Sheeran and N. Rodley (eds), *Routledge Handbook of International Human Rights Law* (London and New York: Routledge 2013) 643; and Wilde, 'Triggering State Obligations Extraterritorially: The Spatial Test in Certain Human Rights Treaties' 516.
56 *Bankovic and Others v Belgium and Others* App no 52207/99 (ECtHR, 12 December 2001) para 75.
57 *Issa v Turkey* App no 31821/96 (ECtHR, 16 November 2004) para 75.
58 *Catan and Others v Moldova and Russia* App nos. 43370/04, 8252/05 and 18454/06 (ECtHR, 19 October 2012) para 107; and *Chiragov and others v Armenia* App no 13216/05 (ECtHR, 16 June 2015) para 169.
59 *Ilaşcu and Others Moldova and Russia* para 392 (emphasis added).
60 *Catan and Others v Moldova and Russia* para 122 (emphasis added).
61 *Chiragov and others v Armenia* para 186.
62 Thus:

the obligation to secure, in such an area, the rights and freedoms set out in the Convention, derives from the fact of such control, whether it be exercised directly, through the Contracting State's own armed forces, or through a subordinate local administration'.

Al-Skeini v United Kingdom para 138.

63 According to Moreno-Lax and Giuffre: '"decisive influence" constitutes, it is posited, a form of indirect but nonetheless effective control that amounts "jurisdiction" under Article 1 ECHR, thus triggering the responsibility of Member States under the Convention in case of human rights violations'. Violeta Moreno-Lax and Mariegiulia Giuffré, 'The Rise of Consensual Containment: From "Contactless Control" to "Contactless Responsibility" for Migratory Flows' in S Juss (ed), *Research Handbook on International Refugee Law* (Elgar Elgar, 2019) 106.
64 *Issa v Turkey* para 71; and Milanovic, 'From Compromise to Principle: Clarifying the Concept of State Jurisdiction in Human Rights Treaties' 423.
65 Anna Liguori, 'Some Observations on the Legal Responsibility of States and International Organizations in the Extraterritorial Processing of Asylum Claims' (2016) 25 The Italian Yearbook of International Law Online 135, 149.
66 Gammeltoft-Hansen and Hathaway concur, providing:

the personal control jurisprudence is an especially valuable means of challenging some critical forms of cooperation-based non-entrée under which the role of the extraterritorial state in interdiction or enforcement can be characterised as amounting to de facto control over the refugees themselves.

Thomas Gammeltoft-Hansen and James C Hathaway, 'Non-Refoulement in a World of CooperatRive Deterrence' (2014) 53 Columbia Journal of Transnational Law 235, 266.

67 Marko Milanovic, 'Al-Skeini and Al-Jedda in Strasbourg' (2012) 23 European Journal of International Law 121, 122; Wouters and Den Heijer, 'The Marine I Case: a Comment' 10.
68 Committee Against Torture, *General Comment* 2 para 16.
69 *JHA v Spain* para 8.2.
70 Gammeltoft-Hansen and Hathaway, 'Non-Refoulement in a World of Cooperative Deterrence' 271.
71 *Bankovic and Others v Belgium and Others* para 59; and Karen Da Costa, *The Extraterritorial Application of Selected Human Rights Treaties* (Martinus Nijhoff Publishers 2012) 249.
72 *Medvedyev and others v France* App no 3394/03 (ECtHR, 29 March 2010) para 65; *Bankovic and Others v Belgium and Others* para 73; *Al-Skeini v United Kingdom* para 73; and *Hirsi Jamaa and Others v Italy* para 75.
73 *X v Germany* App no 1611/62 (European Commission of Human Rights, 25 September 1965) 168.
74 *W.M. v Denmark* App no 17392/90 (European Commission of Human Rights, 14 October 1992).
75 *"B" and Others v Secretary of State for the Foreign & Commonwealth Office* [EWCA] Civ 1344 para 66.
76 *Xhavara and Others v Italy and Albania* App no 39473/98 (ECtHR, 11 January 2001).
77 *Hirsi Jamaa and Others v Italy*; and Violeta Moreno-Lax, 'Hirsi Jamaa and Others v Italy or the Strasbourg Court versus Extraterritorial Migration Control?' (2012) 12 Human Rights Law Review 574, 577–8.
78 *Hirsi Jamaa and Others v Italy* para 77 (references omitted).
79 *Isaak v Turkey* App no 44587/98 (admissibility decision) (ECtHR, 28 September 2006); and Da Costa, *The Extraterritorial Application of Selected Human Rights Treaties* 206.
80 *Issa v Turkey* para 71 (emphasis added).
81 *Pad and others v Turkey* App no 60167/00 (ECtHR, 28 June 2007); *Solomou and others v Turkey* App no 36832/97 (ECtHR, 18 May 1999).
82 Marko Milanovic, 'Jurisdiction and Responsibility: Trends in the Jurisprudence of the Strasbourg Court' in Anne van Aaken and Iulia Motoc (eds), *European Convention on Human Rights and General International Law* (Oxford University Press 2018) 100.
83 *Al-Saadoon and Mufdhi v United Kingdom* App no 61498/08 (admissibility decision) (ECtHR, 30 June 2009) para 88.
84 *Hassan v United Kingdom* App no 29750/09 (ECtHR [GC], 16 September 2014) para 136.
85 *Al-Skeini v United Kingdom* para 136.
86 *Medvedyev v France.*
87 *Hirsi Jamaa and Others v Italy* para 81.
88 *Medvedyev v France*; *JHA v Spain* para 8.2; and *Hirsi Jamaa and Others v Italy* para 81.
89 An apparent outlier case is *Women on Waves v Portugal*, in which a Portuguese warship prevented a Dutch NGO vessel from entering Portuguese territorial waters. The ECtHR assumed Portugal's jurisdiction and found the conduct in

breach of Article 10 ECHR. *Women on Waves v Portugal* App no 31276/05 (ECtHR, 3 February 2009).

90 *JHA v Spain* para 8.2.

91 *Al-Skeini v United Kingdom* para 135 (citations removed).

92 Gammeltoft-Hansen and Hathaway, 'Non-Refoulement in a World of Cooperative Deterrence' 268.

93 According to Tzevelekos:

> Instead of its classic test of effectiveness, the ECtHR sets a presumption. States exercising public authority (especially if they do so willingly, as a consequence of a military invasion) are automatically presumed to exercise control leading to the expansion of their jurisdiction beyond their own territory, that is, over the territory under their authority.
>
> Vassilis P Tzevelekos, 'Reconstructing the Effective Control Criterion in Extraterrestrial Human Rights Breaches: Direct attribution of Wrongfulness, Due Diligence, and Concurrent Responsibility' (2014) 36 Michigan Journal of International Law 129, 150.

94 For example, the range of bilateral agreements between Australia and, respectively, Nauru, Papua New Guinea and Cambodia, fall under the category of 'other agreements'.

95 *Al-Skeini v United Kingdom* para 135.

96 International Law Commission, Articles on Responsibility of States for Internationally Wrongful Acts, Report of the ILC on the Work of its 53rd Session, UN Doc. A/56/10 (2001a) (ARSIWA) art 2.

97 ARSIWA art 6.

98 *Al-Skeini v United Kingdom* para 149.

99 *Jaloud v The Netherlands* App no 47708/08 (ECtHR, 20 November 2014) paras 139–53.

100 *Jaloud v The Netherlands* para 152.

101 Sari, 'Untangling Extra-Territorial Jurisdiction from International Responsibility in Jaloud v Netherlands: Old Problem, New Solutions?' 15.

102 Gammeltoft-Hansen and Hathaway conclude:

> We thus believe that reliance on the public powers approach definition of *an additional* basis of jurisdiction has the potential to serve as an important tool in the fight against cooperative variants of non-entrée, allowing liability to be imposed in a number of circumstances that arguably fall outside either the territorial or the personal mode of jurisdiction.
>
> Gammeltoft-Hansen and Hathaway, 'Non-Refoulement in a World of Cooperative Deterrence' 271–2.

103 Moreno-Lax and Giuffré, 'The Rise of Consensual Containment: From "Contactless Control" to "Contactless Responsibility" for Migratory Flows'.

104 Gammeltoft-Hansen, *Access to Asylum* 124–5.

105 Gammeltoft-Hansen, *Access to Asylum* 152.

106 Rick Lawson, 'Life after Bankovic: On the Extraterritorial Application of the European Convention on Human Rights' in F Coomans and M T Kamminga (eds), *Extraterritorial Application of Human Rights Treaties* (Intersentia 2004) 86, 104.

107 *Al-Skeini v United Kingdom*, concurring opinion of Judge Bonello para 12. Judge Bonello lays out five core functions of human rights law under the ECHR: not violating human rights; having in place systems which prevent breaches of human rights; investigating complaints of human rights abuses; scourging those of their agents that infringe human rights; and compensating the victims of breaches of human rights.

108 Savitri Taylor, 'Australian Funded Care and Maintenance of Asylum Seekers in Indonesia and PNG: All Care But No Responsibility?' (2010) 33 University of New South Wales Law Journal 337, 350.
109 *Armando Alejandre Jr. and Others v Cuba ('Brothers to the Rescue')* Case 11589, (Inter-American Commission on Human Rights, 29 September 1999) para 25.
110 Milanovic, 'Al-Skeini and Al-Jedda in Strasbourg' 129.
111 Notably *Al-Skeini v United Kingdom* and *Jaloud v The Netherlands*. Milanovic observes a shift towards a 'more factual and... more expansive approach' to extraterritorial jurisdiction in the jurisprudence of the ECtHR. Milanovic, 'Jurisdiction and Responsibility: Trends in the Jurisprudence of the Strasbourg Court' 99.
112 Tom De Boer, 'Closing Legal Black Holes: The Role of Extraterritorial Jurisdiction in Refugee Rights Protection' (2014) 28 Journal of Refugee Studies 118, 129.
113 *Lopez Burgos v Uruguay* CCPR/C/13/D/52/1979 (Human Rights Committee, 29 July 1981) para 12.2.
114 Human Rights Committee, *General comment 36* para 63.
115 Committee against Torture, *Concluding observations on the fourth and fifth periodic reports of Australia* CAT/C/AUS/CO/4-5 (26 November 2014).
116 Human Rights Committee, *Concluding observations on the sixth periodic report of Australia* CCPR/C/AUS/CO/6 (9 November 2017).
117 Human Rights Committee, *General Comment 31* para 10; and Human Rights Committee, *General comment 36* para 63.
118 *Regina v Immigration Officer at Prague Airport and Another, Ex parte European Roma Rights Centre and Others*.
119 *M.N. and Others against Belgium* App no. 3599/18 (ECtHR [GC], 5 May 2020.
120 *M.N. and Others against Belgium* para 118. See further Nikolas Feith Tan and Thomas Gammeltoft-Hansen, 'Adjudicating old questions in refugee law: MN and Others v Belgium and the limits of extraterritorial refoulement' (EU Immigration and Asylum Law and Policy, 26 May 2020) https://eumigrationlawblog.eu/adjudicating-old-questions-in-refugee-law-mn-and-others-v-belgium-and-the-limits-of-extraterritorial-refoulement/ accessed 16 August 2024.
121 *X. and X. v Belgian State* ECLI:EU:C:2017:173; C638/16 (CJEU [GC], 7 March 2017) para 51.
122 For an analysis of resettlement interviews and jurisdiction under the ECHR, see Tom de Boer and Marjoleine Zieck, 'The Legal Abyss of Discretion in the Resettlement of Refugees: Cherry-Picking and the Lack of Due Process in the EU' (2020) International Journal of Refugee Law 54.
123 *Corfu Channel Case (United Kingdom v Albania)* ICJ Reports 1949 (9 April 1949) 22.
124 Exceptions are Peter Vedel Kessing, 'Transnational operations carried out from a State's own territory: armed drones and the extraterritorial effect of international human rights conventions' in Thomas Gammeltoft-Hansen and Jens Vedsted-Hansen (eds), *Human Rights and the Dark Side of Globalisation* (Routledge 2016); Tilmann Altwicker, 'Transnationalizing Rights: International Human Rights Law in Cross-Border Contexts' (2018) 29 European Journal of International Law 581; and Thomas Gammeltoft-Hansen, 'International Cooperation on Migration Control: A Legal Research Agenda' (2018) 20(4) European Journal of Migration and Law 373.

125 Kessing, 'Transnational operations carried out from a State's own territory: armed drones and the extraterritorial effect of international human rights conventions' 89.
126 Altwicker, 'Transnationalizing Rights: International Human Rights Law in Cross-Border Contexts' 586.
127 *Trail Smelter Arbitration (United States v Canada)* 3 RIAA 1905 (1938 and 1941).
128 *Andreou v Turkey* App no 45653/99 (admissibility decision) (ECtHR, 3 June 2008).
129 Kessing, 'Transnational operations carried out from a State's own territory: armed drones and the extraterritorial effect of international human rights conventions' 94–5.
130 Gammeltoft-Hansen, 'International Cooperation on Migration Control: A Legal Research Agenda' 382–3.
131 Altwicker, 'Transnationalizing Rights: International Human Rights Law in Cross-Border Contexts' 590–4.
132 Gammeltoft-Hansen and Hathaway, 'Non-Refoulement in a World of Cooperative Deterrence' 244.
133 *Ilaşcu and Others v Moldova and Russia.*
134 *Öcalan v Turkey* para 93.
135 *El-Masri v The Former Yugoslav Republic of Macedonia* App No 39630/09 (ECtHR, 13 December 2012) para 221: 'Having regard to the manner in which the applicant was transferred into the custody of the US authorities, the Court considers that he was subjected to "extraordinary rendition", that is, "an extra-judicial transfer of persons *from one jurisdiction or State to another*, for the purposes of detention and interrogation outside the normal legal system, where there was a real risk of torture or cruel, inhuman or degrading treatment" (emphasis added). See further *Husayn (Abu Zubaydah) v Poland* App no 7511/13 (ECtHR, 24 July 2014); and *Al Nashiri v Poland* App no 28761/11 (ECtHR, 24 July 2014).
136 *JHA v Spain.*
137 *Namah v Pato (Minister for Foreign Affairs and Immigrations) and ors* (2016) PJSC 13 para 74.
138 According to Rygnaert, 'the system of international jurisdiction allows for the exercise of concurrent jurisdiction by more than one state'. Cedric Ryngaert, *Jurisdiction in international law* (Oxford University Press 2008) 146.
139 According to Shaw, 'Many countries, particularly those with a legal system based upon the continental European model, claim jurisdiction over crimes committed by their nationals, notwithstanding that the offence may have occurred in the territory of another state'. Malcolm Shaw, *International Law* (Cambridge University Press 2008) 663.
140 See for example Mark Gibney and Sigrun Skogly, *Universal Human Rights and Extraterritorial Obligations* (University of Pennsylvania Press 2012) 5; Gammeltoft-Hansen and Hathaway, 'Non-Refoulement in a World of Cooperative Deterrence' 272; and Niels Frenzen, 'The Practice of Shared Responsibility in relation to Extraterritorial Refugee Protection' in A Nollkaemper and I Plakokefalos (eds), *The Practice of Shared Responsibility in International Law* vol 2 (Cambridge University Press 2016).
141 Gammeltoft-Hansen, *Access to Asylum* 151.
142 Anja Klug and Tim Howe, 'The Concept Of State Jurisdiction And The Applicability Of The Non-Refoulement Principle To Extraterritorial Interception Measures' in Bernard Ryan and Valsamis Mitsilegas (eds), *Extraterritorial Immigration Control* (Brill 2010) 99.

143 Gammeltoft-Hansen, *Access to Asylum* 152–3.
144 *Legal Consequences of the Construction of a Wall in the Occupied Palestinian Territory* para 112.
145 *Samuel Lichtensztejn v Uruguay* CCPR/C/18/D/77/1980 (Human Rights Committee, 31 March 1983) para 6.2.
146 *Al-Skeini* para 137; *Hirsi Jamaa and Others v Italy* para 75.
147 For example, neither Libya nor Indonesia are party to the Refugee Convention.
148 *Loizidou v Turkey*; *Ilaşcu and Others v Moldova and Russia.*
149 *Al-Skeini v United Kingdom* para 137.
150 Charter of Fundamental Rights of the European Union [2016] OJ C 202/389 (EUCFR) art 51(1) provides:

> The provisions of this Charter are addressed to the institutions, bodies, offices and agencies of the Union with due regard for the principle of subsidiarity and to the Member States only when they are implementing Union law. They shall therefore respect the rights, observe the principles and promote the application thereof in accordance with their respective powers and respecting the limits of the powers of the Union as conferred on it in the Treaties.

151 Sergio Carrera and others, 'Offshoring Asylum and Migration in Australia, Spain, Tunisia and the US: Lessons learned and feasibility for the EU' (Open Society 2018).
152 Netherlands Advisory Committee on Migration Affairs, *External Processing: Conditions applying to the Processing of Asylum Applications outside the European Union* (2010) 30–6; Sergio Carrera and others, 'Offshoring Asylum and Migration in Australia, Spain, Tunisia and the US: Lessons learned and feasibility for the EU' (CEPS Research Report, September 2018) 50–1.
153 Daniel Thym, 'Legal Framework for Entry and Border Controls' in K Hailbronner and D Thym (eds), *EU Immigration and Asylum Law: A Commentary* (2nd edn C.H. Beck 2016).
154 Directive 2013/32/EU of the European Parliament and of the Council of 26 June 2013 on common procedures for granting and withdrawing international protection (emphasis added). According to Article 3(2), the Directive shall not apply to requests for diplomatic or territorial asylum.
155 Directive 2013/33/EU of the European Parliament and of the Council of 26 June 2013 laying down standards for the reception of applicants for international protection (recast) (emphasis added).
156 Daniel Thym, 'Legal Framework for Entry and Border Controls' in K Hailbronner and D Thym (eds), *EU Immigration and Asylum Law: A Commentary* (2nd edn C.H. Beck 2016) 49.
157 According to Thym:

> Against this background, it would be possible, from a legal perspective, for the EU legislature to establish by means of future legislation the conditions for relocating asylum seekers to a safe country or transit zones on the basis of agreements providing for credible guarantees for fair treatment, if necessary by supporting third states or international organisations in guaranteeing an adequate treatment of the returnees through financial or administrative support. On this basis, asylum reception centres could be established outside the EU territory but in compliance with the principle of non refoulement
>
> Daniel Thym, 'Legal Framework for Entry and Border Controls' 49.

158 Directive 2011/95/EU of the European Parliament and of the Council of 13 December 2011 on standards for the qualification of third-country nationals or stateless persons as beneficiaries of international protection, for a uniform status

for refugees or for persons eligible for subsidiary protection, and for the content of the protection granted (recast).

159 With respect to the European Convention on Human Rights, see *Amuur v France* App no 19776/92 (ECtHR, 10 June 1996).

160 Directive 2011/95/EU of the European Parliament and of the Council of 13 December 2011 on standards for the qualification of third-country nationals or stateless persons as beneficiaries of international protection, for a uniform status for refugees or for persons eligible for subsidiary protection, and for the content of the protection granted art 35.

161 Jens Vedsted-Hansen, 'Asylum procedures directive 2013/32/EU' in Kay Hailbronner and Daniel Thym (eds), *EU Immigration and Asylum Law* (Nomos 2016) 1356–7.

162 James Crawford, *State Responsibility: The General Part* (Cambridge University Press 2013) 64.

163 Ulf Linderfalk, 'State responsibility and the primary-secondary rules terminology – The role of language for an understanding of the international legal system' (2009) 78 Nordic Journal of International Law 53.

164 Thus, according to the International Law Commission (ILC) Commentaries to the Articles on Responsibility of States for Internationally Wrongful Acts (ARSIWA)"

> The emphasis is on the secondary rules of State responsibility: that is to say, the general conditions under international law for the State to be considered responsible for wrongful actions or omissions, and the legal consequences which flow therefrom. The articles do not attempt to define the content of the international obligations, the breach of which gives rise to responsibility. This is the function of the primary rules, whose codification would involve restating most of substantive customary and conventional international law.
>
> ILC, *Draft Articles on Responsibility of States for Internationally Wrongful Acts, with commentaries* 31.

165 Ian Brownlie, *Principles of Public International Law* (7th edn, Oxford University Press 2008) 457.

166 In 1988, Noyes and Smith found: 'The scholarly literature is surprisingly devoid of reference to the circumstances or consequences of multiple state responsibility. Judicial or arbitral decisions addressing a state's assertions that other states share responsibility are essentially unknown'. John E Noyes and Brian D Smith, 'State responsibility and the principle of joint and several liability' (1988) 13 Yale Journal of International Law 225.

167 Tom Dannenbaum, 'Public Power and Preventive Responsibility: Attributing the Wrongs of International Joint Ventures' in A Nollkaemper and D Jacobs (eds), *Distribution of Responsibilities in International Law* (Cambridge University Press 2015) 192.

168 See André Nollkaemper, 'Introduction' in A Nollkaemper and I Plakokefalos (eds), *Principles of Shared Responsibility in International Law: An Appraisal of the State of the Art*, vol 1 (Cambridge University Press 2014).

169 ILC, *Draft Articles on Responsibility of States for Internationally Wrongful Acts, with commentaries* 64 para 2.

170 André Nollkaemper and Dov Jacobs, 'Shared responsibility in international law: a conceptual framework' (2012) 34 Michigan Journal of International Law 359, 366–8.

171 André Nollkaemper, 'Shared responsibility for human rights violations: A relational account' in Thomas Gammeltoft-Hansen and Jens Vedsted-Hansen (eds), *Human Rights and the Dark Side of Globalisation* (Routledge 2017) 35.

172 André Nollkaemper, 'Introduction' in André Nollkaemper and Ilias Plakokefalos (eds), *Principles of Shared Responsibility in International Law: An Appraisal of the State of the Art* (Cambridge University Press 2014) 6–7.
173 Maarten den Heijer, 'Shared Responsibility Before the European Court of Human Rights' (2013) 60 Netherlands International Law Review 411, 412 fn 2.
174 Ineke Boerefijn, 'Establishing State Responsibility for Breaching Human Rights Treaty Obligations: Avenues under UN Human Rights Treaties' (2009) 56 Netherlands International Law Review 167.
175 Maarten den Heijer, 'The Practice of Shared Responsibility in Relation to Refoulement' in A Nollkaemper, I Plakokefalos and J Schechinger (eds), *The Practice of Shared Responsibility in International Law* (Cambridge University Press 2017) 481–505.
176 Nollkaemper, 'Shared responsibility for human rights violations: A relational account'.
177 den Heijer, 'Shared Responsibility Before the European Court of Human Rights'.
178 Izabella Majcher, 'Human Rights Violations During EU Border Surveillance and Return Operations: Frontex's Shared Responsibility or Complicity?' (2015) 7 Silesian Journal of Legal Studies 45.
179 Mariagiulia Giuffré, 'State Responsibility Beyond Borders: What Legal Basis for Italy's Push-backs to Libya?' (2013) 24 International Journal of Refugee Law 692.
180 Francesca Mussi and Nikolas Feith Tan, 'Comparing cooperation on migration control: Italy–Libya and Australia–Indonesia' in Siobhán Mullally (ed), *Irish Yearbook of International Law* (Hart-Bloomsbury 2017).
181 Liguori, 'Some Observations on the Legal Responsibility of States and International Organizations in the Extraterritorial Processing of Asylum Claims'; and Nikolas Feith Tan, 'State responsibility and migration control: Australia's international deterrence model' in Thomas Gammeltoft-Hansen and Jens Vedsted-Hansen (eds), *Human Rights and the Dark Side of Globalisation: Transnational law enforcement and migration control* (Routledge 2017).
182 Natalia Szablewska and Ratana Ly, 'Regional Collaborative Responses to the Global Migration Crisis: Refugee Law, Human Rights and Shared State Responsibility: The Australia-Cambodia Refugee Resettlement Agreement' (2017) 91 Australian Law Journal 186.
183 André Nollkaemper, 'Issues of shared responsibility before the International Court of Justice' in E Rieter and H de Waele (eds), *Evolving Principles of International Law: Studies in Honour of Karel C Wellens* (Martinus Nijhoff 2012).
184 Nollkaemper, 'Introduction' 10.
185 Frenzen, 'The Practice of Shared Responsibility in relation to Extraterritorial Refugee Protection'.
186 *United States Diplomatic and Consular Staff in Tehran (United States of America v Iran)* para 56.
187 ILC, *Draft Articles on Responsibility of States for Internationally Wrongful Acts, with commentaries* 125 para 8.
188 Pierre d'Argent, 'Reparation, cessation, assurances and guarantees of non-repetition' in A Nollkaemper and I Plakokefalos (eds), *Principles of Shared Responsibility in International Law: An Appraisal of the State of the Art*, vol 1 (Cambridge University Press 2014) 211–2.
189 ILC, *Draft Articles on Responsibility of States for Internationally Wrongful Acts, with commentaries* 67–9, 124 para 2. Article 17 deals with the exercise of direction and control by one State over the commission of an internationally wrongful act by another. Under Article 17, 'a State which directs and controls

another in the commission of an internationally wrongful act is responsible for the act itself, since it controlled and directed the act in its entirety'. Moreover, the directed or controlled state may still be internationally responsible.

190 ILC, *Yearbook of the International Law Commission* (vol II, 1978) 99. Thus:

> the conduct of the common organ cannot be considered otherwise than as an act of each of the States whose common organ it is. If that conduct is not in conformity with an international obligation, then two or more States will concurrently have committed separate, although identical, internationally wrongful acts.

191 *Certain phosphate lands in Nauru (Nauru v Australia)* (Preliminary Objections), ICJ Rep 240 (26 June 1992); and *Eurotunnel Arbitration (The Channel Tunnel Group Ltd & France-Manche S.A. v United Kingdom & France)* Partial Award, PCA (Permanent Court of Arbitration) (30 January 2007).

192 *Certain phosphate lands in Nauru* para 47; Andreea Manea, 'At the corner of "if" and "maybe": A (possible) joint state responsibility perspective for human rights and humanitarian law violations arising out of the use of private military and security companies' (Master, Utrecht University 2016) 11.

193 Dennanbaum puts forward the concept of Joint Public Enterprises (JPE) as encompassing both common organs (as in the *Nauru Case)* and multilateral arrangements where states place their organs at the disposal of states or international organization, such as peace operations: 'JPEs arise when multiple states or international organisations cooperate to form a public organ or venture with partially merged processes of decision-making and action. Unlike international organisations, however, JPEs lack full legal personality, and are ordinarily temporary'. Tom Dannenbaum, 'Public Power and Preventive Responsibility: Attributing the Wrongs of International Joint Ventures' in Andre Nollkaemper and Dov Jacobs (eds), *Distribution of Responsibilities in International Law* (Cambridge University Press 2015) 194–5.

194 *Eurotunnel Arbitration* para 179 (emphasis added).

195 *Ilse Hess v the United Kingdom* App no 6231/73 (European Commission on Human Rights, 28 May 1975).

196 See further den Heijer, *Europe and Extraterritorial Asylum* 90.

197 *Ilse Hess v the United Kingdom* 176.

198 *Ilaşcu and Others v Moldova and Russia.* On *Hess*, see Lawson, 'Life after Bankovic: On the Extraterritorial Application of the European Convention on Human Rights' 90–2.

199 Memorandum of Understanding between the Republic of Nauru and the Commonwealth of Australia, relating to the Transfer to and Assessment of Persons in Nauru, and Related Issues (signed 3 August 2013) art 22; Madeline Gleeson, *Offshore: Behind the wire on Manus and Nauru* (NewSouth 2016) 202.

200 Memorandum of Understanding between the Government of the Independent State of Papua New Guinea and the Government of Australia, relating to the transfer to, and assessment and settlement in, Papua New Guinea of certain persons, and related issues (signed and entered into force 6 August 2013) art 23.

201 'Libya and Italy to set up operations room to tackle migrant smuggling' (*Reuters*, 9 December 2017) https://www.reuters.com/article/us-europe-migrants-libya/libya-and-italy-to-set-up-operations-room-to-tackle-migrant-smuggling-idUSKBN1E30L8 accessed 21 June 2018.

202 den Heijer, *Europe and Extraterritorial Asylum* 88.

203 d'Argent, 'Reparation, cessation, assurances and guarantees of non-repetition' 244.

204 International Law Commission, *Draft Articles on Responsibility of States for Internationally Wrongful Acts, with commentaries* 124 para 3 (emphasis added).

205 den Heijer, *Europe and Extraterritorial Asylum* 89.

206 *Case Concerning Oil Platforms (Islamic Republic of Iran v United States of America)* ICJ 4 (6 November 2003) (separate opinion of Judge Simma) para 76 (emphasis added).
207 *Saddam Hussein v Albania and twenty other states* App no 23276/04 (Admissibility decision) (ECtHR, 19 March 2006). See further *Ilse Hess v the United Kingdom.*
208 Helmut Philipp Aust, *Complicity and the Law of State Responsibility* (Cambridge University Press 2011), *Complicity and the Law of State Responsibility*; Miles Jackson, *Complicity in International Law* (Oxford University Press 2015); and Vladyslav Lanovoy, *Complicity and its Limits in the Law of International Responsibility* (Bloomsbury 2016).
209 Giuffré, 'State Responsibility Beyond Borders: What Legal Basis for Italy's Push-backs to Libya?' 725.
210 The ILC Commentaries thus note 'Under article 16, aid or assistance by the assisting State is not to be confused with the responsibility of the acting State. In such a case, the assisting State will only be responsible to the extent that its own conduct has caused or contributed to the internationally wrongful act'. ILC, *Draft Articles on Responsibility of States for Internationally Wrongful Acts, with commentaries* 66 para 1.
211 den Heijer, *Europe and Extraterritorial Asylum* 92.
212 Article 17 relates to situations where one state assumes direction and control over another state in committing an internationally wrongful act. Article 18 relates to situations of coercion.
213 *Application of the Convention on the Prevention and Punishment of the Crime of Genocide (Bosnia and Herzegovina v Serbia and Montenegro)* ICJ Reports 2007 (*Genocide Case*) para 420. Nolte and Aust are more circumspect, finding that state practice 'suggests that there does indeed exist a secondary rule prohibiting aid or assistance to internationally wrongful conduct, although its exact scope remains unclear. It remains to be determined how far Article 16 is the proper articulation of this norm'. Georg Nolte and Helmut Philipp Aust, 'Equivocal Helpers—Complicit States, Mixed Messages and International Law' (2009) 58 International and Comparative Law Quarterly 1, 10.
214 Legomsky, 'Secondary Refugee Movements and the Return of Asylum Seekers to Third Countries: The Meaning of Effective Protection' 620.
215 den Heijer, *Europe and Extraterritorial Asylum* 91–101; and Maarten den Heijer, 'Europe Beyond Its Borders: Refugee And Human Rights Protection In Extraterritorial Immigration Control' in Bernard Ryan and Valsamis Mitsilegas (eds), *Extraterritorial Immigration Control: Legal Challenges* (Brill 2010) 194.
216 Giuffré, 'State Responsibility Beyond Borders: What Legal Basis for Italy's Push-backs to Libya?' 725–32.
217 Gammeltoft-Hansen and Hathaway, 'Non-Refoulement in a World of Cooperative Deterrence' 282.
218 Nora Markard, 'The Right to Leave by Sea: Legal Limits on EU Migration Control by Third Countries' (2016) 27 European Journal of International Law 591, 'The Right to Leave by Sea: Legal Limits on EU Migration Control by Third Countries' 615.
219 Moreno-Lax and Giuffré, 'The Rise of Consensual Containment: From "Contactless Control" to "Contactless Responsibility" for Migratory Flows'.
220 den Heijer, *Europe and Extraterritorial Asylum* 95.
221 ILC, *Draft Articles on Responsibility of States for Internationally Wrongful Acts, with commentaries* 66 para 5 (emphasis added).
222 den Heijer, *Europe and Extraterritorial Asylum* 95.
223 ILC, *Draft Articles on Responsibility of States for Internationally Wrongful Acts, with commentaries* 66 para 9.

224 ILC, *Yearbook of the International Law Commission* (vol I, 1978) 239.
225 Georg Nolte and Helmut Philipp Aust, 'Equivocal Helpers—Complicit States, Mixed Messages and International Law' (2009) 58 International and Comparative Law Quarterly 1and Aust, 'Equivocal Helpers—Complicit States, Mixed Messages and International Law' 10.
226 ILC, *Draft Articles on Responsibility of States for Internationally Wrongful Acts, with commentaries* 65–6; and Vladyslav Lanovoy, 'Complicity in an Internationally Wrongful Act' in A Nollkaemper and I Plakokefalos (eds), *Principles of Shared Responsibility in International Law: An Appraisal of the State of the Art*, vol 1 (Cambridge University Press 2014) 144.
227 Markard, 'The Right to Leave by Sea: Legal Limits on EU Migration Control by Third Countries' 615.
228 ILC, *Draft Articles on Responsibility of States for Internationally Wrongful Acts, with commentaries* 66 para 5 (emphasis added).
229 Aust, *Complicity and the Law of State Responsibility* 235.
230 ILC, *Draft Articles on Responsibility of States for Internationally Wrongful Acts, with commentaries* 66 para 9 (emphasis added).
231 Lanovoy, 'Complicity in an Internationally Wrongful Act' 150.
232 Aust, *Complicity and the Law of State Responsibility* 233.
233 ILC, *Yearbook of the International Law Commission* 235–8.
234 Aust, *Complicity and the Law of State Responsibility* 235.
235 Nolte and Aust, 'Equivocal Helpers – Complicit States, Mixed Messages and International Law' 7.
236 *Genocide Case* para 421.
237 Nolte and Aust, 'Equivocal Helpers – Complicit States, Mixed Messages and International Law' 14.

238 'In most cases it may be extremely difficult, if not impossible, to prove that a State did not only know that its assistance will be used for illegal purposes, but that it had been supplied just for that purpose, that is with the intention to facilitate the commission of the wrongful act'.

Bernhard Graefrath, 'Complicity in the law of international responsibility' (1996) 29 Revue Belge de Droit International 370, 375.

239 Lanovoy, 'Complicity in an Internationally Wrongful Act' 152.
240 Paolo Palchetti, 'State Responsibility for Complicity in Genocide' in Paola Gaeta (ed), *The UN Genocide Convention: A Commentary* (Oxford University Press 2009) 389.
241 Jackson, *Complicity in International Law* 161. See further Harriet Moynihan, *Aiding and assisting: Challenges in armed conflict and counterterrorism* (Chatham House 2016).
242 Moreno-Lax and Giuffré, 'The Rise of Consensual Containment: From "Contactless Control" to "Contactless Responsibility" for Migratory Flows'.
243 Gammeltoft-Hansen and Hathaway, 'Non-Refoulement in a World of Cooperative Deterrence' 280.
244 Shepson, 'Jurisdiction in Complicity Cases: Rendition and Refoulement in Domestic and International Courts' 713.
245 *El-Masri v The Former Yugoslav Republic of Macedonia*; and Lanovoy, 'Complicity in an Internationally Wrongful Act' 155.
246 Article 16 ARSIWA is also mentioned in *Al Nashiri v Poland*; and *Husayn (Abu Zubaydah) v Poland*.
247 Nolte and Aust, 'Equivocal Helpers—Complicit States, Mixed Messages and International Law' 16.

248 ILC, *Draft Articles on Responsibility of States for Internationally Wrongful Acts, with commentaries* 114–5. The Commentaries provide that Article 41(1):

> prohibits States from rendering aid or assistance in maintaining the situation created by a serious breach in the sense of article 40. This goes beyond the provisions dealing with aid or assistance in the commission of an internationally wrongful act, which are covered by article 16. It deals with conduct "after the fact" which assists the responsible State in maintaining a situation "opposable to all States in the sense of barring erga omnes the legality of a situation which is maintained in violation of international law". It extends beyond the commission of the serious breach itself to the maintenance of the situation created by that breach, and it applies whether or not the breach itself is a continuing one. As to the elements of "aid or assistance", article 41 is to be read in connection with article 16. In particular, the concept of aid or assistance in article 16 presupposes that the State has "knowledge of the circumstances of the internationally wrongful act.

249 Nolte and Aust, 'Equivocal Helpers – Complicit States, Mixed Messages and International Law' 17.

250 ILC, *Draft Articles on Responsibility of States for Internationally Wrongful Acts, with commentaries* 66 para 6.

251 On this question, see Aust, *Complicity and the Law of State Responsibility* 261–6; and Lanovoy, *Complicity and its Limits in the Law of International Responsibility* 240–58.

252 ILC, *Draft Articles on Responsibility of States for Internationally Wrongful Acts, with commentaries* 66 para 6.

253 Crawford, *State Responsibility: The General Part* 410.

254 Accordingly:

> many partner states not bound by the Refugee Convention or Protocol are nonetheless parties to other human rights instruments that contain a cognate duty of non-refoulement (though the scope of same may not in all cases be identical) – thus providing the required basis for a finding of international wrongfulness.
>
> Gammeltoft-Hansen and Hathaway, 'Non-Refoulement in a World of Cooperative Deterrence' 282.

255 Jackson, *Complicity in International Law* 162.

256 van Berlo, 'The Protection of Asylum Seekers in Australian-Pacific Offshore Processing: The Legal Deficit of Human Rights in a Nodal Reality' 58.

257 Former Australian immigration minister Scott Morrison thus declared, 'it is my instruction to those who run these centres that that's the level of care and support that needs to be provided'. Geoff Thompson and Karen Michelmore, 'Difficult to Ensure Safety on Manus at All Times: Morrison' (*ABC News*, 28 April 2014) http://www.abc.net.au/news/2014-04-28/manus-island-safety-difficult-to-ensure-at-all-times-morrison/5414272 accessed 17 November 2018.

258 van Berlo points out the range of functions carried out by private entities in third country processing, noting with regard to the Nauru RPC:

> the service providers providing safety and garrison services may be considered as exercising a traditional core function of sovereignty, and as such governmental authority, but this is less obvious with, for example, service providers providing accommodation, welfare or construction services'.
>
> van Berlo, 'The Protection of Asylum Seekers in Australian-Pacific Offshore Processing: The Legal Deficit of Human Rights in a Nodal Reality' 59.

259 *Genocide Case* para 406.

4

PRE-ENTRY PROCESSING

4.1 Introduction

Pre-entry processing is an umbrella term for pre-arrival asylum procedures carried out by the authorities of a destination country or regional entity in a partner state. This use of 'proactive' extraterritorial asylum processing in a transit state or first country of asylum has the potential to create safe and controlled access to protection, relieve pressure on external borders and share responsibility for refugees.[1] In contrast to third country processing, discussed at length in the next chapter, pre-entry processing takes place *before* arrival in the destination state's jurisdiction or territory and is generally associated with sharing, not shifting, responsibility for refugees.

Pre-entry processing is defined here as *the full or preliminary pre-arrival processing of an asylum claim by the authorities of a destination country or region in a partner state*. Such a procedure could take place in an open asylum facility or a destination state's embassy. This definition builds on similar concepts of 'extraterritorial', 'transit' or 'regional' processing or 'externalised asylum processing'.[2] Garlick described the approach as 'practices whereby a protection claim is examined to some extent before arrival in an asylum country'.[3] UNHCR has previously referred to 'joint processing carried out by several transit or destination States'.[4] In the EU context, a 2010 Dutch study defined extraterritorial processing as 'the processing of the merits of an application for international protection by and/or subject to the responsibility of the EU or one of its member states which takes place at a location outside the borders of that state or of the EU'.[5]

The chapter focuses on three forms of pre-entry processing, ranging from preliminary profiling and referral into safe and legal pathways to

DOI: 10.4324/9781003463146-4

implementation of full asylum procedures at a pre-entry processing facility. First, pre-entry processing may be conceived as profiling before arrival. This form of pre-entry processing does not include substantive status determination but rather aims to identify and differentiate between people on the move through information provision, counselling, questionnaires or informal interviews to establish a preliminary profile of likely refugees.[6] Such profiling is often combined with referral to safe and legal routes, such as resettlement.

Second, pre-entry processing may also take the form of humanitarian visas, which involve the preliminary assessment of a protection claim by a destination state. Following this preliminary assessment, short-term visas allow for entry to a destination state and access to national asylum procedures.[7] Humanitarian visas are issued at present by a range of European states, including Belgium, France, Italy, Germany, Spain and Switzerland.[8] Outside of Europe, Brazil has launched humanitarian visas specifically for protection seekers from Syria, Afghanistan and Ukraine.[9]

Third, pre-entry processing may take the form of full in-merits procedures, where the entire asylum procedure is undertaken before arrival. The establishment of regional processing facilities that asylum seekers can reach before arriving in a destination state or region may hold the potential to expand rather than restrict access to protection. Such a facility would involve destination state authorities conducting an asylum procedure as well as providing humanitarian assistance and shelter while a claim is being processed.

Pre-entry processing facilities should provide open arrangements, a fair and effective asylum procedure and adequate reception conditions, possibly including temporary accommodation. Such facilities should be accessible only to asylum seekers who have crossed an international border, in line with the alienage requirement contained in Article 1A(2) of the Refugee Convention. This delimitation will also act to mitigate the risk of overwhelming asylum facilities in the hosting partner state.

This chapter outlines previous proposals for and practice of pre-entry processing since the 1980s before unfolding scholarly work on pre-entry processing. Finally, the chapter sets out common standards for pre-entry processing, drawn from international legal obligations and policy lessons learned from previous practice.

4.2 Proposals and practice relating to pre-entry processing

The concept of pre-entry processing dates back at least to 1986, when Denmark introduced a draft UN General Assembly Resolution calling for the establishment of 'regional United Nations processing centres' for the purpose of conducting asylum procedures and administering resettlement.[10] The draft resolution never received the requisite support of other states and was abandoned.

The Comprehensive Plan of Action (CPA), a multilateral framework in place from 1989 to 1997, contained elements of pre-entry processing. The CPA provided solutions for persons displaced in Southeast Asia, with asylum procedures being conducted in countries of first asylum in cooperation with UNHCR, followed by resettlement of refugees to states in the Global North.[11] The CPA had five objectives encompassing the reduction of irregular migration and smuggling, temporary asylum for all protection seekers, asylum procedures in line with international standards, refugee resettlement and repatriation of those not in need of international protection.[12] In this way, the CPA provided controlled access to protection for hundreds of thousands of Indochinese refugees via a procedure in a first country of asylum,[13] though the CPA did not include pre-entry processing by destination states' own asylum authorities.

In Europe, there has been a long line of political proposals for pre-entry processing. The UK's 2003 'New Vision for Refugees' proposed the establishment of both 'regional protection areas' and 'transit processing centres' for asylum seekers.[14] Regional protection areas were envisioned as sites for the processing of asylum seekers in transit states *en route*, with refugees to be resettled by a quota system within the EU. According to Léonard and Kaunert, proposed partner states included Albania, Romania, Croatia, Russia, Turkey, Ukraine, Iran, Somalia and Morocco.[15] At the 2003 European Council meeting, the proposal received insufficient support and was subsequently abandoned.

In 2004–2005, the German interior ministry explored the feasibility of establishing 'safe zones' in North Africa in apparent support of the UK's vision.[16] This proposal included a pre-arrival component, envisioning a facility for asylum seekers who would otherwise risk the journey across the Mediterranean, with a procedure to identify those in need of international protection. The proposal included voluntary European commitments to provide protection, but no guarantee of access to protection in Europe.[17]

In 2009, France and Italy suggested partnerships with countries of origin and of transit to find 'innovative solutions for access to asylum procedures' by, *inter alia*, taking people back to Libya to process their claims extraterritorially.[18] This discussion reignited after the boat tragedy of Lampedusa in October 2013, when hundreds of people lost their lives trying to reach the EU. In 2014, the Italian Prime Minister called for the establishment of refugee camps in Libya,[19] and the German Interior Minister suggested the creation of 'welcome centres' in transit states in North Africa.[20]

In 2017, UNHCR launched its Emergency Transit Mechanism (ETM), with EU financial support, to facilitate the evacuation of vulnerable protection seekers from detention in Libya to Niger, based on an MoU with the Government of Niger.[21] As of April 2024, 4242 protection seekers had been evacuated to Niger.[22] A similar ETM for evacuations from Libya to Rwanda was initiated in 2019. As of April 2024, approximately 2242 people had been evacuated to Rwanda.[23] Under the ETMs, asylum procedures are conducted by UNHCR, with resettlement screenings subsequently undertaken by destination countries.[24]

Also in 2017, French President Macron called for the establishment of asylum 'hotspots' in North Africa.[25] Indeed, while asylum processing centres did not eventuate, from late 2017, France began screening asylum applications on a small scale in Niamey, Niger. Asylum seekers evacuated from Libya to Niger under the ETM are considered by French asylum authorities. Asylum seekers granted international protection are then resettled in France.[26]

Thus far, at the EU level, pre-entry processing has not been implemented. While the EUAA has a mandate to assist member states in conducting asylum procedures, the capacity to process asylum claims remains with member state authorities, thus rendering a fully-fledged EU-run pre-entry asylum facility legally unworkable under current rules. The possibility of a truly EU-run pre-entry asylum facility would likely require an asylum decision-making mandate on the part of the EUAA or a mechanism to make joint asylum decisions between EU member states.[27]

Notwithstanding, in 2018, a joint proposal by UNHCR and the International Organisation for Migration (IOM) for 'regional disembarkation arrangements' once more revived EU discussions on pre-entry processing. The proposal included the establishment of UNHCR-operated regional processing centres outside the EU for asylum seekers rescued at sea by third countries.[28] The European Commission considered the implementation of the UNHCR–IOM proposal, but the approach was never taken up.

In the Americas, the Protection Transfer Arrangement (PTA) includes some elements of pre-entry processing. The PTA was initiated in 2016 by the US and UNHCR in response to the increasing number of people fleeing El Salvador, Honduras and Guatemala.[29] The PTA offered 200 nationals from the three countries transit through Costa Rica at any one time, for a maximum period of six months. The PTA was first piloted by UNHCR in collaboration with El Salvador as the country of origin, Costa Rica as the country of transit and the US as the country of resettlement. The scheme was based on a MoU between UNHCR, IOM and Costa Rica and had three aims: to provide protection to individuals at high risk, to spare them from undertaking dangerous flight routes and risks of trafficking and to foster regional responsibility-sharing.[30] However, the PTA was an ad hoc and highly selective pre-entry processing scheme, with only refugees at 'heightened risk' afforded access.

A recent example of large-scale pre-entry processing is the evacuation of individuals from Afghanistan by the US to transit states since the takeover of the Taliban in August 2021. In the following months, over 130,000 people were evacuated from Afghanistan by the US,[31] however, not all of the Afghans landed on US soil. Instead, a range of other countries, with various levels of experience hosting refugees and some with no ties to the conflict in

Afghanistan, announced that they would temporarily host evacuated Afghans on behalf of the US.[32] In these transit sites, Afghans are screened for both protection needs and security risks by US authorities.

The 2021 German government coalition agreement includes a brief and opaque reference to pre-entry processing. The key paragraph reads:

> The asylum application of people who arrive in the EU or are already here must be examined in terms of content. The EU and Germany must not be open to blackmail. We want to prevent people from being instrumentalised for geopolitical or financial interests. That is why we are committed to migration agreements with third countries based on the rule of law and within the framework of European and international law. To this end, we will examine whether it is possible to establish protection status in third countries in exceptional cases while respecting the Refugee Convention and the ECHR.[33]

The reference to instrumentalisation relates to the actions of Belarus in deliberately sending a group of mostly Iraqi asylum seekers to the borders of Latvia, Lithuania and Poland in the latter months of 2021 in an effort to place pressure on these member states and the EU as a whole.[34] Whether the German mention of extraterritorial processing will be concretised remains to be seen. In February 2023, the German government floated plans to establish pre-entry processing centres for protection seekers en route to Europe.[35]

Most recently, the US government created Safe Mobility Offices in cooperation with the governments of Colombia, Costa Rica, Ecuador and Guatemala. The offices carry out profiling and referral of people on the move to resettlement and legal pathways, ranging from labour mobility to humanitarian parole.[36] Safe Mobility Offices presently allow individuals to register via an online platform for profiling by IOM and UNHCR. Individuals who are identified with potential protection needs are then put into resettlement or humanitarian parole proceedings. The Canadian and Spanish governments have also joined this initiative by offering additional avenues for refugee resettlement and labour mobility.

4.3 Scholarly approaches to pre-entry processing

A number of authors have considered the protective potential of pre-entry processing. In 2015, Garlick carefully indicated that the possibility of pre-entry processing should be revisited in Europe, stating:

> … a well-informed discussion could clarify whether the European Union and Member States are ready to invest what would be required to make this a lawful and viable course – or whether other channels could result in

> safer and better managed routes to protection. Discussions should include rigorous cost–benefit analysis, considering states' interests but based also on protection principles and fundamental rights.[37]

More recently, Moodley has put forward a 'multilateral formulation of regional processing' repurposing lessons from the CPA in the context of EU regional cooperation. According to Moodley:

> ... for regional processing to be successful the most critical requirement is that the sum of all its components – including admission, shelter, humanitarian assistance, refugee status determination and repatriation – must be firmly grounded within a human rights and international protection framework. This would require all states, including those not party to key refugee and human rights law instruments, to agree nonetheless to respect key international and human rights law principles.[38]

In a policy brief on three approaches to pre-entry processing – humanitarian visas, emergency evacuation and pre-entry asylum processing centres – de Oliviera and Tan concluded that, while such approaches can offer safe routes to protection through shifting not only control but also access to protection to the extraterritorial context, pre-entry processing arrangements should include adequate procedural rights in line with international human rights and refugee law standards.[39]

At a more theoretical level, Ayelet Shachar proposed a form of pre-entry processing as a response to 'shifting border' policies that push migration control activities far beyond the physical border.[40] Such an approach uses the methods and technologies of the shifting border to open up deterritorialised access to protection. Thus:

> Instead of having to reach Europe (or another other desired destination) through irregular and increasingly deadly routes of passage, humanitarian-visa applications can in theory be accepted anywhere en route: in countries of origin or transit, via embassies, upon encounter with official agents of border enforcement...[41]

Shachar sets out two shifts required to fulfil this idea. First, core human rights law obligations should follow the shifting border, on the basis of a functional approach to extraterritorial jurisdiction.[42] Second, the link between territory and protection should be minimised, thus 'relaxing the fixation on territorial access as a precondition for securing refuge'.[43] However, Shachar acknowledges that this vision is 'currently more aspirational than applied' and does not suggest concrete arrangements nor a roadmap to advance this idea.[44]

4.4 Pre-entry processing standards

The following elements and standards are key to any pre-entry processing model to ensure the rights of asylum seekers under human rights and refugee law are respected. These standards reflect both international legal obligations incumbent upon states and policy lessons learned from practice and proposals in this area.

4.4.1 Relationship with territorial asylum in the destination state

A fundamental question arising in any pre-entry processing model is the relationship between the processing of an asylum claim in the partner state and access to territorial asylum in the same destination state or region. This issue will arise when an asylum seeker goes through a pre-entry procedure, receives a negative decision and subsequently arrives at the border of the destination state. While ideally, pre-entry processing would be entirely without prejudice to the right to seek asylum in the destination state,[45] governments will likely be sceptical of the concept if such an approach only results in greater numbers of asylum seekers.[46] As a result, any pre-entry processing model will likely have the objective of contributing to a decrease in irregular arrivals of asylum seekers at a destination country's or region's borders.

As a matter of international law, pre-entry processing cannot wholesale replace the right to seek asylum on a state's.[47] The principle of non-refoulement gives rise to a procedural obligation requiring that an asylum seeker arriving within a state's jurisdiction receives an individual assessment of their asylum claim.[48] Relatedly, the prohibition against collective expulsion under European human rights law requires that each asylum seeker receive an opportunity to argue against their expulsion to the competent authorities and be provided with an individual removal decision.[49] Further human rights obligations can limit the ability of a destination state to simply reject an asylum seeker's claim on its territory, for example, the right to family life and best interests of the child considerations for unaccompanied children.[50]

Where the asylum seeker has already been through a fair and efficient pre-entry procedure with procedural rights and guarantees, including the right to appeal, and subsequently applies for asylum upon arrival in the territory of the same destination state, an accelerated two-instance screening at the border will be sufficient. Such a screening could be narrowed down to assessing any *new* risks or a change of circumstances since the pre-entry procedure as well as an assessment of any risk of refoulement in the transit state. Where an asylum seeker does present evidence of new risks or a change of circumstances, they should then be afforded access to a full asylum procedure on the destination state's territory.

The territorial screening process set out above should only be mandated a fairly short time after the pre-entry procedure, as new reasons for flight may arise. The proposed EU Resettlement Regulation, for example, bars refugees from reapplying for resettlement in the EU for five years.[51] The use of rapid border screening processes for three years after a pre-entry procedure may be a reasonable period to balance between border control interests and the possibility that new grounds for flight will arise.

In sum, the relationship between pre-entry processing and seeking asylum in the destination state is crucial to the legality and potential of pre-entry processing. While ideally, pre-entry processing would be entirely without prejudice to the right to seek asylum in the destination state, governments will likely be sceptical of the concept if such an approach only results in greater numbers of refugees.[52] On the other hand, under international law, pre-entry processing cannot replace the right to seek asylum on a state's territory. The principled and pragmatic solution here is for asylum seekers who are screened out of a pre-entry asylum facility and subsequently arrive at a destination state border to be provided with an accelerated two-instance screening at the border, thus upholding the state's obligations with respect to non-refoulement while preventing onwards movement after a fair and effective pre-entry procedure has been carried out.

4.4.2 The applicability of international and regional human rights law

A second key question relevant to any pre-entry processing scheme is the applicability of human rights obligations over a pre-entry processing facility. As explored at length in the previous chapter, jurisdiction is the threshold requirement for the application of state obligations stemming from international human rights law.[53] The jurisdiction of the territorial state will be presumed to exist even where that state exercises no control over a pre-entry processing facility. Where jurisdiction is not triggered, a state owes no legal obligations towards asylum seekers in a pre-entry processing arrangement.[54] In any pre-entry processing arrangement, there should be clarity as to which state/s exercises jurisdiction over the facility.

Whether a destination state holds extraterritorial jurisdiction depends on the legal and factual involvement of the state's agents in pre-entry processing. Extraterritorial jurisdiction is triggered when a state exercises 'effective control' over a defined territory or 'authority and control' over asylum seekers.[55] For example, where a destination state exercises force or other physical control, such as detention, over asylum seekers, it exercises extraterritorial jurisdiction.[56] Currently, as a matter of European law, a state's extraterritorial jurisdiction is not triggered by the processing of a visa application.[57]

Existing pre-entry processing arrangements may fall on either side of the threshold for triggering extraterritorial obligations. Afghans evacuated by the US to third states, for example, are clearly under the US's extraterritorial jurisdiction as its agents exercised authority and control over individuals and, in some cases, state vessels during evacuation. Under the PTA, in contrast, UNHCR retained responsibility for the transfer of vulnerable individuals from El Salvador, Honduras and Guatemala to the transit facility in Costa Rica before resettlement in the US or elsewhere.[58] Similarly, under the ETMs, UNHCR is responsible for the transfer of asylum seekers from Libya to Niger and Rwanda, with destination state involvement limited to resettlement interviews and decisions that presently do not trigger international human rights or refugee law obligations.[59]

Under EU law, fundamental rights stemming from the EU Charter are potentially applicable in the context of pre-entry processing. The EU Charter is binding on EU agencies at all times and EU member states wherever EU law is being implemented, including in a third state.[60] Whether the EU Charter applies turns on the question of whether EU law is being implemented – that is whether there is EU law governing the respective issue.[61] Where the EU Charter does apply, EU member states are, *inter alia*, extraterritorially bound to respect the principle of non-refoulement and the right to an effective remedy.[62]

In some cases, where destination state involvement with a pre-entry processing facility falls short of the control required to trigger extraterritorial jurisdiction, pre-entry processing arrangements will not enliven the human rights obligations of the destination state. Nevertheless, while such pre-entry processing arrangements may fall outside the scope of formal human rights law, adequate safeguards should be in place, including respect for the principle of non-refoulement, safeguards related to the asylum procedure (including the right to an interview, access to an interpreter, written reasons for a decision and the right appeal if the application is rejected), freedom from arbitrary detention and adequate reception conditions in line with international standards.[63]

4.4.3 Relationship with the partner state asylum system

Any pre-entry processing model should operate without prejudice to the territorial state's national asylum framework. In other words, protection seekers who do not meet the criteria for international protection in the pre-entry procedure, maintain the right to seek asylum in the territorial state. Depending on the modalities, joint processing arrangements could be undertaken between destination and partner states, based on harmonisation of interpretation of key international and regional refugee law definitions, such as those relating to inclusion and exclusion.[64]

A further key consideration is to mitigate against overwhelming the resources of both the pre-entry procedures facility and the partner state's national asylum system. Pre-entry processing arrangements should only be accessible to asylum seekers in the partner state and not nationals of that country or individuals already receiving international protection. Moreover, regional asylum quotas could be used to ensure responsibility-sharing and maintain the capacity of the national asylum system and pre-entry asylum facility.

4.4.4 The nature and quality of the asylum procedure

Pre-entry processing facilities may provide either a full procedure or an initial screening procedure or profiling. Where a full asylum procedure is provided at the pre-entry facility, this must include an appeal instance As discussed above, any subsequent limitations on territorial asylum in the destination state are only permissable where a fair and effective process is provided at the pre-entry stage.

There are also a number of modalities possible with respect to asylum authorities. For example, pre-entry processing may be carried out solely by the asylum authorities of one destination state. Other models may include regional pre-entry processing arrangements, such as an EU pre-entry processing site with multiple European asylum authorities conducting asylum procedures, with support from EU agencies, such as the EUAA and Frontex. Still, another model may include joint processing between destination and partner state, with the allocation of responsibility for refugee protection shared between cooperating states.

The availability of fair and effective asylum procedures in line with human rights and refugee law standards is critical to the success of a pre-entry processing model. International law requires that asylum seekers receive an individual asylum procedure fully in line with human rights and refugee law guarantees, including the right to an appeal. Where the pre-entry procedure falls short of these standards, a full territorial procedure in the destination state or region will be required.

4.4.5 Legal status in the partner state

Asylum seekers accessing a pre-entry procedure require a sufficiently certain legal status throughout the asylum process to prevent forced return before a decision has been made. Status as an asylum seeker or temporary humanitarian entrant, either registered by partner state authorities or UNHCR, will generally be sufficient.

4.4.6 Duration of pre-entry processing arrangements

Pre-entry processing arrangements should be relatively fast, with clear time limits on the duration of asylum procedures. Three to six months would seem to be a reasonable time limit for a fair and effective pre-entry asylum procedure. For example, the PTA provides for a six-month stay in Costa Rica, during which asylum procedures and resettlement referrals take place.[65] More concerningly, Afghans evacuated by the US to Albania were expected to remain in the country for more than one year, awaiting passage to the US.[66]

In the ETM context, despite initial estimates that asylum seekers would be in transit for six months, there are no formal time limits set for how long asylum seekers evacuated from Libya are expected to wait for either an asylum procedure or eventual resettlement.[67] As a result, the duration of both asylum processing and resettlement screening has ballooned, reaching an average time of 235 days in Rwanda and 677 days in Niger by June 2021.[68] As a result, a clear time limit of three to six months for pre-entry processing should be established at the outset of any such arrangement.

4.4.7 Access to solutions for refugees

To provide a genuine alternative to unauthorised migration to reach destination state borders, pre-entry processing should lead directly to solutions for those asylum seekers found to require international protection. In general, pre-entry processing should lead to protection in the destination state carrying out the pre-entry procedure. Following a pre-entry screening or full asylum procedure, asylum seekers in need of protection should be promptly and safely transferred to the destination state or region.

In other cases, refugees may be provided protection elsewhere; for example, via a regional distribution mechanism, in the case of a multilateral pre-entry processing facility, or via resettlement to a third country. Whatever the modalities, access to protection following the pre-entry procedure should be safe, rapid and informed, taking into account the interests of the individual to the extent possible.

Some examples of existing practice are too closely linked to resettlement, thus substantially limiting the number of refugees receiving protection via pre-entry processing. Both the PTA, in Central America, and the ETMs, in Niger and Rwanda, for example, are entirely reliant on UNHCR resettlement places to provide solutions to refugees in destination states. While resettlement is an important durable solution, it remains firmly in the policy domain with no binding obligations to resettle refugees.[69] To form a meaningful alternative to spontaneous asylum, pre-entry processing arrangements should provide direct access to protection.

4.4.8 Solutions for persons not in need of international protection

Finally, the destination state or region will need to provide political, financial and operational support in cooperation with the partner state to ensure the return of rejected asylum seekers from the pre-entry facility. While the partner state retains the sovereign power to grant and withdraw immigration status, including the ability to expel rejected asylum seekers,[70] operationalising returns from the facility must be a joint responsibility.

In the context of pre-entry procedures, rejected asylum seekers also require a solution following the asylum procedure. Policymakers must thus ensure that rejected asylum seekers either have access to regularised immigration status in the partner state or are safely returned to their country of origin, in line with the principle of non-refoulement.

4.5 Conclusions: pre-entry processing as responsibility-sharing?

This chapter has set out legal and policy standards for pre-entry processing, an umbrella term for pre-arrival asylum procedures carried out by the authorities of a destination country or regional entity in a partner state. Pre-entry processing has the potential to contribute to responsibility-sharing provided it is implemented in line with international human rights and refugee law obligations and shares rather than shifts responsibility for refugee protection.[71] Pre-entry processing allows for the controlled arrival of refugees in destination states and can prevent abuse of national asylum systems through asylum procedures before arrival.

Notwithstanding the protective potential of pre-entry processing, current and historical approaches generally do not include procedural rights for protection seekers.[72] Irrespective of whether extraterritorial jurisdiction is established or not, this chapter argued for minimum procedural rights in line with international standards as essential for a pre-entry processing scheme to operate in a protection-sensitive way.

Pre-entry processing is the most promising form of transnational asylum in terms of responsibility-sharing. In principle, the pre-entry processing of asylum applications prior to arrival in a particular destination country or region can offer significant protection opportunities. If implemented in a way that respects the rights of individuals under international human rights and refugee law, pre-entry processing can share responsibility with states hosting a significant number of refugees while mitigating the pressures of spontaneous arrivals at a destination state's borders.[73]

Pre-entry processing offers a number of potential protective possibilities in line with destination states' desire for control over the arrival of refugees, allowing destination states to conduct security and health screenings and prepare national reception and integration before arrival.[74] In this way, pre-entry processing can serve as a mechanism to provide controlled access to protection in cooperation with partner countries.[75] While pre-entry asylum centres have been proposed multiple times in a range of regions, as discussed, they have hitherto never been implemented at scale.[76] A full-scale pre-entry processing facility fully in line with international legal obligations has the potential to minimise the risks associated with irregular journeys, combat smuggling and trafficking and alleviate pressure on the external borders of destination states and regions.[77]

In an ideal world, pre-entry processing would operate alongside access to territorial asylum as an additional form of access to asylum. However, in the current political climate, pre-entry processing is highly unlikely to be implemented in isolation without the prospect that it will result in a decrease in spontaneous arrivals, combat smuggling and trafficking and strengthen return policies.[78] As a result, any pre-entry processing model is likely to be conditional upon restrictions on access to territorial asylum and thus employed in combination with third country processing or protection, as discussed in the coming chapters.

Notes

1 Riona Moodley, Rethinking 'Regional Processing': Could the Lessons Learned from the Comprehensive Plan of Action for Indochinese Refugees (CPA) Offer a Roadmap for International Cooperation in Response to 'Regional' Refugee Situations? (UNSW Law Research Paper, 2022). See also Pauline Endres de Oliveira and Nikolas Feith Tan, External Processing: A Tool to Expand Protection or Further Restrict Territorial Asylum? (Migration Policy Institute, 2023).

2 Jane McAdam, 'Extraterritorial Processing in Europe: Is "Regional Protection" the Answer, and If Not, What Is?' (Kaldor Centre for International Refugee Law policy brief, 2015).

3 Madeline Garlick, The Potential and Pitfalls of Extraterritorial Processing of Asylum Claims (Migration Policy Institute, 2015) http://www.migrationpolicy.org/news/potential-and-pitfalls-extraterritorial-processing-asylum-claims accessed 13 August 2024.
Netherlands Advisory Committee on Migration Affairs, 'External Processing: Conditions Applying to the Processing of Asylum Applications Outside the European Union' (2010). Building on this definition, see Riona Moodley, 'Regional Processing in Europe: Pathways to Protection through International Cooperation and Responsibility Sharing' presented at the University of London, Refugee Law Initiative (RLI) 30 June 2022.

4 UNHCR, 'Protection Policy Paper: Maritime Interception Operations and the Processing of International Protection Claims: Legal Standards and Policy Considerations with Respect to Extraterritorial Processing' (2010) para 14.

5 Netherlands Advisory Committee on Migration Affairs, 'External Processing: Conditions Applying to the Processing of Asylum Applications Outside the European Union'.

6 UNHCR, 'Protection Policy Paper: Maritime Interception Operations and the Processing of International Protection Claims: Legal Standards and Policy Considerations with Respect to Extraterritorial Processing' (2010) para 15.
7 UNHCR, 'Complementary Pathways for Admission of Refugees to Third Countries: Key considerations' (2019).
8 See, for example, International Bar Association, 'A Model Instrument for an Emergency Evacuation Visa' (2019).
9 de Oliveira and Tan, External Processing: A Tool to Expand Protection or Further Restrict Territorial Asylum? 11.
10 UN General Assembly, 'International procedures for the protection of refugees: draft resolution/ Denmark' (U.N. Doc. A/C3/41/L.51, 12 November 1986); Gregor Noll, 'Visions of the exceptional: legal and theoretical issues raised by transit processing centres and protection zones' (2003) 5 European Journal of Migration and Law 303, 312.
11 W Courtland Robinson, 'The comprehensive plan of action for Indochinese refugees, 1989–1997: Sharing the burden and passing the buck' (2004) 17 Journal of refugee Studies 319; Richard Towle, 'Processes and Critiques of the Indo-Chinese Comprehensive Plan of Action: An Instrument of International Burden-Sharing?' (2006) 18 International Journal of Refugee Law 537; and Alexander Casella, 'Managing the "Boat People" Crisis: The Comprehensive Plan of Action for Indochinese Refugees' (International Pease Institute, October 2016).
12 United Nations General Assembly, Declaration and Comprehensive Plan of Action of the International Conference on Indo-Chinese Refugees, Report of the Secretary-General (A/44/523), 22 September 1989, A/44/523.
13 Moodley, *Rethinking 'Regional Processing': Could the Lessons Learned from the Comprehensive Plan of Action for Indochinese Refugees (CPA) Offer a Roadmap for International Cooperation in Response to 'Regional' Refugee Situations?*
14 United Kingdom, 'New Vision for Refugees' (2003).
15 Sarah Léonard and Christian Kaunert, 'The extra-territorial processing of asylum claims' (2016) Forced Migration Review 48.
16 German Interior Ministry, Effektiver Schutz für Flüchtlinge, wirkungsvolle Bekämpfung illegaler Migration – Überlegungen des Bundesministers des Innern zur Einrichtung einer EU-Aufnahmeeinrichtung in Nordafrika, 9 September 2005.
17 Madeline Garlick, 'The EU Discussions on Extraterritorial Processing: Solution or Conundrum?' (2006) 18 International Journal of Refugee Law 601, 619.
18 Council of the European Union, 'The migration situation in the Mediterranean: Establishing a partnership with migrants' countries of origin and of transit, enhancing Member States' joint maritime operations and finding innovative solutions for access to asylum procedures' (Council doc. 13205/09, Brussels 11 September 2009), 11; see further Anna Liguori, 'The extraterritorial processing of asylum claims' (JMCE Migrants Working Papers, Jean Monnet Centre of Excellence on Migrants' Rights in the Mediterranean 2015), 4.
19 ANSAmed, 'Italian Premier Renzi calls for UN refugee camps in Libya' *ANSAMed News* (20 May 2014).
20 'Die haben gelernt zu töten: Interview with Thomas de Maizière' Die Freie Presse (27 November 2014).
21 Laura Lambert, 'Extraterritorial asylum processing: the Libya-Niger emergency transit mechanism' (2021) 68 Forced Migration Review 18.
22 UNHCR, Flash Update: Emergency Transit Mechanism (ETM) (April 2024), https://reporting.unhcr.org/niger-and-rwanda-emergency-transit-mechanism-etm-flash-update-8493 accessed 13 August 2024.

23 UNHCR, 'First evacuation flight of 2022 from Libya to Rwanda brings over 100 asylum seekers to safety' (30 March 2022) https://www.unhcr.org/rw/news/first-evacuation-flight-2022-libya-rwanda-brings-over-100-asylum-seekers-safety accessed 13 August 2024.

24 UNHCR, Flash Update: Emergency Transit Mechanism (ETM) (April 2024).

25 BBC, 'EU migrant crisis: France plans asylum "hotspots" in Libya' (27 July 2017) https://www.bbc.com/news/world-europe-40738199 accessed 22 March 2022. The EU hotspot approach was a Union–member state hybrid method on the registration, identification and filtering of new arrivals into asylum and return procedures in Italy and Greece. See Danish Refugee Council, *Fundamental Rights and the EU Hotspot Approach* (2017).

26 Anja Palm, 'A French Processing Centre in Niger: The first step towards extraterritorial processing of asylum claims or (just) good old resettlement?' (Aspenia Online, 18 April 2018) https://aspeniaonline.it/a-french-processing-centre-in-niger-the-first-step-towards-extraterritorial-processing-of-asylum-claims-or-just-good-old-resettlement-2/ accessed 8 August 2024.

27 Guy Goodwin-Gill has suggested the creation of a European Protection Agency in the following terms:

> what is needed, as a matter of logic and coherence, is a European refugee status built on Member States' international obligations and supplemented with the broad community benefits of EU law, including freedom of movement; it is a long shot, but a European Protection Agency competent for refugees and migrants in need of protection would be a good start, for many issues are common to both. Such a comprehensive re-organization of responsibilities, if it could be achieved, would need to be complemented by an external competence, through which the EU could engage positively and constructively with other States confronted with the phenomenon of people on the move, though always consistently with EU law, international legal obligations, and the European Convention on Human Rights.
>
> Guy S. Goodwin-Gill, 'The MediterraneaRn Papers: Athens, Naples and Istanbul' (2016) 28 International Journal of Refugee Law 276, 277.

28 UNHCR and IOM, Proposal for a regional cooperative arrangement ensuring predictable disembarkation and subsequent processing of persons rescued-at-sea (2018).

29 See further UNHCR, Evaluation of effectiveness of the Protection Transfer Arrangement in Central America (Evaluation Report, December 2018).

30 UNHCR, Evaluation of effectiveness of the Protection Transfer Arrangement in Central America (Evaluation Report, December 2018).

31 See Department of Homeland Security, Operation Allies Welcome – Afghan Evacuee Report, December 2021.

32 This list includes Albania, Bahrain, Canada, Colombia, Costa Rica, Chile, Ecuador, Guyana, India, Kuwait, Mexico, Netherlands, North Macedonia, Poland, Portugal, Qatar, Rwanda, Singapore, Uganda and the United Arab Emirates.

33 Government of Germany coalition agreement 2021 https://www.bundesregierung.de/breg-de/service/gesetzesvorhaben/koalitionsvertrag-2021-1990800 accessed 13 August 2024 (unofficial translation from German).

34 See further Julia Kienast, '"Crisis Rhetoric" and Derogations from the AFSJ: Is EU Asylum Policy Discriminatory or does its Implementation Reflect the Rule of Law?' *Cuadernos Europeos de Deusto* 06 (2022) 117–43.

35 Ben Knight, 'Germany Mulls Sending Refugees to Africa' (Deutsche Welle, 10 February 2023) https://www.dw.com/en/new-german-migration-official-aims-to-send-refugees-to-africa/a-64667296 accessed 13 August 2024.
36 US Department of Homeland Security, 'Fact Sheet: US Government Announces Sweeping New Actions to Manage Regional Migration' (27 April 2023) https://www.dhs.gov/news/2023/04/27/fact-sheet-us-government-announces-sweeping-new-actions-manage-regional-migration accessed 13 August 2024.
37 Garlick, The Potential and Pitfalls of Extraterritorial Processing of Asylum Claims.
38 Riona Moodley's doctoral thesis explores the concept of EU pre-arrival processing and provides an in-depth legal feasibility study on its potential use as a complementary legal pathway to protection: see Riona Moodley, Regional Processing by the European Union - A Bridge Over Troubled Water? (University of New South Wales, 2024).
39 de Oliveira and Tan, 'External Processing: A Tool to Expand Protection or Further Restrict Territorial Asylum?' 25–6.
40 Ayelet Shachar, *The shifting border: Legal cartographies of migration and mobility* (Manchester University Press 2020) 5.
41 Shachar 76.
42 See Chapter 3.
43 Shachar, 74–88.
44 Shachar 74.
45 Moodley, *Rethinking 'Regional Processing': Could the Lessons Learned from the Comprehensive Plan of Action for Indochinese Refugees (CPA) Offer a Roadmap for International Cooperation in Response to 'Regional' Refugee Situations?* 3.
46 Garlick, The Potential and Pitfalls of Extraterritorial Processing of Asylum Claims.
47 Garlick.
48 Jens Vedsted-Hansen, 'The asylum procedures and the assessment of asylum requests' in Vincent Chetail and Céline Bauloz (eds), *Research Handbook on International Law and Migration* (Edward Elgar 2014); Álvaro Botero and Jens Vedsted-Hansen, 'Asylum Procedures' in Michelle Foster, J McAdam and Cathryn Costello (eds), *The Oxford Handbook of International Refugee Law* (Oxford University Press 2021) 597–606.
49 Article 4 of Protocol 4 to the ECHR.
50 Article 3 of the Convention on the Rights of the Child; Article 8 of the ECHR.
51 European Commission, Proposal for a Regulation establishing a Union Resettlement Framework and amending Regulation (EU) No. 516/2014.
52 Garlick, The Potential and Pitfalls of Extraterritorial Processing of Asylum Claims.
53 See Chapter 3.
54 International Law Commission, *Draft Articles on Responsibility of States for Internationally Wrongful Acts, with commentaries* (Yearbook of the International Law Commission, Volume II, 2001) arts 16, 17 and 18. See further Chapter 3.
55 Marko Milanovic, 'From Compromise to Principle: Clarifying the Concept of State Jurisdiction in Human Rights Treaties' (2008) 8 Human Rights Law Review 411, 417; Samantha Besson, 'The Extraterritoriality of the European Convention on Human Rights: Why Human Rights Depend on Jurisdiction and What Jurisdiction Amounts to' (2012) 25 Leiden Journal of International Law 857, 860.
56 See, for example, *JHA v Spain*, Communication no 323/2007 (Committee Against Torture, 21 November 2008) para 8.2; *Hassan v United Kingdom* App no 29750/09 (ECtHR [GC], 16 September 2014) para 136.
57 *X. and X. v Belgian State* ECLI:EU:C:2017:173; C638/16 (CJEU [GC], 7 March 2017); ND and NT v Spain App nos 8675/15 and 8697/15 (ECtHR [GC], 13 February 2020).

58 UNHCR, Evaluation of effectiveness of the Protection Transfer Arrangement in Central America (Evaluation Report, December 2018).
59 Tom de Boer and Marjoleine Zieck, 'The Legal Abyss of Discretion in the Resettlement of Refugees: Cherry-Picking and the Lack of Due Process in the EU' (2020) 32 International Journal of Refugee Law 54.
60 Article 51(1) of the EU Charter provides that:

> The provisions of this Charter are addressed to the institutions, bodies, offices and agencies of the Union with due regard for the principle of subsidiarity and to the Member States only when they are implementing Union law. They shall therefore respect the rights, observe the principles and promote the application thereof in accordance with their respective powers and respecting the limits of the powers of the Union as conferred on it in the Treaties.

61 *Fransson*, Case C-617/10 Åklagaren v Hans Åkerberg Fransson [2013] ECLI:EU:C:2013:280.
62 Articles 4 and 19(2) and 47, respectively.
63 European Council for Refugees and Exiles, 'Protection in Europe: Safe and Legal Access Channels: ECRE's Vision on Europe's Role in the Global Refugee Protection Regime' (Policy Paper 1, February 2017), 16; de Oliveira and Tan, *External Processing: A Tool to Expand Protection or Further Restrict Territorial Asylum?*
64 For example, the definitions of refugeehood under the Organisation of African Union Convention and the Cartagena Declaration are broader than the 1951 Convention. See further Nikolas Feith Tan and Julia Kienast, *The Right of Asylum in Comparative Regional Perspectives: Access, Procedures and Protection* (ASILE working paper, 2022).
65 UNHCR, Evaluation of effectiveness of the Protection Transfer Arrangement in Central America (Evaluation Report, December 2018).
66 Andrew Higgins, 'From Taliban Terror to Beach Resort: A Strange Journey for Some Refugees', *The New York Times*, 13 September 2021.
67 Altai Consulting, Case Study: Emergency Transit Mechanism (June 2021) 27.
68 Altai Consulting, Case Study: Emergency Transit Mechanism (June 2021) 21.
69 de Boer and Zieck, 'The Legal Abyss of Discretion in the Resettlement of Refugees: Cherry-Picking and the Lack of Due Process in the EU'.
70 Netherlands Advisory Committee on Migration Affairs, *External Processing: Conditions applying to the Processing of Asylum Applications outside the European Union* 44.
71 Moodley, *Rethinking 'Regional Processing': Could the Lessons Learned from the Comprehensive Plan of Action for Indochinese Refugees (CPA) Offer a Roadmap for International Cooperation in Response to 'Regional' Refugee Situations?*
72 See further de Oliveira and Tan, External Processing: A Tool to Expand Protection or Further Restrict Territorial Asylum?
73 For a proposal on 'regional processing' in the context of the EU, see Moodley, *Rethinking 'Regional Processing': Could the Lessons Learned from the Comprehensive Plan of Action for Indochinese Refugees (CPA) Offer a Roadmap for International Cooperation in Response to 'Regional' Refugee Situations?*
74 de Oliveira and Tan, External Processing: A Tool to Expand Protection or Further Restrict Territorial Asylum?
75 Nikolas Feith Tan, (2021) 'The Temporary Hosting of Evacuated Afghans in Third Countries: Responsibility Sharing or Externalisation?' (RLI Blog on Refuge Law and Forced Migration, 15 September 2021) https://rli.blogs.sas.ac.uk/2021/09/15/the-temporary-hosting-of-evacuated-afghans-in-third-countries-responsibility-sharing-or-externalisation/ accessed 13 August 2024.

76 While the CPA was a large-scale processing scheme, it did not involve asylum procedures carried out by destination states.

77 Moodley, *Rethinking 'Regional Processing': Could the Lessons Learned from the Comprehensive Plan of Action for Indochinese Refugees (CPA) Offer a Roadmap for International Cooperation in Response to 'Regional' Refugee Situations?*

78 Garlick, The Potential and Pitfalls of Extraterritorial Processing of Asylum Claims.

5

THIRD COUNTRY PROCESSING

5.1 Introduction

Third country processing involves the *transfer of an asylum seeker from the territory or jurisdiction of a destination state to a partner state for the purpose of processing their asylum claim*. Pre-entry processing – discussed at length in the previous chapter – and third country processing share common legal, policy and operational elements; however, there are also crucial distinctions, most notably that pre-entry processing relates to processing of an asylum claim *before arrival*, while third country processing involves the transfer of an asylum seeker to a partner state *after arrival* in the jurisdiction of a destination state.

This chapter proceeds in four sections. First, the chapter sets out three different models of third country processing drawn from practice in terms of the law of jurisdiction.[1] Second, the chapter outlines previous proposals and practices on third country processing, tracing the rise and fall of the concept in various jurisdictions over the last 30 years. Third, the chapter explores scholarly responses to third country processing. In general, scholars have been deeply sceptical of third country processing, variously criticising the approach in terms of exceptionality, legal obstacles, ineffectiveness and shifting of responsibility. Finally, the chapter sets out standards for any policy of third country processing, drawn from legal obligations and policy lessons learned from two iterations of third country processing in the Pacific.

5.2 Models of third country processing

First, third country processing may be conceived of on the basis of *exclusive partner state jurisdiction*. Cooperation is largely focused on the transfer of

DOI: 10.4324/9781003463146-5

asylum seekers from one state to another. After transfer, the partner state assumes complete responsibility for the asylum seeker, including the asylum procedure and reception conditions. The EU–Turkey Statement is an example of this model, whereby Turkey assumes responsibility for asylum seekers returned from the Aegean islands on the basis of the safe third country concept.[2] Similarly, the US–Guatemala Asylum Cooperative Arrangement (ACA) was based on sole Guatemalan jurisdiction over transferred individuals.

Second, third country processing may take place on the basis of *joint jurisdiction* between destination and partner state, characterised by a high level of destination state involvement in the reception or processing of asylum seekers. In such scenarios, the jurisdiction of the destination state endures after transfer, creating a situation of joint or shared jurisdiction over asylum seekers. Crucially, jurisdiction is a question of fact and may differ from the stated intentions of cooperating states. Despite the denials of the Australian government, the Manus Island RPC is an apt example of joint jurisdiction. In contrast, some proposals in Europe explicitly acknowledge the jurisdiction of the destination state alongside that of the partner State.[3]

Finally, in rare cases, third country processing may take place on the basis of *exclusive destination state jurisdiction.* Such a situation will only take place where the partner state's role is limited to offering the use of its territory to the destination state. However, in general, the presence of asylum seekers in a state's territory will trigger jurisdiction, except where a territorial lease or military occupation, war or rebellion displaces the presumption.[4] For example, the US's transfers to centres in Cuba and Panama, discussed below, took place under territorial leases granting exclusive control to the US.

The jurisdiction of the destination state *at the point of transfer* in situations of third country processing is not in question. In such situations, the individuals will be under the authority and control of the destination state following interception at sea, or under that state's territorial jurisdiction on land. The jurisdiction of the partner state is enlivened as soon as the transfer occurs or at the moment at which the individual reaches its territory. What is in question is whether destination state jurisdiction continues *after transfer* to the partner country – an assessment that depends on the individual cooperation modalities. Where the site is exclusively run by partner state authorities, the jurisdiction of the destination state will cease with the transfer.

However, a number of bases for *continued* destination state jurisdiction are possible. First, where the destination state exercises authority or control over persons in an asylum processing facility through its agents, jurisdiction will be enlivened. For example, where destination state authorities are responsible for the day-to-day management of the facility and carrying out the asylum procedure, the destination state's jurisdiction is relatively clear. In particular, destination state detention of asylum seekers in a third country processing facility will certainly trigger jurisdiction.[5] Jurisdiction in such instances will be established notwithstanding the shared jurisdiction of the territorial state, whose agents may also be involved in the management and operations of the facility.[6]

Second, in rare cases, the destination state may exercise effective control over the territory upon which the facility is located. While the US's jurisdiction over Guantanamo Bay in Cuba is one prominent example, the likelihood of similar territorial lease arrangements is remote. It is difficult to conceive of a European state, for example, holding such a high level of overt control over the territory of the third state.

Third, the jurisdiction of the destination state may conceivably fall under the public powers approach. Certainly, asylum processing is a public power closely linked to the sovereign prerogative of controlling migration and borders. Moreover, third country processing requires the existence of a bilateral agreement between cooperating states. However, situations in which any violations of international obligations will be exclusively attributable to the destination state are less clear-cut, given the presumption of partner state territorial jurisdiction. The public powers approach may come into play where the authorities of the partner state are effectively inactive or non-functional, such as to afford the partner state a comparable level of control over the facility as an occupying power or peacekeeping force.[7]

Finally, under a functional approach, jurisdiction may be triggered by a number of factors that amount to power over an individual sufficient to create a jurisdictional link. As discussed above, human rights treaty bodies have established that the cumulative effect of a number of interventions by a destination state in the context of third country processing can reach the necessary standard. In particular, a combination of causing establishment of a facility, transfer of individuals there, financial backing and choice of contractors may amount to jurisdiction.[8]

In sum, therefore, whether jurisdiction over asylum seekers transferred to a third country processing facility endures after transfer will depend on the facts. Where the partner state is exclusively responsible for the management and asylum processing at the facility, destination state jurisdiction will be extinguished after transfer.[9] However, where the destination state exercises authority or control over persons or effective control over territory, jurisdiction will adhere.

5.3 Proposals for and practice of third country processing

Third country processing, in various forms, has been proposed and, in some cases, implemented by states for some time.[10] In 1986, Denmark put forward a draft United Nations General Assembly resolution for the establishment of 'regional United Nations processing centres administrating resettlement' and requested a study into the allocation of resettlement places according to states' gross domestic product.[11] The draft resolution never received the requisite support of other states and was abandoned.

In 1991, in response to the exodus of Haitian asylum seekers following the fall of 'Papa Doc' Duvalier, the US began using Guantanamo Bay, Cuba, as an asylum processing centre. There, US immigration officials assessed the claims of transferred asylum seekers. The US exercises complete control and jurisdiction over Guantanamo Bay under a perpetual lease agreement with Cuba.[12] Under the Migrant Interdiction Program (MIP), the US continues to intercept and transfer irregular migrants to Guantanamo Bay, on a small scale, to this day.[13]

In 1993, the Dutch government returned to the concept of asylum processing in the region of origin, proposing the establishment of asylum processing centres near countries of origin. The concept was tabled in the Intergovernmental Consultation on Asylum, Refugees and Migration (ICG), but not taken up.[14]

In 1994, following the exodus of some 30,000 Cubans by boat, the US embarked on its 'Safe Havens' program, under which thousands of Cubans were transferred to Guantanamo Bay and Howard Air Force Base in the US-controlled area of the Panama Canal Zone on a temporary basis.[15] Rather than a focus on asylum *processing*, the Safe Havens program was focused on the provision of temporary protection for all irregular migrants, irrespective of refugee status.[16]

In 2001, following the MV Tampa standoff, Australia began transferring asylum seekers arriving by boat to Nauru and, later, Papua New Guinea. The 'Pacific Solution' remained in place until 2007 and was later restored in 2012 in its current form as part of Operation Sovereign Borders. As discussed in Chapter 3, both iterations of the policy include the interception and transfer of asylum seekers bound for Australia to Nauru and Papua New Guinea for the purposes of asylum processing.

The UK's 2003 'New Vision for Refugees' proposed the establishment of both 'regional protection areas' and 'transit processing centres' for asylum seekers also included a post-arrival component.[17] The proposal included processing of asylum seekers in transit states to the EU, with refugees to be resettled by a quota system within the EU. Functionally, asylum seekers could either apply for asylum in regional protection areas or be transferred after arrival in the EU, presumably on the basis of the safe third country concept.[18]

In 2004, the German and Italian interior ministers called for the establishment of asylum processing centres in North Africa.[19] The proposal envisioned the interception of irregular migrants crossing the Mediterranean and transferring to a partner state where a pre-screening procedure would occur. Rather than a full asylum procedure, this pre-screening would identify likely refugees for transfer to Europe and likely migrants for channelling into national immigration procedures. According to a Netherlands Advisory Committee, the concept was rejected without a formal examination.[20]

Since the European migrant and refugee crisis in 2015, proposals for third country processing, either on behalf of the EU or individual member states, have intensified.[21] In 2018, for example, the Danish Social Democrats put forward a policy platform that proposed removing any asylum seeker arriving on Danish territory to a third country for the processing of their claim for international protection.[22] A subsequent joint Austrian–Danish vision paper proposed increased use of EU hotspots at the external borders and regional disembarkation for those arriving by sea with no access to an asylum procedure or subsequent resettlement in Europe and the establishment of Mobile Protection Teams to identify refugees for resettlement.[23]

An approach including both pre-entry processing and third country processing elements, a UNHCR–IOM proposal for a regional disembarkation mechanism revived the discussions on extraterritorial processing once more. The proposal included the transfer of individuals rescued at sea to third states and the processing of asylum claims there.[24] The European Council agreed to consider the introduction of 'regional disembarkation platforms' in third countries to filter irregular migrants intercepted in the Mediterranean. According to media reporting, the EU considered Algeria, Egypt, Libya, Tunisia, Niger and Morocco as possible partners.[25]

In 2019, the Trump Administration entered into a bilateral ACA under which non-Guatemalan asylum seekers may be transferred from the US to Guatemala without the chance to claim asylum.[26] Between November 2019 and March 2020, 939 asylum seekers were transferred under the ACA, though only 30 people applied for asylum in Guatemala. The operation of the ACA was suspended in March 2020 due to the COVID-19 pandemic.[27] The US also entered into similar bilateral arrangements with Honduras and El Salvador, but transfers were never activated.

In June 2021, Denmark's parliament passed L226, a legislative amendment inserting a new paragraph in the Aliens Act allowing for the transfer of asylum seekers to a third country outside the EU for the purposes of both asylum processing and protection of refugees in the third country.[28] Transfers must take place under an international agreement between Denmark and the third country and that asylum seekers are to be transferred 'unless it would be in breach of Denmark's international obligations'. While the Danish government has referred to negotiations with a handful of countries, notably Rwanda, no concrete agreement is yet in place.[29]

In April 2022, the UK and Rwanda signed a five-year MoU providing for an APA.[30] Under the APA, asylum seekers reaching the UK were subject to transfer to Rwanda, following a screening procedure by UK authorities. Upon arrival, Rwandan authorities would assume responsibility for the asylum procedure. Asylum seekers found to be refugees were to be offered protection in Rwanda, while those not in need of protection were to be returned or provided with leave to remain in Rwanda. The APA included the formation of an independent Monitoring Committee, though its powers to influence the APA's operation (such as the suspension of transfers) were not spelt out.

In November 2023, Italy and Albania concluded a non-binding protocol for the transfer of persons rescued by Italian vessels in the Mediterranean Sea to Albania for asylum processing.[31] The Protocol provides that Italy will have exclusive jurisdiction and control over certain 'areas' in Albania where Italy will construct facilities to receive disembarked people with asylum and return procedures carried out by Italian authorities (Article 3). Italy is responsible for almost all activities under the Protocol, including all financial costs, carrying out border and return procedures in the areas (Article 4(3)), health care inside the areas and transferring persons out of Albania following border and return procedures (Article 9(1)). No reference is made to solutions for those found to require international protection, though it is clear that Italy retains responsibility for removing persons from Albania following asylum/return procedures (Article 9(1)). The Protocol is limited to 3000 persons present in Albania at any one time (Article 4), and the agreement runs for five years.

The Italy-Albania arrangement is quite distinct from the UK-Rwanda APA and suggests destination states are learning from the failure of UK-Rwanda. Rather than seeking to externalise asylum processing for all irregular arrivals, the Italy-Albania protocol only applies to persons with likely unfounded claims from a list of prescribed safe countries of origin. Furthermore, the Italy-Albania protocol is limited to asylum processes only, with those found to require international protection provided access to protection in Italy. Moreover, rather than delegating responsibility for these asylum processes to a third country, under the agreement Italian authorities carry out asylum procedures extraterritorially, on Albanian soil.

5.4 Scholarly approaches to third country processing

In general, refugee law scholars have been highly critical of third country processing. Scholarship ranges from analyses of exceptionality, legal obstacles, ineffectiveness and state responsibility vis-à-vis the approach. As den Heijer puts it:

> Within the sphere of refugee advocacy, the external processing and protection of refugees has raised a multitude of concerns, especially as regards the use of detention as a necessary auxiliary instrument and the lack of safeguards against the onward removal to potentially unsafe countries. On a more fundamental note, it is feared that schemes of external protection may render refugees 'beyond the domain of justice' and create 'rights-free zones' where neither domestic nor international legal obligations apply.[32]

There are a number of strands to this criticism, explored below First, a number of scholars have focused on the *exceptional* nature of third country processing as a dangerous departure from the traditional territorial approach to asylum. Third country processing, it is argued, risks placing refugees in 'legal black holes' beyond the reach of justice.[33] In 2003, in his exploration of the Danish and UK proposals for asylum processing centres outside Europe, Noll saw these policies as part of a 'paradigm shift' placing the refugee beyond the rule of law. The title of his article, 'Visions of the exceptional', indicates the radical nature of third country processing and the inherent dangers to such an approach: 'This is precisely what the state of exception is all about. The vision will introduce a permanent state of exception in asylum and migration policies'.[34].

Also in 2003, Crisp argued that third country processing proposals represented 'an important shift in the asylum paradigm', signalling the end of reactive reception of asylum seekers on state territory, to migration management based on control and organised movement.[35] Similarly, den Heijer reflects on the departure that third country processing represents in the following terms:

> ... policies of external reception represent a fundamental shift from the traditional paradigm that asylum is granted inside the state's territory. Instead, asylum seekers are granted a temporary safe haven in a foreign location, allowing for the determination of their status and the arrangement of more durable solutions.[36]

Afeef discussed the paradoxical role of strengthened human rights cultures in developed states in pushing asylum policy into third states. Rather than labelling offshore asylum policies as exceptional, Afeef emphasised the central role such approaches play in the policymaking of developed states, observing: 'Offshore asylum policies are here to stay. They are likely to fundamentally shape future asylum policies and they are already changing the way asylum is conceptualised, especially in western states'.[37]

Second, particularly in Europe, scholars have discussed the *legal obstacles* to third country processing, emphasising the additional layers of protection afforded asylum seekers and refugees contained in the EU asylum *acquis*. In 2006, Garlick traced the European debate surrounding third country processing, concluding that the policy was unjustified and unfeasible at the time.[38] Moreno-Lax, in 2015, argued against the implementation of third country processing on the part of the EU, citing a number of practical and legal obstacles, and concluding that meeting these legal requirements was an 'impossibility'.[39]

In 2017, Carrera and Guild raised a multitude of questions critical to the success of third country processing, noting:

> There is substantial legal opinion that offshoring asylum procedures is not compatible with the member states' obligations under the UN

> convention relating to the status of refugees [sic] 1951 and its 1967 Protocol and that the inevitable deterioration of conditions in centres where such offshoring may take place is contrary to the member states' human rights obligations.[40]

Similarly, McAdam highlighted the practical and legal barriers to EU third country processing, putting forward a 'protection toolkit' as an alternative to a third country processing model.[41]

Third, scholars argue that third country processing is *ineffective* in protecting asylum seekers and refugees. In relation to the first and second iterations of the Pacific Solution, a number of scholars have addressed human rights violations in Nauru and Papua New Guinea. In 2006, Taylor set out the distinction between burden sharing and burden shifting in Australian-led cooperation arrangements, labelling the policy a 'counterfeit' form of international cooperation.[42] In 2007, Kneebone argued that conditions in Nauru and Papua New Guinea did not amount to 'effective protection', concluding that third country processing required 'durable solutions and freedom from arbitrary detention, penalties, discrimination and refoulement'.[43] Similarly, Francis warned policymakers in Europe that efforts to provide 'effective protection' in Nauru and Papua New Guinea had failed, stating that 'extraterritorial processing schemes are anathema to protection under the Refugee Convention while they retain their fundamental objective of preventing and deterring direct access to fair and effective processing in-country'.[44] In 2016, Dastyari and O'Sullivan discussed the decision of the Papua New Guinea Supreme Court in *Namah v Pato*, which ordered the closure of the Manus Island centre, concluding 'extraterritorial processing in PNG is not a sustainable, long-term solution to refugee protection in the region'.[45]

Fourth, scholarship explores *responsibility* and, to a lesser extent, accountability in third country processing arrangements. The risk identified here is that extraterritorial conduct may take place beyond the reach of courts and other oversight mechanisms. In 2007, Goodwin-Gill located third country processing as an expression of state exploitation of the gap between the right to asylum and the principle of non-refoulement, approaches operating 'in the grey, unregulated areas of international law'.[46] Goodwin-Gill also sketched the outline of a framework of responsibility for third country processing, concluding that 'international law may not prevent states from seeking "new" solutions to old problems, but it does set the parameters'.[47] In 2016, Liguori highlighted the importance of the law of state responsibility in third country processing arrangements, including the possible complicity of any European state aiding or assisting asylum processing outside the EU. However, Liguori also acknowledges the 'Achilles heel' of remedies in regard to state responsibility, where extraterritorial jurisdiction is not triggered.[48]

In a 2016 assessment of the Pacific RPCs, Nethery and Holman conclude there is 'substantial and incontrovertible evidence that the human rights outcomes of Australia's offshore detention centres are devastating'.[49] In 2017, Van Berlo outlined the complexity of 'nodal governance' in relation to asylum processing in Nauru, highlighting the lack of accountability mechanisms provided by human rights law.[50]

Finally, a small group of scholars have expressed *cautious openness* to third country processing, considering how the approach could provide solutions for both states and refugees. Thym and Hailbronner, for example, have suggested that the establishment of third country processing centres can be in compliance with the non-refoulement obligation.[51]

The marked scepticism of refugee lawyers towards third country processing is sound. The approach represents a departure from the principle of territorial asylum, a long-established state practice in dealing with asylum seekers. Third country processing faces a number of serious legal obstacles, requiring that states secure obligations owed to individuals beyond their borders. In practice, too, the approach has resulted in repeated violations of human rights law and an often intentional lack of clarity as to crucial questions of jurisdiction and state responsibility.[52]

5.5 Third country processing standards

The following standards for the use of third country processing reflect both international legal obligations incumbent upon states engaged in third country processing and policy lessons learned from recent practice and proposals in this area.

5.5.1 A robust pre-transfer procedure

International refugee and human rights law requires an individual pre-transfer procedure for all asylum seekers who reach a destination state's jurisdiction to assess whether that state's international obligations prevent transfer. This imperative is required by a number of international obligations, notably the principle of non-refoulement, the prohibition against collective expulsion, the right to family life and the best interests of the child. While a destination state is not necessarily obliged to hear an asylum seeker's claim for international protection, it does have obligations before sending a person to a third country.

This pre-transfer procedure should take place within the destination state's territory. While in theory, such assessments could take place extraterritorially (e.g., on board a vessel or aircraft), previous practice has shown this approach routinely falls short of international law standards.[53]

Such an assessment must also meet the procedural requirements imposed by international obligations related to procedural fairness, including the prohibition against collective expulsion and the right to an effective remedy.[54] The prohibition against collective expulsion requires that each asylum seeker slated for transfer be provided with an individual decision for their transfer and an opportunity to argue against their transfer to competent authorities.[55] The right to an effective remedy guarantees a right of appeal to an independent decision-making body with respect to the decision to transfer.[56] Thus, according to the Michigan Guidelines on Protection Elsewhere:

> Any person to be transferred to another state under a protection elsewhere policy must be able to contest the legality of the proposed transfer before it is effected. The sending state shall notify any person to be transferred of this entitlement, and shall consider in good faith any challenge to the legality of transfer under a procedure that meets international standards of procedural fairness. Such procedure must in particular afford an effective remedy bearing in mind the nature of the rights alleged to be at risk in the receiving state.[57]

In terms of substance, the pre-transfer procedure must assess whether the transfer would breach the destination state's international obligations. First and foremost, the procedure must consider the risk of direct or indirect refoulement as a result of the transfer. Second, the procedure must assess whether the person slated for transfer has a legal basis to enter or remain in the destination state, such as the right to family life.[58] Third, the procedure must assess whether there are other international or domestic rules which would prevent the transfer, such as the best interests of the child for children seeking asylum, either arriving with family or unaccompanied.[59]

The Refugee Law Initiative Declaration on Externalisation and Asylum also sets out a number of practical considerations that should be taken into account.

> Such pre-transfer assessments should also consider the following practical elements in order to evaluate whether the individual transfer of the asylum seeker is reasonable on the facts:
>
> i any risk that the asylum seeker will not be admitted to the receiving country.
> ii any lack of prior connection of the person with the receiving country, especially where the arrangement envisages the provision of asylum in the receiving State.
> iii any special needs of the person, including on the basis of their gender or other protected characteristics, and the capacity of the receiving State to meet those needs.
> iv wider conditions in the receiving country and their stability, including any armed conflict or generalised violence, exposure to serious disasters and/or patterns of widespread violations of human rights, especially if on a discriminatory basis pertinent to the person concerned.[60]

5.5.2 Partner state ratification of international treaties

A further element to support lawful third country processing arrangements is the ratification of relevant international treaties on the part of partner states. This is an important step towards comparable levels of protection for asylum seekers subject to third country processing, though not decisive.[61] Accession to and ratification of the Refugee Convention, CAT and the ICCPR are important safeguards for the rights of asylum seekers and bring the levels of international commitment between the two states closer together.[62]

Obviously, a destination state cannot control the sovereign prerogative of a partner state in acceding to or ratifying international treaties. Nevertheless, when negotiating third country processing arrangements, destination states wield some influence over the policymaking of partner states. There is some relevant past practice in this regard. In 2011, for example, Nauru ratified the Refugee Convention just one year before the resumption of asylum processing in cooperation with Australia.[63]

In a similar vein, the removal of reservations held by partner states narrows the gap between obligations on the part of cooperating states. Papua New Guinea, a party to the Refugee Convention since 1986, had entered reservations against seven articles of the convention, relating to wage-earning employment, housing, public education, freedom of movement, refugees unlawfully in the country of refuge, expulsion and naturalisation.[64] Under the 2013 Refugee Resettlement Agreement, the Papua New Guinea government committed to 'immediately take steps to withdraw its reservations to the Refugee Convention, with respect to persons transferred by Australia'.[65] This undertaking formally broadens protections for only a limited number of asylum seekers and refugees in Papua New Guinea, with no benefit to West Papuan refugees in the country.[66]

The fundamental point here is that it is in the interests of destination states and asylum seekers for wider ratification of core human rights and refugee law instruments. While ratification of the Refugee Convention will not ipso facto render third country processing lawful, it does signify a commitment to key norms of refugee protection.[67] As discussed below, ratification must also be complemented by a national legal framework to conduct a fair and effective asylum procedure and provide protection in accordance with the Convention framework.

5.5.3 Attachment to the third country?

As a matter of international law, there is no requirement that there exists a connection between the individual asylum seeker and the third state; however, at the level of EU law, the APD requires a connection between the asylum seeker and the third country, and it would be reasonable for that person to go to that country. As a result, EU member states can only transfer asylum seekers under the safe third country concept where there exists a sufficient connection between the individual and the third state.

The operation of the EU–Turkey Statement has tested the limits of the safe third country concept under the APD. The Greek Appeals Committee has held that asylum seekers arriving in the Aegean islands could not be returned on the basis of the safe third country concept after short transits in Turkey. For example, in two separate 2017 decisions, the Appeals Committees held that the mere fact of transiting through Turkey does not create a sufficient connection with the country. One case concerned a Syrian man who spent eight days in Turkey and had no family or social networks in the country.[68] Another related to a family of four who had spent 15 days in Turkey before travelling to Greece.[69] In both cases, the Appeal Committees found that the applicants could not be returned under the safe third country concept.

5.5.4 Clear lines of jurisdiction and responsibility

Any third country processing arrangement should clearly articulate areas of state responsibility. A lack of clarity in relation to legal and operational responsibilities creates accountability gaps that make human rights violations more likely and effective international cooperation more remote.[70] The complexity of two sovereign actors involved in carrying out asylum procedures requires a clear division of responsibility over the various aspects of third country processing arrangements.

As discussed in Chapter 3, where a destination state exercises extraterritorial jurisdiction, it owes human rights law obligations to asylum seekers under its authority and control or to the geographic area under its effective control. Thus, the Refugee Law Initiative Declaration on Externalisation and Asylum holds:

> Where a transferring State operates asylum facilities in a third country, those facilities are subject to the same international law standards that govern such functions in its own territory. Those standards apply to any externalised asylum facilities over which the transferring State retains extraterritorial jurisdiction, including through effective control over the person transferred or over the location of the facilities, or where conduct by that State forms part of a chain of action that directly exposes an individual to a breach of protected human rights.[71]

In contrast, where a destination state does not exercise the requisite level of control to trigger jurisdiction, the partner state will retain territorial jurisdiction over any third country processing facility.

MoUs in the Pacific have resulted in confusion over the respective roles of state and private actors. Cooperation has included opaque, complex governance structures, with a number of public and private actors playing a part in asylum processing. In 2012, following the opening of the Nauru processing centre, UNHCR reported a 'lack of clarity as to the legal and operational roles and responsibilities of the two States party to the transfer arrangements'.[72] In relation to the Nauru processing centre, van Berlo notes, 'with a myriad of actors cooperating, contesting and conflicting, it is difficult to discern what the involvement of the Australian and Nauruan authorities is in relation to specific conduct'. [73] Further, Australia has at times appeared to assume responsibility for conditions in the Nauru and Papua New Guinea centres. For example, the Australian government rejected an offer from New Zealand to resettle 150 refugees from partner states, calling into question the proposition that refugees were the responsibility of the Papua New Guinea government.[74]

Under the agreements, Nauru and Papua New Guinea are considered to have ultimate responsibility, in a legal and practical sense, for the operations at the processing centre. Australia, on the other hand, provides substantial aid and assistance but is not legally responsible for centre operations.[75] However, this formal arrangement has not matched reality. In addition to the presence of Australian and Nauru state authorities at the centres, the Australian government has contracted a range of private actors to provide medical, welfare and garrison (security, catering and cleaning) services at the centres, who report to the Australian government under their respective contractual arrangements. The involvement of a multitude of private actors in the day-to-day operations of the centres has contributed to confusion over administrative arrangements and accountability for violations against asylum seekers.

Questions of jurisdiction have also lacked clarity. While Australia acknowledges the possibility of the extraterritorial application of international treaties, the Australian government has repeatedly denied that its involvement in the processing centres in Nauru and Papua New Guinea reaches the threshold of control required to trigger jurisdiction under human rights law.[76] A multitude of UN bodies reject this position, including the Committee Against Torture,[77] Human Rights Committee[78] and UNHCR,[79] creating greater confusion over responsibility for the Nauru and Papua New Guinea RPCs.

5.5.5 Partner state legal framework and capacity

Proposals for and practice of third country processing are characterised by policy 'on the run' made in the midst of a perceived migration crisis, rather than preparedness on the part of cooperating states. Third country processing proposals generally lack detail in regard to partner states, operations, scale and legal framework. Even when implemented, third country processing policies have been characterised by reactive 'emergency' measures, without adequate planning. This almost complete lack of preparedness increases the risk of violations against asylum seekers in third country processing and undermines the provision of durable solutions for those found to be refugees.

In the Pacific, both iterations of third country processing began as ad hoc, emergency measures to curtail asylum-seeking by boat, only later hardening into long-term policy. In 2001, the Tampa crisis triggered the reception of asylum seekers in Nauru, while in 2012, an expert report on asylum seekers recommended the reopening of the Nauru and Papua New Guinea centres as 'circuit breakers' in response to increasing numbers of arrivals.

This lack of preparedness had significant impacts on the provision of a fair and efficient asylum procedure. Asylum seekers in Nauru, where transfers resumed in September 2012, experienced years-long wait times for a determination of their asylum applications. The Nauruan government began processing asylum claims in March 2013, with the first group of refugees being recognised and released into the community in May 2014. This was likely due to a lack of capacity on the part of Nauruan officials to carry out RSD, with UNHCR reporting a complete lack of experienced decision-makers. The following year, UNHCR reported that 'the current expertise and experience of the Nauruan officials is not at a level where they are able to conduct fair and accurate assessments of refugee claims without substantial input from Australian officials'.[80]

The Papua New Guinea centre reopened in November 2012, and asylum procedures began in July 2013. The Papua New Guinea government began handing down initial assessments one year later, but final status determinations were not forthcoming until the middle of 2015, almost two-and-a-half years after the arrival of the first asylum seekers. Critically, Papua New Guinea lacked an appropriate framework at the time of resumption of asylum processing, with no regulations transposing Article 1A(2) of the Refugee Convention into national law and no legal framework governing the asylum procedure. In 2013, UNHCR reported: 'PNG is drafting regulations to establish RSD procedures, but that these have not yet been finalised, and that no time frame for the operationalisation of such procedures has been identified'.[81]

Asylum procedures in both Nauru and Papua New Guinea improved in subsequent years with the development of national legal frameworks and capacity to carry out asylum procedures; however, the years-long delays do not meet the standard of a 'fair and effective' procedure.[82]

Elsewhere, the existence of a national asylum system has not been matched by sufficient capacity to provide fair and effective procedures. Under the US–Guatemala ACA, for example, 939 asylum seekers were transferred to

Guatemala for the purposes of asylum processing, while Guatemala's asylum system only had six employees. At the time of the ACA's suspension due to the COVID-19 pandemic in March 2020, Guatemalan asylum officers had not finalised any asylum decisions.[83]

Under the UK–Rwanda APA, Rwanda was to assume responsibility for the asylum procedure following transfer from the UK. While Rwanda has a national asylum framework in compliance with international standards, the 127,000 refugees residing in Rwanda have almost all received protection on a prima facie basis.[84] According to UNHCR, in 2020, Rwanda had just one eligibility officer, suggesting its asylum system is ill-equipped to conduct the individual asylum procedures foreseen under the APA.[85]

The key lessons here are that policy made 'on the run' raises the risk of violations where a fair and effective asylum procedure needs to be established after the fact. A national asylum system and sufficient capacity to operate this system increase the chance of sustainable cooperation on third country processing while providing vital procedural guarantees for asylum seekers.

5.5.6 Avoiding detention

Proposals for and practice of third country processing commonly involve the long-term detention of asylum seekers while their claim for international protection is being assessed. This connection should be rejected, however, as the detention element of third country processing exponentially raises the likelihood of violations of international law. As discussed, detention in closed centres that is considered arbitrary will violate the right to liberty and security of person.[86]

The European hotspot approach, involving the containment of asylum seekers in the Aegean Islands since the operation of the EU–Turkey Statement in March 2016, signals the risks of a policy of detention even at the borders of a destination state. In Greece, Law 4375/2016 provides detention should be carried out exceptionally, following an individual assessment and as a measure of last resort where no alternative measures can be applied.[87] However, in practice, new arrivals have been systematically prevented from leaving the hotspots for 25 days, a policy that amounts to detention.[88] The obvious question emerging from the hotspot approach is whether the EU or one of its member states could establish asylum processing centres that uphold the rights of asylum seekers in a third state outside European territory.

In the Pacific, the use of mandatory, indefinite and arbitrary detention in the Nauru and Papua New Guinea centres has been the major source of violations of international law. Multiple UN bodies, including the Committee Against Torture and the Human Rights Committee, have indicated that the conditions of detention breach international law.[89] Further, a number of scholars have addressed the harms of detention in Nauru and Papua New Guinea.[90] Finally, and crucially, litigation in relation to the legality of detention has had emphatic impacts on the approach adopted in Nauru and Papua New Guinea. In October 2015, after three years of closed detention and with litigation testing the legality of the centre in the Australian High Court imminent, the Nauruan government announced that the facility would become an open centre, with asylum seekers free to come and go at all hours of the day.[91] In April 2016, after four years of closed detention, the Papua New Guinea Supreme Court in *Namah* ordered the closure of the Manus Island RPC, on the basis that the detention of asylum seekers and refugees there was in contravention of the right to liberty in the Constitution.

The use of long-term detention in third country processing policies creates numerous legal risks for asylum seekers and states. Asylum seekers face increased risks of a range of human rights violations, while states are exposed to the risk of litigation and liability for harm. Detention in this context should be avoided, except in those narrow circumstances permitted by human rights and refugee law.

5.5.7 Transparency and independent oversight

Third country processing policies should be subject to proper transparency and oversight. Transparency is an important element for democratic oversight of the actions of elected governments, requiring that information about the modalities and conditions in third country processing arrangements be publicly available in both destination and partner states.

Oversight, in this context, relates to access of independent monitoring bodies to third country processing settings.[92] A common objection to third country processing is that such remoteness and an absence of national (territorial) safeguards render these sites and individuals 'out of sight, out of mind'.[93] Transparency and independent oversight go some way to remedying this concern. UNHCR would be well placed to monitor third country processing arrangements, given its international protection mandate. The Michigan Guidelines on Protection Elsewhere thus provide in part:

> At a minimum, such an agreement should… grant UNHCR the right to be present in the receiving state and to enjoy unhindered access to transferred refugees in order to monitor compliance with the receiving state's responsibilities towards them; and to abide by a procedure (whether established by the agreement or otherwise) for the settlement of any disagreement arising out of interpretation or implementation of the agreement.[94]

The Refugee Law Initiative Declaration on Externalisation and Asylum further provides:

> International agreements concerning third country processing must take a form suitable for protecting transferees' rights and ideally be binding

> under international law. Their content must detail the applicable substantive and procedural standards... and include an effective supervision mechanism to ensure that the legal rights of transferred asylum seekers are respected during implementation and to correct the situation if they are not. These agreements should be published and open to scrutiny by democratic and judicial mechanisms.[95]

In the Pacific, transparency in regard to third country processing has been thwarted by government secrecy. Because asylum seekers arriving by boat were considered a 'national emergency' eliciting a military-led response, the Australian government considers 'on-water operations' a confidential matter of national security. The rationalisation for this position is that public information on boat turnbacks and transfers of asylum seekers would fuel people smuggling operations.[96]

In relation to the centres in Nauru and Papua New Guinea, transparency is problematic for a number of reasons. First, their remote location, in small islands in the Pacific, makes physical access to the sites difficult.[97] Second, for some years the sites operated as closed detention centres, requiring authorisation for entry. Third, staff at the centres are bound by confidentiality agreements. Finally, there appear to have been deliberate attempts by the cooperating governments to prevent transparency. For example, Nauru increased the cost of journalist visas from $A200 to $A8000 in 2014.[98] In this vein, van Berlo describes the Nauru centre as:

> ... characterised by limited transparency and openness. This is on the one hand due to the walls of governance that are erected: many of the bilateral and contractual arrangements between the various public and private actors involved remain secret and the corporate actors involved act without much public scrutiny. On the other hand, the lack of transparency and openness enhanced by the physical and procedural remoteness of the Centre.[99]

Oversight is a persistent issue in the Pacific, with a number of Australian and international observers denied access to the processing centres. For example, Australia's national human rights institution, the Australian Human Rights Commission, was denied access to Nauru in 2014. The UN Special Rapporteur for the Human Rights of Migrants cancelled a visit to the RPCs in 2015 on the basis that Australian regulations prevented him from 'fully and freely carrying out his duties'.[100]

The UK–Rwanda APA provided for an independent Monitoring Committee with a mandate to monitor the 'entire relocation process' encompassing the four phases outlined above (para 15). The Monitoring Committee wide access to both individuals and facilities under the APA, though crucially there was no provision setting out the powers of the Monitoring Committee (e.g., to request the return of individuals to the UK or to suspend transfers to Rwanda where breaches of international law are uncovered), nor a mechanism for the Monitoring Committee to report its findings.[101]

The key point here is that destination states committed to meeting their international obligations while implementing third country processing must allow sufficient scrutiny of their policies. Transparency, as a democratic principle, requires a reasonable degree of openness about asylum policies undertaken in a third state. Oversight, in turn, is a necessary safeguard for the rights of asylum seekers and the reputations of states engaged in third country processing.

5.5.8 Solutions for refugees

Any third country processing approach requires the provision of solutions for those asylum seekers found to be refugees. Too often, third country processing proposals and practices overlook this basic imperative. If third country processing is, in fact, undertaken as a way to reduce the risks associated with irregular journeys and to prevent migrants with no need of protection reaching destination states, the approach must include the provision of solutions, in particular resettlement.

Within Europe, the failure of the EU relocation scheme indicates that willingness to accept a quota of resettled refugees remains relatively low. Relocation, introduced in 2015, was a mechanism to relieve the pressure on frontline states Italy and Greece during the European migrant and refugee crisis. However, only around one third of the 98,000 asylum seekers slated for relocation were transferred in the program's two-year operation.

In the Pacific, a lack of solutions for refugees has rendered third country processing in Nauru and Papua New Guinea unsustainable. The Australian government has ruled out the possibility of resettlement of refugees in the country, closing off the most obvious form of protection for refugees in Nauru and Papua New Guinea.[102] The key lesson from the Pacific experience is that a failure to secure durable solutions for refugees has undermined the effectiveness of international cooperation and placed refugees in limbo for years on end.

5.5.9 Solutions for persons not in need international protection

Finally, third country processing must take into account the situation of rejected asylum seekers. While refugee law does not protect persons who do not meet the definition of Article 1A(2) of the Refugee Convention, human rights law provides additional layers of protection and any returns from a partner state would be subject to the principle of non-refoulement. Depending on the modalities of the processing arrangements, jurisdiction over a rejected asylum seeker may lie with the partner state, destination state or, more likely, both states. In any case, the partner state retains the sovereign power to grant and withdraw immigration status, including the ability to expel rejected asylum seekers.[103]

The key point here is that rejected asylum seekers subject to third country processing also require a solution following the asylum procedure. Clearly, remaining in the facility is untenable. Policymakers must therefore ensure that rejected asylum seekers either have access to residence in the partner state, where return would violate the principle of non-refoulement, or are safely returned to their country of origin.

5.6 Conclusions: third country processing as responsibility-sharing?

While not unlawful per se, third country processing poses clear challenges to the traditional model of territorial asylum. This chapter has traced the various proposals for and practice of third country processing dating back to the 1980s, as well as surveying scholarly responses to the approach. The chapter further sets out standards to ensure the protection of the rights of asylum seekers and refugees, drawn from both legal obligations and policy lessons. The standards applied to third country processing in this chapter do not represent ideal levels of protection but rather minimum standards. Any future third country processing arrangements should adhere to these standards in providing a fair and effective asylum procedure and solutions to those asylum seekers found to be refugees.

In terms of responsibility-sharing, while adherence to these standards may render third country processing *internationally lawful*, this does not mean such approaches should be considered a form of responsibility-sharing. Indeed, current proposals and practices focused on third country processing in isolation, such as the UK–Rwanda APA and Danish legislation for the externalisation of asylum processing and protection, amount to responsibility-shifting, not responsibility-sharing.

Any third country processing approach should be accompanied by pre-entry processing and/or binding obligations to resettle refugees already present in the partner state at scale. Third country processing may, for example, play a role in responsibility-sharing arrangements where it is used to filter asylum applicants or reserved only for asylum seekers likely to have unfounded claims.[104]

Notes

1 This typology is drawn from Nikolas Feith Tan, 'The Manus Island Regional Processing Centre: A legal taxonomy' (2018), 20 European Journal of Migration and Law 427–51.

2 An abortive 2011 people swap agreement between Australia and Malaysia left jurisdiction over transferred asylum seekers in Malaysia's hands alone. Michelle Foster, 'The Implications of the Failed 'Malaysian Solution': The Australian High Court and Refugee Responsibility Sharing at International Law' (2012) 13 Melbourne Journal of International Law 1.

3 Retfærdig og realistisk: En udlændingepolitik, der samler Danmark, February 2018 (in Danish); Protocol between the Government of the Republic of Italy and the Council of Ministers of the Republic of Albania for the Strengthening of Cooperation in Migration Matters, 2023.

4 *Ilascu and Others v. Moldova and Russia* 48787/99 App no 48787/99 (ECtHR, 8 July 2004), para 312; Kees Wouters and Maarten Den Heijer, 'The Marine I Case: a Comment' (2010), 22 International Journal of Refugee Law 1, 11.

5 *Hassan v United Kingdom* App no 29750/09 (ECtHR [GC], 16 September 2014) para 136; United Nations General Assembly, *Report of the Special Rapporteur on torture and other cruel, inhuman or degrading treatment or punishment, Juan E. Méndez* A/70/303 (7 August 2015) para 38.

6 UNHCR, *UNHCR monitoring visit to the Republic of Nauru 7 to 9 October 2013*. Similarly, in relation to the Papua New Guinea RPC, see UNHCR, *UNHCR Mission to Manus Island, Papua New Guinea 15–17 January 2013* 7.

7 *Al-Skeini v United Kingdom* App no 55721/07 (ECtHR, 7 July 2011) para 149.

8 Committee against Torture, *Concluding observations on the fourth and fifth periodic reports of Australia* CAT/C/AUS/CO/4-5 (26 November 2014); and Human Rights Committee, *Concluding observations on the sixth periodic report of Australia* CCPR/C/AUS/CO/6 (9 November 2017).

9 As noted at above, however, the end of jurisdiction does not rule out responsibility for subsequent *refoulement* from the partner state.

10 This account of proposals and practice draws on Tan, 'The Manus Island Regional Processing Centre: A legal taxonomy' 430–3.

11 Penelope Mathew and Tristan Harley, *Refugees, Regionalism and Responsibility* (Edward Elgar 2016) 115.

12 Harold Hongju Koh, 'America's Offshore Refugee Camps' (1994) 29 University of Richmond Law Review 139.

13 According to Dastyari, 425 people were transferred to Guantánamo Bay for asylum processing between 1996 and 2014. The majority of those requiring protection are resettled in third countries, not the US. Azadeh Dastyari, *United States Migrant Interdiction and the Detention of Refugees in Guantánamo Bay* (Cambridge University Press 2015) 4.

14 Gregor Noll, 'Visions of the exceptional: legal and theoretical issues raised by transit processing centres and protection zones' (2003) 5 European Journal of Migration and Law 303.

15 Daniel Ghezelbash, *Refuge Lost: Asylum Law in an Interdependent World* (Cambridge University Press 2018) 110.

16 Sartori Maria E Sartori, 'The Cuban Migration Dilemma: An Examination of the United States' Policy of Temporary Protection in Offshore Safe Havens' (2000) 15 Georgetown Immigration Law Journal 319.

17 Noll, 'Visions of the exceptional: legal and theoretical issues raised by transit processing centres and protection zones'.

18 Jane McAdam, *Extraterritorial processing in Europe* (Kaldor Centre for International Refugee Law policy brief, 2015).

19 Noll, 'Visions of the exceptional: legal and theoretical issues raised by transit processing centres and protection zones' 303; and McAdam, *Extraterritorial processing in Europe* 4.

20 Netherlands Advisory Committee on Migration Affairs, *External Processing: Conditions applying to the Processing of Asylum Applications outside the European Union* (2010) 17.
21 According to one scholar, 'Politicians in the UK, France, Holland, Denmark, Austria and Belgium have advocated for an Australian-style approach' to asylum. Daniel Ghezelbash, 'Why Europe shouldn't follow Australia's lead on asylum seekers' (*The Conversation*, 27 March 2018) https://theconversation.com/why-europe-shouldnt-follow-australias-lead-on-asylum-seekers-90304 accessed 5 April 2018.
22 Retfærdig og realistisk: En udlændingepolitik, der samler Danmark, February 2018 (in Danish).
23 Austria and Denmark, *Vision for a Better Protection System in a Globalized World* (2018).
24 European Commission, 'Non-paper on regional disembarkation arrangements', June 2018 https://ec.europa.eu/home-affairs/sites/homeaffairs/files/what-we-do/policies/european-agenda-migration/20180724_non-paper-regional-disembarkation-arrangements_en.pdf accessed 30 August 2018.
25 European Council, Conclusions – 28 June 2018 http://www.consilium.europa.eu/media/35936/28-euco-final-conclusions-en.pdf accessed 30 August 2018; and European Commission, 'Non-paper on regional disembarkation arrangements'.
26 Agreement Between the Government of the United States of America and the Republic of Guatemala on Cooperation Regarding the Examination of Protection Claims (26 July 2019).
27 Refugees International and Human Rights Watch, *Failure of Protection under the US-Guatemala Asylum Cooperative Agreement* (2020).
28 L 226 Forslag til lov om ændring af udlændingeloven og hjemrejseloven (Indførelse af mulighed for overførsel af asylansøgere til asylsagsbehandling og eventuel efterfølgende beskyttelse i tredjelande), Lovforslag som vedtaget, 3 June 2021.
29 Nikolas Feith Tan, 'Visions of the Realistic? Denmark's Legal Basis for Extraterritorial Asylum' (2022) 91 Nordic Journal of International Law 172.
30 Memorandum of Understanding between the government of the United Kingdom of Great Britain and Northern Ireland and the government of the Republic of Rwanda for the provision of an asylum partnership arrangement (13 April 2022).
31 Protocol between the Government of the Republic of Italy and the Council of Ministers of the Republic of Albania for the Strengthening of Cooperation in Migration Matters (2023).
32 Maarten den Heijer, *Europe and Extraterritorial Asylum* (Bloomsbury 2012) 260–1.
33 Koh, 'America's Offshore Refugee Camps' 14; and Itamar Mann, 'Maritime Legal Black Holes: Migration and Rightlessness in International Law' (2017) 29 European Journal of International Law 347, 349.
34 Noll, 'Visions of the exceptional: legal and theoretical issues raised by transit processing centres and protection zones' 338.
35 Jeff Crisp, 'A New Asylum Paradigm?: Globalization, Migration and the Uncertain Future of the International Refugee Regime' (2003) 1 St Antony's International Review 39, 51.
36 den Heijer, *Europe and Extraterritorial Asylum* 260.
37 Karin Fathimath Afeef, 'The Politics of Extraterritorial Processing: Offshore Asylum Policies in Europe and the Pacific' (Refugee Studies Centre Working Paper, 2006) 27.

38 Madeline Garlick, 'The EU Discussions on Extraterritorial Processing: Solution or Conundrum?' (2006) 18 International Journal of Refugee Law 601.
39 Violeta Moreno-Lax, *Europe in Crisis: Facilitating Access to Protection, (Discarding) Offshore Processing and Mapping Alternatives for the Way Forward* (Red Cross EU Office, 2015) 31.
40 Sergio Carrera and Elspeth Guild, 'Offshore processing of asylum applications Out of sight, out of mind?' (CEPS, 2017).
41 McAdam, *Extraterritorial processing in Europe* 12.
42 Savitri Taylor, 'Pacific Solution or a Pacific Nightmare: The Difference between Burden Shifting and Responsibility Sharing' (2005) 6 Asian-Pacific Law & Policy Journal 1, 43.
43 Susan Kneebone, 'The Pacific Plan: The Provision of "Effective Protection"?' (2006) 18 International Journal of Refugee Law 696, 720.
44 Angus Francis, 'Bringing Protection Home: Healing the Schism between International Obligations and National Safeguards Created by Extraterritorial Processing' (2008) 20 International Journal of Refugee Law 273.
45 Azadeh Dastyari and Maria O'Sullivan, 'Not for Export: The Failure of Australia's Extraterritorial Processing Regime in Papua New Guinea and the Decision of the PNG Supreme Court in Namah' (2016) 42 Monash University Law Review 308.
46 Guy S Goodwin-Gill, 'The Extraterritorial Processing of Claims to Asylum or Protection: The Legal Responsibilities of States and International Organisations' (2007) 9 UTS Law Review 26.
47 Goodwin-Gill 40.
48 Anna Liguori, 'Some Observations on the Legal Responsibility of States and International Organizations in the Extraterritorial Processing of Asylum Claims' (2016) 25 The Italian Yearbook of International Law Online 135.
49 Amy Nethery and Rosa Holman, 'Secrecy and human rights abuse in Australia's offshore immigration detention centres' (2016) 20 The International Journal of Human Rights .
50 Patrick van Berlo, 'The Protection of Asylum Seekers in Australian-Pacific Offshore Processing: The Legal Deficit of Human Rights in a Nodal Reality' (2017) 17 Human Rights Law Review 33.
51 Daniel Thym and Kay Hailbronner, 'Legal Framework for EU Asylum Policy' in Kay Hailbronner and Daniel Thym (eds), *EU Immigration and Asylum Law: Commentary* (2nd edn, C.H. Beck 2016) 1048; and Daniel Thym, 'Legal Framework for Entry and Border Controls' in Kay Hailbronner and Daniel Thym (eds), *EU Immigration and Asylum Law: Commentary* (2nd edn, C.H. Beck 2016) 40.
52 See, for example, Nikolas Feith Tan, 'State responsibility and migration control: Australia's international deterrence model' in Thomas Gammeltoft-Hansen and Jens Vedsted-Hansen (eds), *Human Rights and the Dark Side of Globalisation: Transnational law enforcement and migration control* (Routledge 2017); Madeline Gleeson and Natasha Yacoub, 'Cruel, Costly and Ineffective: the Failure of Offshore Processing in Australia' (Kaldor Centre Policy Brief No. 11, 2021); and Liguori, 'Some Observations on the Legal Responsibility of States and International Organizations in the Extraterritorial Processing of Asylum Claims'.
53 Azadeh Dastyari and Daniel Ghezelbash, 'Asylum at Sea: The Legality of Shipboard Refugee Status Determination Procedures' (2020) 32 International Journal of Refugee Law 1. See further Refugee Law Initiative Declaration on Externalisation and Asylum (2022) para 18.
54 For an example of pre-transfer procedures falling short of such procedural standards, see AAA and others v Secretary of State for the Home Department [2022] EWHC 3230 (Admin) in which the UK High Court held the UK-Rwanda APA

to be lawful policy, but quashed all eight individual transfer decisions on the basis of procedural errors on the part of the UK Home Office.

55 The prohibition of collective expulsion can be found, *inter alia*, article 4 Protocol 4 to the ECHR and article 22 International Convention on the Protection of the Rights of All Migrant Workers and Members of their Families (adopted 18 December 1990, entered into force 1 July 2003) 2220 UNTS 3 (ICRMW). The only exception to the obligation, at least in the Council of Europe, is where a large group of aliens creates a dangerous situation by using force to enter a state. See *ND and NT v Spain* App Nos 8675/15 and 8697/15 (ECtHR, 13 February 2020).

56 The right to an effective remedy is contained notably in Article 13 ECHR.

57 'The Michigan Guidelines on Protection Elsewhere' (2006) 28 Michigan Journal of International Law para 12.

58 See, for example, *Osman v Denmark* App No 38058/09 (ECtHR, 14 June 2011).

59 Articles 3 and 37 Convention on the Rights of the Child. See further Refugee Law Initiative Declaration on Externalisation and Asylum (2022) para 19.

60 Refugee Law Initiative Declaration on Externalisation and Asylum (2022) para 20.

61 *Hirsi Jamaa and Others v Italy* App no. 27765/09 (ECtHR, 23 February 2012) para 128.

62 On the effect of ratification, see Oona A Hathaway, 'Do human rights treaties make a difference?' (2002) Yale Law Journal 1935; and Eric Neumayer, 'Do international human rights treaties improve respect for human rights?' (2005) 49 Journal of conflict resolution 925.

63 Kirsty Needham, 'Nauru signs UN refugee convention' (*The Sydney Morning Herald*, 18 June 2011) https://www.smh.com.au/national/nauru-signs-un-refugee-convention-20110617-1g830.html accessed 27 March 2018.

64 Refugee Convention arts 17(1), 21, 22(1), 26, 31, 32 and 34.

65 Regional Resettlement Arrangement between Australia and Papua New Guinea (signed and entered into force 19 July 2013) art 7.

66 Diana Glazebrook, 'Papua New Guinea's refugee track record and its obligations under the 2013 Regional Resettlement Arrangement with Australia' (2014) 11.

67 Around the Mediterranean basis, for example, only Libya and Lebanon are not party to the 1951 Convention. Turkey maintains a geographical limitation.

68 9th Appeals Committee, Decision 15602/2017, 29 September 2017.

69 11th Appeals Committee, Decision 14011/2017, 29 September 2017.

70 Nethery and Holman, 'Secrecy and human rights abuse in Australia's offshore immigration detention centres'.

71 Refugee Law Initiative Declaration on Externalisation and Asylum (2022) para 22.

72 UNHCR, *UNHCR Mission to the Republic of Nauru 7 to 9 October 2013* 1.

73 van Berlo, 'The Protection of Asylum Seekers in Australian-Pacific Offshore Processing: The Legal Deficit of Human Rights in a Nodal Reality' 61.

74 Kirsten McConnachie, 'Refugee Protection and the Art of the Deal' (2017) 9 Journal of Human Rights Practice 190, 193.

75 According to the Australian government, therefore: 'Nauru owns and administers the Nauru Regional Processing Centre, under Nauruan law. Australia provides capacity building and funding for Government of Nauru's operation of the centre and coordinates the contract administration process'. Select Committee on the Recent allegations relating to conditions and circumstances at the Regional Processing Centre in Nauru, *Taking responsibility: conditions and circumstances at Australia's Regional Processing Centre in Nauru* 9. In relation to the PNG centre, since closed, the Australian government stated: 'The administrator of PNG's ICSA, the Immigration and Citizenship Service Authority, is responsible for the centre. There is an operational manager who is also an officer of PNG ICSA and controls the day-to-day operations of the centre. Then there is

a coordinator who was appointed by the Australian government and assists the operation manager through the provision of reports and information from service providers to manage the various contracts' and Senate Legal and Constitutional Affairs References Committee, *Incident at the Manus Island Detention Centre from 16 February to 18 February 2014* 18.

76 For example, the Australian government has stated: 'Australia does not exercise the degree of control necessary in regional processing countries to enliven Australia's international obligations'. Select Committee on the recent allegations relating to conditions and circumstances at the Regional Processing Centre in Nauru, *Taking responsibility: conditions and circumstances at Australia's Regional Processing Centre in Nauru* 15.

77 Committee Against Torture, *Concluding observations on the fourth and fifth periodic reports of Australia* para 17.

78 Human Rights Committee, *Concluding observations on the sixth periodic report of Australia* para 35.

79 UNHCR reported in 2013 in relation to the Nauru centre:

Australia has retained a high degree of control and direction in almost all aspects of the bilateral transfer arrangements. The Government of Australia funds the refugee status determination process which takes place in Nauru, seconds Australian immigration officials to undertake the processing and effectively controls most operational management issues'.

UNHCR, *UNHCR monitoring visit to the Republic of Nauru 7 to 9 October 2013* 23. Similarly, in relation to the PNG centre, see UNHCR, *UNHCR Mission to Manus Island, Papua New Guinea 15-17 January 2013* 7.

80 UNHCR, *UNHCR monitoring visit to the Republic of Nauru 7 to 9 October 2013* 8.

81 UNHCR, *UNHCR monitoring visit to Manus Island, Papua New Guinea, 23 to 25 October 2013* 8.

82 Thym and Hailbronner, 'Legal Framework for EU Asylum Policy' 1048.

83 Refugees International and Human Rights Watch, *Failure of Protection under the US-Guatemala Asylum Cooperative Agreement* (2020).

84 Matthew Albert, 'Governance and Prima Facie Refugee Status Determination: Clarifying the Boundaries of Temporary Protection, Group Determination, and Mass Influx' (2010) 29 Refugee Survey Quarterly 61.

85 UNHCR), *UNHCR Submission for the Universal Periodic Review - Rwanda - UPR 37th Session (2021)*, July 2020 4.

86 UNHCR, *Protection Policy Paper: Maritime interception operations and the processing of international protection claims: legal standards and policy considerations with respect to extraterritorial processing* (2010) para 26.

87 Article 46(2).

88 Asylum Information Database (AIDA), 'Country Report: Greece, 2016 update – March 2017' 94; and Danish Refugee Council, *Fundamental Rights and the EU Hotspot Approach* (2017) 1.

89 Committee Against Torture, *Concluding observations on the fourth and fifth periodic reports of Australia* para 17; and Human Rights Committee, *Concluding observations on the sixth periodic report of Australia* para 35.

90 Sharon Pickering and Leanne Weber, 'New Deterrence Scripts in Australia's Rejuvenated Offshore Detention Regime for Asylum Seekers' (2014) 39 Law & Social Inquiry 1006; Azadeh Dastyari, 'Detention of Australia's Asylum Seekers in Nauru: Is Deprivation of Liberty by Any Other Name Just as Unlawful?' (2015) 38 University of New South Wales Law Journal 669; Nethery and Holman, 'Secrecy and human rights abuse in Australia's offshore immigration detention centres'; and Lisa Jane Archbold, 'Offshore Processing of Asylum

Seekers – Is Australia Complying With Its International Legal Obligations' (2015) 15 QUT Law Review.

91 Republic of Nauru, 'Regional processing – Open Centre' (2 October 2015) http://www.abc.net.au/news/2015-10-03/letter-from-republic-of-nauru-about-open-centre/6825366 accessed 18 February 2016.

92 Nethery and Holman, 'Secrecy and human rights abuse in Australia's offshore immigration detention centres'.

93 Carrera and Guild, 'Offshore processing of asylum applications Out of sight, out of mind?'.

94 'The Michigan Guidelines on Protection Elsewhere' para 16.

95 Refugee Law Initiative Declaration on Externalisation and Asylum (2022) para 17.

96 James Glenday, 'Asylum Seekers: Releasing Operation Sovereign Borders Details not in the National Interest, Scott Morrison Tells Senate Committee' (*ABC News*, 4 February 2014) http://www.abc.net.au/news/2014–01–31/morrison-appears-before-senate-committee/5230836 accessed 6 April 2018; and Natalie Klein, 'Assessing Australia's Push Bank the Boats Policy Under International Law: Legality and Accountability for Maritime Interceptions of Irregular Migrants' (2014) 15 Melbourne Journal of International Law 414, 418.

97 Nethery and Holman, 'Secrecy and human rights abuse in Australia's offshore immigration detention centres' 10.

98 Joyce Chia, 'Offshore detention removes scrutiny and accountability for those who need it most', (*The Conversation*, 3 September 2015) https://theconversation.com/offshore-detention-removes-scrutiny-and-accountability-for-those-who-need-it-most-46990 accessed 6 April 2018.

99 van Berlo, 'The Protection of Asylum Seekers in Australian-Pacific Offshore Processing: The Legal Deficit of Human Rights in a Nodal Reality' 65–6.

100 Jane Lee, 'UN Cancels Australia Visit over Border Force Laws' (*Sydney Morning Herald*, 26 September 2015).

101 Memorandum of Understanding between the government of the United Kingdom of Great Britain and Northern Ireland and the government of the Republic of Rwanda for the provision of an asylum partnership arrangement, 13 April 2022 para 15.

102 Several hundred asylum seekers who arrived Nauru and PNG between September 2012 and July 2013 were transferred to Australia.

103 Netherlands Advisory Committee on Migration Affairs, *External Processing: Conditions applying to the Processing of Asylum Applications outside the European Union* 44.

104 See Chapter 7.

6

THIRD COUNTRY PROTECTION

6.1 Introduction

The previous chapter considered legal standards applicable to third country processing arrangements. This chapter addresses a distinct but related form of transnational asylum, namely 'third country protection', which involves *the transfer of a refugee from a destination state or region to a partner state for the purpose of receiving international protection.* In some contrast to processing, third country protection entails the long-term integration of refugees in a partner state.

There is some variation in the form of third country protection arrangements. Most clearly, arrangements for the protection of recognised refugees in a third state fall under this category. Refugees transferred to Nauru, for example, receive a five-year visa and a settlement package paid for by the Australian government. Similarly, the Regional Resettlement Arrangement between Australia and Papua New Guinea attempted the local integration of refugees. The Australia–Cambodia MoU attempted to permanently integrate recognised refugees transferred from Nauru.[1] Moreover, other cooperative asylum arrangements for the transfer of asylum seekers may in practice result in third country protection. The EU–Turkey Statement, for example, results in the protection of refugees in Turkey. Similarly, the UK–Rwanda APA and Danish legislation foresee the delegation of both asylum processing and subsequent refugee protection to a third state.[2]

Third country protection arrangements may be understood as either a form of international cooperation, with the potential to increase 'protection space' in bilateral or regional contexts,[3] or as an example of deterrence, by which destination states extend their efforts to avoid responsibility for refugees to the 'outsourcing' of international protection.[4]

DOI: 10.4324/9781003463146-6

In its guidance on transfer agreements, UNHCR calls for arrangements that 'contribute to the enhancement of the overall protection space' in the destination state, partner state or regionally.[5] Whatever the characterisation, third country protection policies raise several legal questions related to refugee rights under Articles 2–34 of the Refugee Convention.[6]

Third country protection is distinct from the durable solution of resettlement.[7] Crucially, resettlement involves countries with greater capacity and resources accepting refugees from states less able to provide protection to refugees.[8] In contrast, third country protection generally involves the transfer of a refugee from the jurisdiction of a destination state in the Global North to receive international protection in a country in the Global South, under a bilateral agreement.

Under its mandate, UNHCR coordinates resettlement as a mechanism to share responsibility for refugees by relieving pressure on hosting states. UNHCR thus describes resettlement as:

> the selection and transfer of refugees from a State in which they have sought protection to a third State which has agreed to admit them – as refugees – with permanent residence status. The status provided ensures protection against refoulement and provides a resettled refugee and his/her family or dependents with access to rights similar to those enjoyed by nationals. Resettlement also carries with it the opportunity to eventually become a naturalised citizen of the resettlement country.[9]

Through its resettlement program, UNHCR submits individuals for resettlement to countries with a resettlement quota. Resettlement countries allocate spots to selected refugees, who then depart the country of asylum for the resettlement country. Historically, some cooperation arrangements have included resettlement on an *ad hoc* basis, often in the face of mass influx situations. The Comprehensive Plan of Action (CPA), for example, saw western states resettle Indochinese refugees in exchange for the cooperation of Southeast Asian countries in providing temporary asylum.[10] The EU's attempt to relocate in Italy and Greece throughout the EU between 2015 and 2017 may also be seen as a form of intra-EU resettlement, with 34,323 people relocated under the scheme.

Moreover, third country protection is distinct from 'safe third country' and 'first country of asylum' concepts in a couple of key respects. Third country protection does not necessarily involve a return to a transit state or a state where the refugee has already received protection.[11] Refugees transferred under third country protection arrangements may have never set foot in the state ultimately providing protection. Further, third country protection involves the *coordinated* provision of international protection under a bilateral agreement, while the safe third country or first country of asylum concepts often are limited to transfer from one state to another.[12]

This chapter proceeds in three sections. First, the chapter traces the proposals for and practices of third country protection. Second, it provides an account of scholarly responses to practice in this area. As third country protection is a relatively recent phenomenon, these opening sections are rather brief. Finally, the chapter sets out standards to promote the legality of third country protection policies in attempted transnational asylum approaches.

6.2 Proposals for and practice of third country protection

In contrast to third country processing, third country protection is a relatively new form of transnational asylum, and thus practice in this area is recent and limited. It is imperative to note that the attempts at third country protection outlined below violate a number of refugee and human rights law obligations and do not meaningfully expand protection space. Any future approaches must learn from the flaws of these attempts to develop a lawful approach that enhances international protection.

The most prominent examples of third country protection actually implemented can be found in the Asia–Pacific, where a series of bilateral agreements formed the basis for the protection of refugees who sought asylum in Australia in developing states. Since 2013, Australia has refused protection to refugees who arrived by boat. With this avenue to asylum off the table, Australia has attempted to craft different durable solutions for refugees transferred to Nauru and Papua New Guinea.

First, refugees may be locally integrated in Nauru. The 2013 MoU between Australia and Nauru provides for the settlement of people found to be refugees in that country 'subject to agreement between the two participants and numbers'.[13] While Nauru has displayed a willingness to locally integrate refugees, the micro state's capacity has thus far been limited to around 100 refugees.

Second, refugees in Papua New Guinea could be locally integrated there under the 2013 Regional Resettlement Arrangement.[14] In practice, the vast majority of refugees in Papua New Guinea live in transit centres on Manus Island and the mainland, due to concerns for their safety in the community while awaiting resettlement.

Thirdly, refugees in Nauru had the option of receiving protection in Cambodia. Under an agreement in operation between 2014 and 2018, Cambodia offered permanent settlement to people found to be refugees in Nauru.

Beyond the Asia–Pacific, Israel entered into secret bilateral agreements with Rwanda and Uganda to accept persons from Sudan and Eritrea on a permanent basis between 2013 and 2018.[15] While the policy notionally related to 'infiltrators' who were not recognised refugees, many of the 4,000, mostly Sudanese and Eritrean nationals transferred, were likely in need of protection, including due to the shortcomings of Israel's asylum procedure.[16]

In 2014, five individuals were transferred from US jurisdiction in Guantanamo Bay to Kazakhstan under a bilateral agreement. The five men, of Yemeni and Tunisian origin, were granted asylum seeker status and began a two-year integration program in Kazakhstan, a party to the Refugee Convention.[17] The arrangement does not amount to a durable solution as there is no legal avenue for their permanent integration in Kazakhstan.[18]

The 2016 EU–Turkey Statement provides for the return of irregular migrants who reach the Greek islands back to Turkey. Those in need of international protection returned under the statement must necessarily receive that protection in Turkey under the Law on Foreigners and International Protection (LFIP).[19] Between April 2016 and April 2020, 2,140 people were returned under the arrangement.[20] Since 2021, the statement has been suspended.

The US-led Asylum Cooperation Agreements (ACA), signed with El Salvador, Guatemala and Honduras, envisaged not only that the asylum procedure would take place in the receiving state but also that any need for protection would be addressed there.[21] Under the UK–Rwanda APA, asylum seekers transferred to Rwanda and found to be refugees were to be offered protection in Rwanda.[22] Similarly, the Danish legislation provides for the transfer of asylum seekers to a third country outside the EU for the purposes of both asylum processing and protection of refugees in the third country.[23]

6.3 Scholarly approaches to third country protection

Given the relative novelty of third country protection approaches, there is little scholarly work on the transfer of *recognised* refugees under third country protection arrangements. However, third country protection has elicited a number of responses from scholars as a final step in externalisation and deterrence, as a form of responsibility-shifting disguised as responsibility-sharing, as an instantiation of deal-making and as a potential responsibility-sharing approach to expand protection space for refugees.

First, third country protection arrangements have been characterised as the logical end-game of externalisation, focused on the attempts of destination states to deter asylum seekers and refugees. In her article comparing Israeli and Australian practices, Bar-Tuvia argues that such approaches are cynical exercises aimed at buying off developing countries to achieve deterrence aims.[24] Failla characterises third country protection as a corollary to third country processing in the Pacific.[25]

Second, third country protection arrangements have been characterised as responsibility-shifting in the guise of responsibility-sharing. The 2006 Michigan Guidelines on Protection Elsewhere encompass situations where refugee protection is 'addressed somewhere other than in the territory of the state where the refugee has sought, or intends to seek, protection'. The Guidelines set out minimum standards for the lawful transfer of a refugee to a third state, acknowledging the potential of such agreements to share responsibility for refugees while expressing concern for refugee rights in practice.[26] Foster, an author of the Guidelines, explored the Australia–Malaysia arrangement as 'an important contribution to our understanding of the limits of the Refugee Convention in accommodating responsibility-sharing regimes'.[27]

Third, scholars have focused on the cooperation element of third country protection. Gammeltoft-Hansen points out that such arrangements have the effect of diluting the *quality* of international protection, by virtue of the very structure of the Refugee Convention.[28] McConnachie considers such policies 'protection bargaining',[29] while Failla observes that responsibility-sharing 'requires more than the provision of monetary compensation for the receipt of responsibility'.[30] With respect to the EU–Turkey Statement, Thym has argued that the arrangement is an exercise of international cooperation to remedy a mass-influx of asylum seekers into the EU.[31]

Finally, some scholars have taken a more pragmatic approach to third country protection arrangements. Writing just prior to the EU–Turkey Statement, Hathaway argued that states enjoy 'substantial latitude to require a refugee to benefit from protection in a state not of the refugee's choosing' and set out three requirements for a transfer from one state to another. According to Hathaway, the receiving state must be a party to the Refugee Convention, must ensure that refugees are recognised in practice and must 'in fact honour refugee rights' with reference to Articles 2–34 of the convention.[32]

Azhigulova presents a rather more positive view of the potential of third country protection to develop into an additional tool for international protection. According to Azhigulova:

> … there are quite a few developing states that may be hardly hosting any refugees and who could potentially participate more in sharing the burden of hosting refugees with other states, both economically developed and developing. Economic development or underdevelopment should not be a criterion for states' participation in burden-sharing mechanisms; to the contrary, the Refugee Convention encourages all states to cooperate in finding a solution to a refugee problem.[33]

Thus, Azhigulova argues that third country protection offers a new form of protection, brokered between states (rather than UNHCR), that may occur across geographic regions with the potential to tap refugee protection in states not party to the Refugee Convention.[34] Clearly, the existing practice of third country protection offers inadequate and often unlawful conditions of protection. The following sets out standards to inform future attempts at such arrangements.

6.4 Third country protection standards

The following sets out standards for the use of third country protection to guarantee the rights of transferred refugees. These standards reflect both the legal obligations incumbent upon states engaged in third country protection and policy lessons learned from recent practice. While the focus is on the Refugee Convention, given its primacy in regulating the protection of refugees, standards from international and regional human rights instruments play an important supplementary role; however, given the great variation of obligations among potential partner states, these are not discussed here.[35]

6.4.1 Ratification of the Refugee Convention

First, as an important preliminary consideration, third country protection should only take place where the partner state in law and practice respects the terms of the Refugee Convention or its 1967 Protocol. As Hathaway points out, the convention drafters believed 'state parties should be free to share out the duty to protect refugees'.[36] While ratification of the Refugee Convention will not ipso facto render third country protection lawful, it is a necessary but not sufficient condition for a suitable partner state, signifying a commitment to the key obligations of refugee protection. Ratification of the convention represents a binding commitment to respect its terms to implement the treaty in practice, over and above mere political commitments.[37] Moreover, transfer to a non-party state would limit UNHCR's ability to oversee protection standards in the country.[38]

According to UNHCR's Summary Conclusions on the Concept of 'Effective Protection' (15.e):

> While accession to international refugee instruments and basic human rights instruments is a critical indicator, the actual practice of States and their compliance with these instruments is key to the assessment of the effectiveness of protection. Where the return of an asylum seeker to a third State is involved, accession to and compliance with the 1951 Convention and/or 1967 Protocol are essential, unless the destination country can demonstrate that the third State has developed a practice akin to the 1951 Convention and/or its 1967 Protocol.[39]

The question of whether a party to the Refugee Convention that maintains a geographical limitation may be a suitable partner state has also arisen with respect to the EU–Turkey Statement. Turkey maintains a geographical limitation, by which it only recognises refugees originating from Europe.[40] Thus, for the vast majority of refugees, including those transferred under the EU–Turkey Statement, Turkey is a non-party state. In 2016, Hathaway argued that the legality of the EU–Turkey Statement turned on Turkey's lifting of its geographical restriction.[41] UNHCR took a more pragmatic approach, arguing that *de facto* compliance with the Refugee Convention was sufficient in the following terms.

> Turkey must allow, in accordance with rules laid down in national law, non-European nationals or stateless persons who had their place of habitual residence outside Europe to request refugee status and to have access to all rights conferred by the 1951 Convention.[42]

Finally, in exceptional cases, a non-party state will be a suitable partner country where domestic law and practice do in fact respect refugee rights.[43] In relation to standards on the safe third country and first country of asylum concepts, for example, UNHCR does not require ratification of the Refugee Convention. As previously mentioned, the 2002 expert roundtable concluded that 'accession to and compliance with the 1951 Convention and/or 1967 Protocol are essential, unless the destination country can demonstrate that the third state has developed a practice *akin* to the 1951 Convention and/or its 1967 Protocol'.[44] In *Plaintiff M70/2011 v Minister for Immigration and Citizenship*, for example, Malaysia's non-party status and lack of a domestic legal framework rendered it an unsuitable protection country. In this vein, Keifel J noted:

> … it is difficult to see how it can be said that a country provides protection, in a concrete sense, if its laws contain no such provisions. It may not be necessary that a country be a party to the Convention in order that it recognise and protect refugees, although it is more likely that a country's domestic laws will provide for that recognition and protection if they are a Contracting State.[45]

Thus, in general, third country protection should only take place where the partner state has ratified the Refugee Convention. Ultimately, what is likely required is that the partner state respect the law and practice the full set of rights contained in the Refugee Convention.[46] As a result, a state party will not be a suitable protection country where refugee rights are not respected in practice. Recent partner states, including Cambodia, Guatemala, Nauru,

Papua New Guinea and Rwanda, though parties to the Refugee Convention, have lacked the capacity to protect refugees in practice.

6.4.2 Non-refoulement over time

Second, and fundamentally, refugees transferred to a partner state under a third country protection arrangement must in practice be protected against direct and indirect refoulement over time. Most obviously, a refugee transferred must not face a real risk of persecution, torture or other ill treatment in the partner state. Moreover, a refugee transferred must be protected from subsequent refoulement from the partner state.[47] Thus, according to the Michigan Guidelines on Protection Elsewhere:

> Because the duty is to avoid acts which result in a refugee's expulsion or return to the frontiers of a territory where life or freedom would be threatened 'in any manner whatsoever', Art. 33 prohibits indirect refoulement of the kind that occurs when a refugee is sent to a state in which there is a foreseeable risk of subsequent refoulement.[48]

The principle of non-refoulement binds both the destination and the partner state engaged in third country protection. Similarly, the Refugee Law Initiative Declaration on Externalisation and Asylum provides:

> Where third country arrangements extend to the provision of international protection by the receiving State, transferred asylum seekers must receive ongoing protection against refoulement in the receiving State.[49]

Relatedly, UNHCR's Summary Conclusions on the Concept of 'Effective Protection' proscribe both direct and indirect refoulement in the following terms.

a The person has no well-founded fear of persecution in the third State on any of the 1951 Convention grounds.
b There will be respect for fundamental human rights in the third State in accordance with applicable international standards, including but not limited to the following:

- there is no real risk that the person would be subject to torture or to cruel, inhuman or degrading treatment or punishment in the third State;
- there is no real risk to the life of the person in the third State;
- there is no real risk that the person would be deprived of his or her liberty in the third State without due process.

c There is no real risk that the person would be sent by the third State to another State in which he or she would not receive effective protection or would be at risk of being sent from there on to any other State where such protection would not be available.[50]

Finally, it is settled law that third country protection arrangements cannot adopt a 'one size fits all' approach for the transfer of refugees between destination and partner states, as the principle of non-refoulement requires an *individual* case-by-case assessment that a partner country is suitable for protection.[51] Thus, a pre-transfer assessment is necessary for each refugee subject to a third country protection arrangement. Where transfer would expose a refugee to persecution or other ill treatment in breach of the principle of non-refoulement, for example, due to vulnerability, religion or sexual orientation, transfer must not take place.[52]

6.4.3 Non-discrimination between and among refugees

Article 3 provides for *freedom of discrimination between and among refugees* on the basis of race, religion or country of origin as soon as a refugee is within a state's jurisdiction.[53] As Hathaway points out, Article 3 'establishes a presumption that differential treatment based on any of the enumerated grounds is illegitimate'[54] and the non-discrimination obligations extend to all rights contained in the Refugee Convention.

In the context of third country protection, Article 3 provides an important ballast ensuring that refugees across the entire country benefit from the non-discrimination principle, including those who are not part of a transnational asylum arrangement. As a result, fundamental to a good faith interpretation of Article 3 is that the 'rising tide' of standards of treatment required of the destination state must 'lift all boats' in the form of non-discrimination between all refugees present in the partner state.

The provision of, for example, improved access to education for refugees transferred under a transnational asylum arrangement should be extended to other refugees in the partner state. Papua New Guinea lifted reservations against seven articles of the Convention, relating to wage-earning employment, housing, public education, freedom of movement, refugees unlawfully in the country of refuge, expulsion and naturalisation under the 2013 Refugee Resettlement Agreement with Australia.[55] However, the withdrawal of restrictions was limited to persons transferred by Australia, thus arguably breaching the state's Article 3 obligations. The undertaking broadened protections for only a limited number of asylum seekers and refugees in Papua New Guinea, with no benefit to West Papuan refugees in the country.[56]

6.4.4 Civil and political rights under the Refugee Convention

Third country protection arrangements will only be lawful where refugees receive those civil and political rights set down in the Refugee Convention. In the context of transnational asylum arrangements, both cooperating states share responsibility for ensuring that these rights are in place. The following sets out the core civil and political rights afforded refugees, with reference to both the standards of treatment and levels of treatment contained in the Refugee Convention. The subsequent analysis proceeds on the basis that refugees in a partner state hold a relatively stable legal status on the basis of lawful presence, lawful stay or durable residence.

Refugees are entitled to *religious freedom* at a standard at least as favourable as that accorded to citizens, upon entering a state's territory.[57] The Refugee Convention places freedom to practice religion and freedom of religious education in pride of place, immediately following the generalised non-discrimination principle. Such was the importance afforded to religious freedom (often a reason for flight in the first place), the Convention requires 'substantive equality of religious freedom for refugees' at least on par with that of nationals.[58]

Article 16 provides refugees with *access to courts* in the state party in absolute terms, granting the right to engage in litigation of all kinds, including enforcing rights under the Convention itself.[59] The Convention thus requires that refugees in any third state 'have unimpeded access to the courts to enforce relevant claims'.[60]

Refugees are further entitled to *freedom of movement* within the asylum state, including the right to choose their place of residence in line with the treatment afforded other aliens.[61] According to Hathaway, therefore, once a refugee has regularised their status, 'all refugee-specific restrictions on the right to move freely and to choose one's residence must end'.[62] Article 26 allows for limitations on freedom of movement to the extent that they are 'applicable to aliens generally'. For example, where the asylum state has created zones around military installations where aliens are not permitted to enter, such prohibition will apply to refugees on equal terms with other non-citizens who are lawfully present.[63]

Finally, the Refugee Convention requires the asylum state to issue *identity papers* to those refugees on their territory not in possession of a valid travel document.[64] According to Hathaway, the goal of Article 27 is to ensure that all refugees are afforded proof of their refugee status, often in expectation of the issuance of a Convention Travel Document under Article 28.[65]

6.4.5 Socio-economic rights under the Refugee Convention

As with the civil and political rights discussed above, the legality of third country protection arrangements will depend on whether refugees can benefit from key socio-economic rights set down in the Refugee Convention. Chief among these is the *right to work*, adhering to refugees lawfully staying in the asylum state at the most favourable treatment accorded to other aliens in the same circumstances.[66] US representative Louis Henkin stated that 'without the right to work all other rights were meaningless. Without that right no refugee could even become assimilated within his country of residence'.[67]

The standard of treatment required by Article 17 means that refugees lawfully staying shall have the same rights as those foreign nationals who are granted the most favourable treatment as regards access to the labour market. Article 17 has been interpreted to cover all kinds of employment.[68] Article 17 is triggered when a refugee is lawfully staying, a level of attachment requiring an ongoing 'settling down' in practical terms, but not an established residence in the asylum state.[69]

Furthermore, the Refugee Convention provides for the *right to education* for refugee children. With respect to public elementary or primary education, Article 22(1) entitles refugee children to the same treatment accorded to nationals as soon as they are within the asylum state's territory.[70] With respect to secondary and further education, Article 22(2) obliges the asylum state to provide refugee children treatment not less favourable than that accorded to aliens generally in the same circumstances.

Refugees lawfully staying are further entitled to *access to housing* where matters related to housing are subject to public control to a standard as favourable as possible and, in any event, not less favourable than aliens generally in the same circumstances.

With respect to public assistance, Article 23 provides a *right to public relief*, while Article 24 guarantees social security for refugees lawfully staying, both in line with the treatment of nationals. The combined result of these articles is simply that refugees are entitled to both unemployment benefits and any public relief paid to those incapacitated or incapable of work.[71]

6.4.6 Rights of solution

Third country protection should deliver durable solutions to transferred refugees. The provision of a durable solution to refugees is a paramount consideration, though not necessarily a binding obligation. As destination states seek to shift away from the traditional approach of territorial asylum and territorial protection, provision for durable solutions is key to effective policymaking.

First, local integration in the partner state should be the explicit aim of any international agreement. Local integration need not be permanent, though it must last for the duration of the need for protection, or until another durable solution is found. Article 34 of the Refugee Convention calls for a conclusive form of long-term stay, requesting contracting states 'as far as possible to facilitate the assimilation and naturalisation of refugees'. Second, a refugee may choose to voluntarily repatriate from the partner state. Clearly, however, repatriation must be truly voluntary and not forced by a lack of rights and protections.

UNHCR's Summary Conclusions on the Concept of 'Effective Protection' provides in part:

> g The person has access to means of subsistence sufficient to maintain an adequate standard of living. Following recognition as a refugee, steps are undertaken by the third State to enable the progressive achievement of self-reliance, pending the realisation of durable solutions.
>
> ...
>
> h If the person is recognised as a refugee, effective protection will remain available until a durable solution can be found.[72]

Previous cooperative asylum policies have not met these standards. In Papua New Guinea, for example, even once refugees were free from detention, many could not integrate into the host community because of religious tensions between the local community and the refugees. [73] Similarly, most asylum seekers and refugees have, in fact, ended up in Australia because of the need for medical care not available in Nauru and Papua New Guinea.[74] Others have been resettled to Canada and Europe because of the lack of durable solutions in Nauru and Papua New Guinea.[75]

Six of the seven refugees transferred to Cambodia chose voluntary repatriation after some time in the country, despite the agreement's stated objective to 'expand protection opportunities and durable solutions for Refugees in the Asia–Pacific region'.[76] The five asylum seekers transferred from Guantanamo Bay to Kazakhstan were left in 'legal limbo' by a lack of legal pathways to refugee permanent residence.[77] Clearly, Rwanda and Uganda were unable or unwilling to provide a durable solution to Sudanese and Eritrean refugees from Israel, as most moved on irregularly or sought asylum further afield.[78] Finally, refugees returned to Turkey receive 'conditional' or temporary protection, but the vast majority do not have access to durable solutions as local integration is not currently available under Turkish law.[79]

Perhaps most fundamentally, the full complement of refugee rights is practically necessary to allow refugees the opportunity to function effectively in partner states. Malaysia was declared an unlawful partner state in part due to its lack of protection framework under either international or domestic law. Moreover, most of the 4,000 asylum seekers and refugees transferred to Rwanda and Uganda did not receive identity documents and were forced to leave. Some travelled to Europe to apply for asylum and, in fact, received international protection.[80] In contrast, Turkey has thus far been held to be a suitable third country protection state on the basis of temporary forms of protection available to Syrian refugees in the country.

6.4.7 Development of partner state integration capacity

As a practical matter, a suitable partner state should have experience in receiving refugees or, absent such experience, substantial assistance in successful integration from the destination state. This requires a functioning legal framework providing for integration and appropriate services to support newly arrived refugees. The development of such integration capacity is necessary in at least three respects.

- First, refugees transferred need every opportunity to reside in the partner state until a durable solution is found.
- Second, integration capacity is essential for the sustainability of any third country protection policy to ensure that refugees do not end up in 'asylum orbit'.
- Third, the development of integration capacity is fundamental to both the protection of those particular individuals transferred and also the future protection of other groups of refugees.

While local integration has been largely unsuccessful in existing practice, an experienced destination state supporting the integration of refugees in a suitable partner state is necessary for any future third country protection arrangement.

6.4.8 Transparency and independent oversight

As with policies of third country processing, transparency before and during cooperation and independent oversight of implementation are important safeguards for refugee rights and cooperating states' reputations. In principle, UNHCR is an apt independent monitor for third country protection arrangements it deems in accordance with the letter and spirit of the Refugee Convention.[81] However, as noted at a 2011 expert roundtable, UNHCR should not be involved in arrangements that 'contribute to a shrinking of protection space'.[82]

The Australia–Cambodia arrangement was negotiated 'without consultation with parliament or civil society in either Australia or Cambodia'.[83] Similarly, Israel's bilateral agreements with Rwanda and Uganda were negotiated and largely implemented in secret, with national authorities refusing to acknowledge the existence of the agreements until court proceedings forced their hand.[84] Moreover, the Australia–Cambodia MoU in fact included a reference to cooperation with UNHCR in its supervisory role, but the agency refused to play a role in the arrangement, labelling it 'a worrying departure from international norms'.[85]

Moreover, third country protection arrangements call for *ongoing* oversight of treatment in the partner state. In *Yogathas*, the House of Lords stressed the duty of the destination state to 'inform itself of the facts and monitor the decisions made by a third country in order to satisfy itself that the third country will not send the applicant to another country otherwise in accordance with the Convention'.[86] The key point here is that states committed to meeting their international obligations while implementing third country protection must allow sufficient scrutiny of their policies before and during implementation.

6.5 Conclusions: third country protection as responsibility-sharing?

This chapter has addressed third country protection, involving the transfer of a refugee to a partner state for the purpose of receiving international protection. Third country protection extends to the provision of international protection between states. The chapter shows how practice in this area has generally failed to provide protection and sets forth standards to inform future efforts, highlighting the imperative that the full suite of civil and political socio-economic rights and rights of solution owed to refugees under the Refugee Convention be provided in the third state.

In terms of responsibility-sharing, while adherence to these standards may render third country protection *internationally lawful*, such approaches are unlikely to amount to responsibility-sharing. However, as discussed in the final chapter, third country protection may be used in limited ways as part of a coherent transnational asylum approach.

Notes

1 Memorandum of Understanding between the Government of the Kingdom of Cambodia and the Government of Australia, Relating to the Settlement of Refugees in Cambodia (26 September 2014).
2 Memorandum of Understanding between the government of the United Kingdom of Great Britain and Northern Ireland and the government of the Republic of Rwanda for the provision of an asylum partnership arrangement, 13 April 2022; L 226 Forslag til lov om ændring af udlændingeloven og hjemrejseloven (Indførelse af mulighed for overførsel af asylansøgere til asylsagsbehandling og eventuel efterfølgende beskyttelse i tredjelande), Lovforslag som vedtaget, 3 June 2021.
3 Khalida Azhigulova, 'Bilateral Resettlement Agreements: Any Promising Future for Expanding Refugee Protection Space? A Case Study of the Guantanamo

ex-Detainees Seeking Asylum in Central Asia' (Refugee Law Initiative Working Paper No 19, 2007).

4 Monique Failla, 'Outsourcing obligations to developing nations: Australia's refugee resettlement agreement with Cambodia' (2016) 42 Monash University Law Review 638; and Shani Bar-Tuvia, 'Australian and Israeli Agreements for the Permanent Transfer of Refugees: Stretching Further the (Il)legality and (Im)morality of Western Externalization Policies' (2018) 30 International Journal of Refugee Law 1.

5 UNHCR, 'Guidance Note on bilateral and/or multilateral transfer arrangements of asylum-seekers' (2013) para 3(iv).

6 Thomas Gammeltoft-Hansen, 'The extraterritorialisation of asylum and the advent of protection lite' (DIIS working paper, 2007).

7 UNHCR, *UNHCR Resettlement Handbook* 28.

8 Madeline Gleeson, 'In Focus: Resettlement of refugees from Nauru to Cambodia' (Kaldor Centre for International Refugee Law, 9 May 2016) http://www.kaldorcentre.unsw.edu.au/news/focus-resettlement-refugees-nauru-cambodia#sthash.jPJ7lIcS.dpuf accessed 17 May 2016.

9 UNHCR, *UNHCR Resettlement Handbook* 3.

10 Towle Richard Towle, 'Processes and Critiques of the Indo-Chinese Comprehensive Plan of Action: An Instrument of International Burden-Sharing?' (2006) 18 International Journal of Refugee Law 537; and Sara Ellen Davies, *Legitimising Rejection: International Refugee Law in Southeast Asia* (Brill 2008) 226.

11 This has given rise to the term 'fourth country transfer'. Bar-Tuvia, 'Australian and Israeli Agreements for the Permanent Transfer of Refugees: Stretching Further the (Il)legality and (Im)morality of Western Externalization Policies' 3.

12 For analysis on the safe third country and first country of asylum concepts, see Guy S Goodwin-Gill, 'Safe Country? Says Who?' (1992) 4 International Journal of Refugee Law 248; Kay Hailbronner, 'The Concept of "Safe Country" and Expeditious Asylum Procedures: A Western European Perspective' (1993) 5 International Journal of Refugee Law 31; Cathryn Costello, 'The Asylum Procedures Directive and the proliferation of safe country practices: deterrence, deflection and the dismantling of international protection?' (2005) 7 European Journal of Migration and Law 35; and Michelle Foster, 'Responsibility Sharing or Shifting? "Safe" Third Countries and International Law' (2008) 25 Refuge 64.

13 Memorandum of Understanding between the Republic of Nauru and the Commonwealth of Australia, relating to the Transfer to and Assessment of Persons in Nauru, and Related Issues (signed 3 August 2013) art 9.

14 Regional Resettlement Arrangement between Australia and Papua New Guinea (signed and entered into force 19 July 2013) art 5.

15 Bar-Tuvia, 'Australian and Israeli Agreements for the Permanent Transfer of Refugees: Stretching Further the (Il)legality and (Im)morality of Western Externalization Policies'.

16 Israel is a party to the Refugee Convention but has not incorporated its provisions in national law. See further Ruvi Ziegler, 'No Asylum for "Infiltrators": The Legal Predicament of Eritrean and Sudanese Nationals in Israel' (2015) 29 Immigration, Asylum and Nationality Law 172.

17 Azhigulova.

18 Azhigulova, 95.

19 Law No. 6458 of 2013 on Foreigners and International Protection (as amended 29 Oct 2016).

20 UNHCR, Returns from Greece to Turkey, 20 April 2020. https://data2.unhcr.org/en/documents/download/75075 accessed 16 December 2020.

21 See, for example, Agreement Between the Government of the United States of America and the Republic of Guatemala on Cooperation Regarding the Examination of Protection Claims, 26 July 2019.
22 Memorandum of Understanding between the government of the United Kingdom of Great Britain and Northern Ireland and the government of the Republic of Rwanda for the provision of an asylum partnership arrangement, 13 April 2022, para 10.
23 L 226 Forslag til lov om ændring af udlændingeloven og hjemrejseloven (Indførelse af mulighed for overførsel af asylansøgere til asylsagsbehandling og eventuel efterfølgende beskyttelse i tredjelande), Lovforslag som vedtaget, 3 June 2021.
24 Bar-Tuvia, 'Australian and Israeli Agreements for the Permanent Transfer of Refugees: Stretching Further the (Il)legality and (Im)morality of Western Externalization Policies' 35.
25 Failla, 'Outsourcing obligations to developing nations: Australia's refugee resettlement agreement with Cambodia' 643.
26 'The Michigan Guidelines on Protection Elsewhere' (2006) 28 Michigan Journal of International Law; Michelle Foster, 'Protection Elsewhere: The Legal Implications of Requiring Refugees to Seek Protection in Another State' (2006) 28 Michigan Journal of International Law 223, 285.
27 Michelle Foster, 'The Implications of the Failed "Malaysian Solution": The Australian High Court and Refugee Responsibility Sharing at International Law' (2012) 13 Melbourne Journal of International Law.
28 Gammeltoft-Hansen, 'The extraterritorialisation of asylum and the advent of protection lite' 7.
29 Kirsten McConnachie, 'Refugee Protection and the Art of the Deal' (2017) 9 Journal of Human Rights Practice 190, 193.
30 Failla, 'Outsourcing obligations to developing nations: Australia's refugee resettlement agreement with Cambodia' 684.
31 Daniel Thym, 'Why the EU-Turkey Deal is Legal and a Step in the Right Direction' (*Verfassungsblog*, 9 March 2016) https://verfassungsblog.de/why-the-eu-turkey-deal-is-legal-and-a-step-in-the-right-direction/ accessed 27 September 2020.
32 James C Hathaway, 'Three legal requirements for the EU-Turkey deal: An interview with James Hathaway' (*Verfassungsblog*, 9 March 2016) https://verfassungsblog.de/three-legal-requirements-for-the-eu-turkey-deal-an-interview-with-james-hathaway/ accessed 27 September 2020.
33 Azhigulova, 87.
34 Azhigulova, 95–6.
35 See extensively James C Hathaway, *The Rights of Refugees under International Law* (2 edn, Cambridge University Press 2021).
36 James C Hathaway, *The Rights of Refugees under International Law* (2 edn, Cambridge University Press 2021) 328.
37 Rosemary Byrne and Andrew Shacknove, 'The Safe Country Notion in European Asylum Law' (1996) 9 Harvard Human Rights Journal 185, 200; and Foster, 'Protection Elsewhere: The Legal Implications of Requiring Refugees to Seek Protection in Another State' 240.
38 Foster, 'Protection Elsewhere: The Legal Implications of Requiring Refugees to Seek Protection in Another State' 241. Foster notes that article 28, providing for ICJ jurisdiction over any subsequent dispute between the parties, offers a potential dispute mechanism.
39 UNHCR, Summary Conclusions on the Concept of 'Effective Protection' in the Context of Secondary Movements of Refugees and Asylum-Seekers (Lisbon Expert Roundtable, 9–10 December 2002), February 2003 para e.
40 Meltem Ineli-Ciger, 'Protecting Syrians in Turkey: A Legal Analysis' (2017) 29 International Journal of Refugee Law 555.

41 'Three legal requirements for the EU-Turkey deal: An interview with James Hathaway'.
42 UNHCR, 'Legal considerations on the return of asylum-seekers and refugees from Greece to Turkey as part of the EU-Turkey Cooperation in Tackling the Migration Crisis under the safe third country and first country of asylum concept' (2016) 6.
43 Foster, 'The Implications of the Failed "Malaysian Solution": The Australian High Court and Refugee Responsibility Sharing at International Law' 11.
44 UNHCR, 'Summary conclusions on the concept of "Effective Protection" in the context of secondary movements of refugees and asylum seekers' para 15(e) (emphasis added).
45 [2011] HCA 32 (High Court of Australia, 31 August 2011) para 92. See further Tamara Wood and Jane McAdam, 'Australian Asylum Policy all at Sea: An analysis of Plaintiff M70/2011 v Minister for Immigration and Citizenship and the Australia–Malaysia Arrangement' (2012) 61 International and Comparative Law Quarterly 274.
46 Refugee Law Initiative Declaration on Externalisation and Asylum (2022) para 24.
47 Failla, 'Outsourcing obligations to developing nations: Australia's refugee resettlement agreement with Cambodia' 660; Maria O'Sullivan, Explainer: does the Cambodia refugee deal comply with the convention? (*The Conversation*, 30 September2014)https://theconversation.com/explainer-does-the-cambodia-refugee-deal-comply-with-the-convention-29639 accessed 17 May 2016.
48 The Michigan Guidelines on Protection Elsewhere para 6.
49 Refugee Law Initiative Declaration on Externalisation and Asylum para 24.
50 UNHCR, Summary Conclusions on the Concept of 'Effective Protection' in the Context of Secondary Movements of Refugees and Asylum-Seekers (Lisbon Expert Roundtable, 9–10 December 2002), February 2003.
51 *MSS v Belgium and Greece* App no 30696/09 (ECtHR [GC], 21 January 2011) para 354; and *R v Secretary of State for the Home Department, ex parte Yogathas* [2002] UKHL 36 947.
52 Wood and McAdam, 'Australian Asylum Policy all at Sea: An analysis of Plaintiff M70/2011 v Minister for Immigration and Citizenship and the Australia–Malaysia Arrangement' 294; and Foster, 'The Implications of the Failed "Malaysian Solution": The Australian High Court and Refugee Responsibility Sharing at International Law' 26–7.
53 Hathaway, *The Rights of Refugees under International Law* 280. Hathaway argues that the limited scope of Article 3 Refugee Convention is remedied by the far broader application of Article 26 ICCPR, which provides for equal protection before the law and protects against discrimination on 'any ground such as race, colour, sex, language, religion, political or other opinion, national or social origin, property, birth or other status'.
54 Hathaway, *The Rights of Refugees under International Law* 280.
55 Regional Resettlement Arrangement between Australia and Papua New Guinea (signed and entered into force 19 July 2013) art 7. Refugee Convention arts 17(1), 21, 22(1), 26, 31, 32 and 34.
56 Diana Glazebrook, 'Papua New Guinea's refugee track record and its obligations under the 2013 Regional Resettlement Arrangement with Australia' (2014) 11.
57 Refugee Convention art 4.
58 Hathaway, *The Rights of Refugees under International Law* 714–6.
59 Hathaway, *The Rights of Refugees under International Law* 800.
60 Hathaway, *The Rights of Refugees under International Law* 800.
61 See further Marjoleine Zieck, 'Refugees and the Right to Freedom of Movement: From Flight to Return' (2018) 39 Michigan Journal of International Law 19, 83.
62 Hathaway, *The Rights of Refugees under International Law* 871.
63 Hathaway, *The Rights of Refugees under International Law* 704–19.

64 Refugee Convention art 27.
65 Hathaway, *The Rights of Refugees under International Law* 772.
66 Refugee Convention art 17. Alongside article 17, the Convention further sets out work-related rights of association and to form trade unions (article 15), liberal professions (article 19), public relief (article 23) and protection of labour legislation (article 25).
67 UN Ad Hoc Committee on Refugees and Stateless Persons, 'Summary Record of the Thirty-Seventh Meeting' (16 August 1950), UN doc E/AC.32.SR.37, 12 (Mr Henkin, US).
68 Hathaway, *The Rights of Refugees under International Law* 747–48; Alice Edwards, 'Article 17', in Andreas Zimmermann (ed), *The 1951 Convention Relating to the Status of Refugees and its 1967 Protocol. A Commentary* (Oxford University Press 2011) 968.
69 Hathaway, *The Rights of Refugees under International Law* 175–86.
70 Paul Weis (ed), *The Refugee Convention, 1951* (Cambridge University Press 1995) 164 and 170; Hathaway, *The Rights of Refugees under International Law* 746.
71 Weis (ed), *The Refugee Convention, 1951* 164 and 170; Hathaway, *The Rights of Refugees under International Law* 1021.
72 UNHCR, Summary Conclusions on the Concept of 'Effective Protection' in the Context of Secondary Movements of Refugees and Asylum-Seekers (Lisbon Expert Roundtable, 9–10 December 2002), February 2003.
73 JC Salyer, 'The Denial of Human Dignity in the Age of Human Rights under Australia's Operation Sovereign Borders' (2020) 32 The Contemporary Pacific 512.
74 Gabrielle Holly, 'Transnational Tort and Access to Remedy under the UN Guiding Principles on Business and Human Rights: Kamasaee v Commonwealth' (2018) 19 Melbourne Journal of International Law 52; and Gabrielle Holly, 'Challenges to Australia's Offshore Detention Regime and the Limits of Strategic Tort Litigation' (2020) 21 German Law Journal 549.
75 Hannah Ryan and Michael Green, 'Suffered more than many': how Canada and Europe are resettling Australia's refugees (*The Guardian*, 16 December 2020) https://www.theguardian.com/australia-news/2020/dec/17/canada-europe-resettling-australia-refugees accessed 16 August 2024.
76 Memorandum of Understanding between the Government of the Kingdom of Cambodia and the Government of Australia, Relating to the Settlement of Refugees in Cambodia (26 September 2014) art 2(a).
77 Azhigulova, 95; and UNHCR, 'Submission by UNHCR for the Office of the High Commissioner for Human Compilation Report Universal Periodic Review: Kazakhstan' (March 2014) http://www.refworld.org/pdfid/5541e1a24.pdf accessed 27 September 2018.
78 Bar-Tuvia, 'Australian and Israeli Agreements for the Permanent Transfer of Refugees: Stretching Further the (Il)legality and (Im)morality of Western Externalization Policies' 35.
79 Ineli-Ciger, 'Protecting Syrians in Turkey: A Legal Analysis' 565.
80 Bar-Tuvia, 'Australian and Israeli Agreements for the Permanent Transfer of Refugees: Stretching Further the (Il)legality and (Im)morality of Western Externalization Policies' 17.
81 UNHCR, *Expert Meeting on International Cooperation to Share Burdens and Responsibilities* 6.
82 UNHCR.
83 Madeline Gleeson, 'The Australia-Cambodia Refugee Relocation Agreement Is Unique, But Does Little to Improve Protection' (*Migration Policy Institute*, 21

September 2016) https://www.migrationpolicy.org/article/australia-cambodia-refugee-relocation-agreement-unique-does-little-improve-protection accessed 27 September 2018.

84 Bar-Tuvia, 'Australian and Israeli Agreements for the Permanent Transfer of Refugees: Stretching Further the (Il)legality and (Im)morality of Western Externalization Policies'.

85 UNHCR, 'UNHCR statement on Australia-Cambodia agreement on refugee relocation' (26 September 2014) http://www.unhcr.org/542526db9.html accessed 25 May 2016.

86 *R v Secretary of State for the Home Department, ex parte Yogathas* para 9 per Lord Bingham.

7

IMPLEMENTING TRANSNATIONAL ASYLUM

This final chapter discusses how transnational asylum can amount to a form of responsibility-sharing before locating transnational asylum alongside those refugee regime reform proposals presented in Chapter 1. The chapter further discusses how such approaches could be operationalised in different regions as a responsibility-sharing framework. Finally, the chapter draws some overall conclusions emerging from the book as a whole.

7.1 Transnational asylum as responsibility-sharing

Does transnational asylum have a role to play in new responsibility-sharing modalities? Arguably, yes. To function as a model for responsibility-sharing, the various forms of cooperation outlined in the preceding chapters would need to be implemented as part of an integrated and comprehensive approach, alongside access to territorial asylum in destination and partner states. Cherry-picking of third country processing and protection models by destination state governments pursuing a deterrence-driven agenda may formally comply with the minimum standards of international law but will never amount to responsibility-sharing.

There are a number of scenarios where transnational asylum approaches, if implemented in line with the standards set out in this book, can amount to responsibility-sharing. First, *pre-entry processing as a means to expand* access *to protection and mitigate pressure on national asylum systems* should be explored. For example, the strategic placement of pre-entry processing facilities along key mixed migration routes could provide access to protection closer to the country of origin, helping to mitigate the loss of life on dangerous flight routes as well as combating smuggling and trafficking. Such pre-entry

DOI: 10.4324/9781003463146-7

processing facilities could carry out full asylum procedures, preliminary processing for the purposes of humanitarian visas or profiling for referral to safe and legal pathways (Model 1).

A crucial risk here is that a pre-entry processing mechanism would create a 'pull factor' for partner states hosting such a facility. Moreover, any pre-entry processing arrangement would need to operate with full respect for any existing national asylum system in the partner state. These two challenges could be addressed through a comprehensive approach involving the establishment of multiple processing facilities along key routes and financial and technical assistance to partner state asylum systems, including through capacity building and, where possible, joint processing. In the short term, to avoid pull factors, a pilot approach could limit access to asylum seekers already present in the partner state.

Such pre-entry processing arrangements would ease stress on destination state asylum systems by linking pre-entry processing to subsequent spontaneous arrival. Under such an approach, asylum seekers who are screened out of a pre-entry asylum process in line with the standards set out in this book and who subsequently arrive at a destination state border within three years would receive an accelerated screening at the border, thus upholding the state's obligations with respect to non-refoulement while preventing onwards movement after a fair and effective pre-entry procedure has been carried out.

Second, an approach combining *pre-entry processing, territorial asylum and third country processing* could be explored (Model 2). Any third country processing approach should be accompanied by pre-entry processing and binding obligations to transfer refugees following the pre-entry procedure to the destination state or region at scale. For example, where a destination state or region has established pre-entry processing procedures en route, third country processing may be implemented for those asylum seekers who, following a negative decision, make their way to a destination state and apply for asylum. These approaches could equally be applied in the context of disembarkation arrangements.

An important form of responsibility-sharing is the provision of substantial financial and technical assistance to partner states to both ensure that standards are met and to improve protection for other asylum seekers and refugees present there.[1] This support could draw on the work of the Asylum Capacity Support Group, a GCR mechanism that builds the capacity of national asylum systems, including on the basis of twinning support.[2] Such an approach would increase the asylum capacity in partner states, thus making refugee protection 'doable' for countries in the Global South,[3] with cooperation codified via a binding international agreement and tied to standards contained in the Refugee Convention and relevant human rights law instruments.

Third, transnational asylum may amount to responsibility-sharing through *large-scale resettlement, territorial asylum and third country processing* of asylum seekers likely to have unfounded claims (Model 3). Under this approach, transnational asylum may play a role in preserving protection space in a particular destination country or region when used as a filtering mechanism while relieving pressure on the partner state's integration capacity. Such approaches may serve to prevent abuse of the asylum system and improve trust among the public that the asylum system is fit for purpose. Provided such an arrangement provides access to protection in the destination state for refugees after asylum procedures in the partner state, the destination state's protection capacity could be maintained and expanded.[4]

A binding agreement with a significant resettlement component would also remedy a weakness in the current protection system, namely that resettlement is widely considered a discretionary policy choice and not a legal obligation.[5] Resettlement is palatable to destination states as a means of providing asylum that meets their control interests in a number of respects. Resettlement involves the orderly movement of recognised refugees across international borders, in contrast to the spontaneous arrival of asylum seekers.[6] Resettlement also involves the predictable allocation of annual quotas, allowing the destination state to predetermine how many refugees receive protection via this route in a given year. Furthermore, resettlement allows destination states to allow access to recognised refugees, thereby avoiding the entry of migrants not requiring international protection. In a number of destination states, admission of refugees under an organised resettlement program tends to be more politically popular than the admission of asylum seekers.[7]

Finally, third country processing or protection may be reasonably considered in mass influx situations. The Refugee Law Initiative Declaration on Externalisation and Asylum finds:

> States are allowed to externalise elements of their asylum functions to a State or entity outside their own territory only where this is done in a way consistent with their own legal obligations and for good faith reasons – to relieve an excessive burden on a country of first asylum in the context of mass influx, for example.[8]

As a result, third country processing or protection arrangements may reasonably be considered as a means to share protection responsibilities where the asylum system of a destination state or region is overwhelmed.

7.2 Transnational asylum models

The following models present examples of how transnational asylum arrangements could function as a form of responsibility-sharing but do not represent an exhaustive prescription for implementing transnational asylum. Rather, the models are designed to illustrate how the various transnational asylum elements could be operationalised and applied in a range of contexts.

MODEL 1 PRE-ENTRY PROCESSING + TERRITORIAL ASYLUM

Element 1: Pre-entry asylum facilities

Pre-entry asylum facilities would be established along key mixed migration routes, providing asylum seekers outside their country of origin with access to destination state asylum procedures closer to their country of origin. Pre-entry asylum facilities would be run by destination state/region authorities, with the support of international organisations. Asylum procedures would be carried out by destination state/region authorities.

Access to the facilities would be managed by a virtual tool that would screen applicants by possible eligibility for international protection (e.g., identity documents proving asylum seeker or refugee status or nationality documents). Asylum seekers accessing the facilities would first access a screening procedure, including biometric registration and registration of their asylum application.

This screening procedure would channel asylum seekers into one of two tracks.

1 Likely well-founded and complex claims, entailing direct transfer to the destination state/region for a full in-merits asylum procedure.
2 Likely unfounded claims, entailing access to a full in-merits asylum procedure at the facility.

Pre-entry processing facilities would further provide reception and temporary accommodation conditions in line with relevant international standards, appeals procedures and legal assistance for applicants with likely unfounded claims, as well as capacity-building between destination state/region authorities and host partner states.

The facilities would operate under the joint jurisdiction of cooperating states and meet relevant international and regional law standards, including those contained in the Refugee Convention and, where relevant, the ECHR and EU Charter. Participating states would coordinate to ensure the lawful and effective return of rejected asylum seekers to their countries of origin.

Element 2: Screening at destination state/region external border

Following the establishment of pre-entry asylum facilities, destination state/region asylum authorities would begin screening at the external border. The screening procedure would operate in a manner that safeguards the right to access territory and seek asylum. As with the pre-entry procedure, the border screening would channel asylum seekers into one of two tracks.

1 Likely well-founded and complex claims, entailing direct access to the destination state/region for a full in-merits asylum procedure.
2 Likely unfounded claims, entailing transfer to a pre-entry processing facility for a full in-merits asylum procedure.

Where an asylum seeker who has previously been found to have a final negative decision at a pre-entry processing facility presents at an external border within three years, they will not have access to the asylum procedure. Instead, a specialised screening will be implemented, assessing any new risk or change of circumstances since the previous screening.

Where an asylum seeker is screened out, they would immediately enter return or readmission proceedings. Where an asylum seeker presents evidence of a new risk or change of circumstances that indicates a likely or possible need for international protection, they would be channelled into the likely well-founded or complex case track.

Element 3: Territorial asylum procedures for well-founded and complex cases

Following screening at the external border or pre-entry asylum facility, asylum seekers with likely well-founded and complex cases would be transferred directly to the territories of participating states for a full in-merits asylum procedure under national asylum law. Recognised refugees would reside in the state that grants protection. Asylum seekers who receive a negative final decision would enter return proceedings in that state.

MODEL 2 PRE-ENTRY PROCESSING + TERRITORIAL ASYLUM + THIRD COUNTRY PROCESSING

Element 1: Pre-entry asylum facilities

Pre-entry asylum facilities would be established along key mixed migration routes, providing asylum seekers and refugees outside their country of origin with access to destination state/region asylum procedures closer to their country of origin. Pre-entry asylum facilities would be run by destination state/region authorities, with the support of international organisations. Asylum procedures would be administered by destination state/region authorities.

Access to the facilities would be managed by a referral system and/or a virtual tool that would screen applicants by possible eligibility for international protection (e.g., identity documents proving asylum-seeker or refugee status or nationality documents). Asylum seekers accessing the facilities would access a screening procedure, including biometric registration and registration of asylum applications.

This screening procedure would channel asylum seekers into one of two tracks:

- Likely well-founded and complex claims, entailing direct transfer to the destination state/region for a full in-merits asylum procedure.
- Likely unfounded claims, entailing access to a full in-merits asylum procedure at the facility.

Pre-entry processing facilities would further provide reception and temporary accommodation conditions in line with relevant international standards, appeals procedures and legal assistance for applicants with likely unfounded claims, as well as capacity-building between destination state/region authorities and host partner states.

The facilities would operate under the joint jurisdiction of cooperating states and meet relevant international and regional law standards, including those contained in the Refugee Convention and, where relevant, the ECHR and EU Charter. Participating states would coordinate to ensure the lawful and effective return of rejected asylum seekers to their country of origin.

Element 2: Screening at destination state/region external border

Following the establishment of pre-entry asylum facilities, destination asylum authorities would begin screening at the external border. The screening procedure would operate in a manner that safeguards the right to access territory and seek asylum. As with the pre-entry procedure, the border screening would channel asylum seekers into one of two tracks.

- Likely well-founded and complex claims, entailing direct access to the destination state/region for a full in-merits asylum procedure.
- Likely unfounded claims, entailing transfer to a third country for a full in-merits asylum procedure.

Where an asylum seeker who has previously been found to have a final negative decision at a pre-entry processing facility presents at an external border within three years, they will not have access to the asylum procedure. Instead, a specialised screening will be implemented, assessing any new risk or change of circumstances since the previous screening.

Where an asylum seeker is screened out, they would enter return or readmission proceedings. Where an asylum seeker presents evidence of a new risk or change of circumstances that indicates a likely or possible need for international protection, they would be channelled into the likely well-founded or complex case track.

Element 3: Third country processing for likely unfounded cases

Following screening at the destination state/region external border and any appeal to their transfer, asylum seekers with likely unfounded claims would be transferred to a third country for full in-merits asylum procedures and return.

Cooperating states would establish and operate processing and return centres in the third country to receive asylum seekers with likely unfounded claims from the external border and, where relevant, carry out returns. The asylum procedure in the third country would be carried out by the destination state acting extraterritorially. The processing and return centres would operate under the joint jurisdiction of cooperating states and meet relevant international and relevant regional law standards, including those enumerated in the Refugee Convention and, where relevant, the ECHR and EU Charter.

Alternatively, asylum procedures could be carried out by authorities of the third country under national law, provided it is fair and effective, with technical and operational support from the destination state/region.

Third country processing would take place under a binding international agreement guaranteeing respect for obligations under human rights and refugee law.

MODEL 3 RESETTLEMENT + TERRITORIAL ASYLUM + THIRD COUNTRY PROCESSING

Element 1: Screening at destination state/region external border

Destination state/region asylum authorities would begin screening at the external border. The screening procedure would operate in a manner that safeguards the right to access territory and seek asylum. This screening procedure would channel asylum seekers into one of two tracks.

- Likely well-founded and complex claims, entailing direct transfer to the destination state/region for a full in-merits asylum procedure.
- Likely unfounded claims, entailing access to a full in-merits asylum procedure in a third country

Element 2: Territorial asylum procedures for well-founded and complex cases

Following screening at the destination state/region external border, asylum-seekers with likely well-founded and complex cases would be afforded access to a full in-merits asylum procedure under national asylum law. Recognised refugees would reside in the state that grants protection. Asylum seekers who receive a negative final decision would enter return proceedings in that state.

Element 3: Third country processing for likely unfounded cases

Following screening at the destination state/region external border and any appeal to their transfer, asylum seekers with likely unfounded claims would be transferred to a third country for full in-merits asylum procedures and, as relevant, information related to legal migration channels and assisted voluntary return.

Cooperating states would establish and operate third country processing and return centres to receive asylum seekers with likely unfounded claims from the external border and, where relevant, carry out returns. The asylum procedure in the third country would be carried out by the destination state/region acting extraterritorially. The processing and return centres would operate under the joint jurisdiction of cooperating states and meet relevant international and relevant regional law standards, including those enumerated in the Refugee Convention and, where relevant, the ECHR and EU Charter.

Alternatively, asylum procedures could be carried out by authorities of the third country under national law, provided it is fair and effective, with technical and operational support from the destination state/region.

Third country processing would take place under a binding international agreement guaranteeing respect for obligations under human rights and refugee law.

Element 4: Resettlement

The binding international agreement would include a mechanism to resettle refugees present in the partner state to the destination state/region at scale, such as to enhance protection in all cooperating states. Such an approach would create obligations of resettlement and increase responsibility-sharing between cooperating states.

7.3 Operationalising transnational asylum

What would be required to operationalise a transnational asylum approach that is both better than the status quo in terms of protection and would amount to responsibility-sharing between cooperating states? As set out in Chapter 1, responsibility-sharing arrangements are forms of international cooperation that comply with international refugee and human rights law obligations and enhance refugee protection.[9] To emerge as a form of responsibility-sharing, a transnational asylum arrangement would thus need to increase protection in cooperating states.

Operationalising transnational asylum arrangements requires a phased approach, set out briefly here, comprising *consultation* between key stakeholders, *piloting* whereby cooperating states test various elements of the approach, *adaptation* between cooperating states with respect to legal standards, drawing on the pilots and, finally, full *implementation* in a specific region or regions.

7.3.1 Phase 1: consultation

The first and immediate phase would be a series of consultations with key stakeholders crucial to the conceptualisation and implementation of transnational asylum, including governments, regional organisations (notably the African Union, the EU and the Organization of American States or OAS), UNHCR, IOM, refugee-led organisations, academics and non-governmental organisations (NGOs). Particular focus should be placed on consultation with partner country governments, who may be sceptical of the good faith intentions of destination states in pursuing transnational asylum arrangements.[10] Consultation would be necessary within and across regions to conceptualise and operationalise transnational asylum approaches on the basis of the principles, standards and models put forward in this book. Consultations could be led by a group of interested governments, a consortium of academics or UNHCR.

7.3.2 Phase 2: pilot

Second, in the short-term, cooperating states would test the transnational asylum building blocks through a number of time-limited pilots implemented in different regions. For example, specific pilots could test, even at a small scale, separate modalities of pre-entry processing and third country processing in two different regions.[11] This testing phase should be expressly identified as taking place within the phased transnational asylum approach to avoid cherry-picking of more restrictive elements, such as third country processing. This phase would need to be overseen by UNHCR.

7.3.3 Phase 3: adaptation

Third, in the medium-term, cooperating states would need to undertake a number of adaptation measures to pave the way for the full implementation of transnational asylum. A primary adaptation would relate to extraterritorial processing where regional variations of the refugee definition exist. Adaptation would not require amendment to respective regional refugee instruments but rather agreement between cooperating states as to which definition is to be applied in a particular transnational asylum setting. For example, where EU authorities carry out asylum procedures in a state party to the 1969 OAU Convention Governing the Specific Aspects of Refugee Problems in Africa (OAU Convention),[12] cooperating states must clarify whether the procedure takes place using the OAU definition or the criteria for protection set out in the EU Qualification Directive.[13] Equally, where US authorities assess protection claims in a Latin American state, the governing agreement may need to address the relevance of the Cartagena Declaration definition of refugeehood.[14]

Regional bodies would play a key role in the adaptation phase. At the AU level, as noted above, no amendment to the OAU Convention is required. At the OAS level, transnational asylum arrangements can lawfully proceed without amendment to the Organisation of American States Charter (OAS Charter) or the 1969 American Convention on Human Rights (ACHR). At the level of EU law, however, legislative amendments to the EU asylum *acquis* may be required in order to fully implement transnational asylum.

First, there is presently no mechanism to allow the EU or its member states to jointly process asylum claims, rendering extraterritorial processing (both pre- and post-arrival) 'technically, legally and practically complicated'.[15] The capacity to determine asylum claims remains with individual member state authorities, with the current mandate of the EUAA limited to assisting member states in conducting asylum procedures, thus rendering a fully-fledged EU-run pre-entry processing or third country processing apparatus presently unworkable.[16] The creation of an EU protection agency, with full asylum decision-making powers and a commensurate appeal system, would require significant amendments to the EU asylum *acquis* and remains a long-term prospect.[17]

Nevertheless, even absent such legislative change, there may be scope for a 'coalition of the willing' of European member states to implement a transnational asylum model involving extraterritorial processing, where such procedures take place in an EU-operated facility with decision-makers from individual European states taking the final decision on asylum claims. Such a coalition approach would involve a group of EU member states and other European countries piloting and funding the operational costs of a first iteration transnational asylum approach. Equally, transnational asylum arrangements could be operationalised in the context of disembarkation, including in the Mediterranean and across the English Channel.

Second, transnational asylum approaches involving third country processing on the part of the EU or its member states may require changes to the APD. Presently, the safe third country concept in Article 38 of the APD requires that there be a connection between the asylum seeker and the third country and it would be reasonable for that person to go to that country. This dual requirement, which acts to limit the ability of EU member states to transfer asylum seekers to third countries, is not reflected in general international law. In the short term, a transnational asylum arrangement with a third country processing component involving the EU or its member states following access to EU territory could only operate to transfer asylum seekers to third states within the constraints of Article 38 of the APD. This connection requirement is currently upheld in the Asylum Procedures Regulations (APR), which will replace the APD as part of the EU Asylum and Migration Pact in 2026.[18]

Third, there is no binding EU mechanism for the resettlement of refugees within the bloc. As the 2016 Proposal for a Regulation on a Union Resettlement Framework remains under negotiation,[19] there is presently no mechanism to coordinate resettlement at the EU level. Instead, resettlement quotas are left to the discretion of individual member states. While the present absence of a coherent and binding EU approach to resettlement limits the responsibility-sharing potential of transnational asylum policies in the short term, there is no reason why a coalition of EU member states and other European countries could not commit to binding resettlement or pre-entry processing quotas through an international agreement with cooperating partner states.

7.3.4 Phase 4: implementation

Finally, drawing on legal, policy and operational lessons from the pilot phase and with the adaptations set out above, transnational asylum modalities would be implemented in full across regions, including Southeast Asia and the Pacific, on both sides of the Mediterranean and in the Americas. Provided such arrangements are implemented in line with the principles and standards set out here, the system would provide greater protection than the status quo. This phase would be overseen by UNHCR, in cooperation with relevant regional bodies, notably the AU, EU and OAS.

7.4 Locating transnational asylum alongside existing reform proposals

How does transnational asylum compare to scholarly reform proposals presented in Chapter 1? The principal premise of transnational asylum is that while states enjoy legal manoeuvre room to transfer asylum seekers and refugees between one another, any such cooperation must meet minimum legal and policy standards, offer genuine access to protection and rights in line with the Refugee Convention and relevant international and regional human rights law and avoid the grave mistakes of past attempts.

While in many ways more limited than previous reform proposals, transnational asylum nevertheless shares certain common features. Notably, Hathaway and Neve's 1997 proposal includes the possibility of extraterritorial processing, provided there are sufficient safeguards in place.[20] A further commonality is the requirement of significant financial and technical assistance on the part of destination states and regions to support the asylum systems of partner states.

There are also crucial differences. Perhaps most notably, transnational asylum does not include a focus on temporary protection for the duration of risk due to the proliferation of protracted displacement crises, normative developments in the right to family and private life and recent bad faith attempts in this direction taken in certain states, notably Denmark.[21] Further, instead of placing the principle of common but differentiated responsibility at the heart of the idea, transnational asylum rests on a series of key legal and policy foundations, including maintaining territorial asylum in destination states, the existence of a binding legal agreement, detailed minimum standards on the quality of asylum procedure and international protection and solutions for refugees.

Transnational asylum equally shares certain commonalities with Hathaway's 2018 global reform proposal,[22] notably a combination of pre-entry processing or binding obligations of resettlement, retained access to territorial asylum for those in need of international protection and limited third country processing. However, while Hathaway's approach seeks to redirect resources from national to international asylum adjudication and provide resettlement to the millions of refugees currently in protracted situations, transnational asylum is more narrowly focused on providing lawful alternatives to current externalisation proposals and policies, as well as remedying the loss of life on routes and governments' concerns around mixed movements.

As a result, Hathaway's wide-ranging vision includes a number of elements beyond the scope of transnational asylum. For example, Hathaway's proposal would end national asylum procedures in favour of an international corps of asylum decision-makers. Given that even under the relatively harmonised EU asylum system, national decision-makers retain adjudicatory powers, such an international cohort of refugee status determination officers seems a remote prospect. Instead, transnational asylum retains national asylum procedures while allowing for their lawful implementation extraterritorially and providing for joint processing in line with international standards.

Hathaway's plan further proposes a massive increase in global resettlement quotas, reaching 1.7 million refugees per year. While transnational asylum proposes the creation of resettlement obligations on destination states, it does not quantify these obligations. Clearly, to amount to responsibility-sharing, transnational asylum arrangements must go well beyond the one-to-one arrangement in place in the EU–Turkey Statement, but to propose such a massive increase in resettlement would risk destination state buy-in.

Transnational asylum equally shares certain characteristics with Schuck[23] and Betts and Collier's proposals.[24] Like these approaches, transnational asylum integrates responsibility-sharing as it relates to the sharing of both people and finances. However, unlike Schuck, it does not put forward a market-based quota system, instead linking responsibility for refugees to binding regional arrangements between destination and partner states. Equally, while Betts and Collier's model emphasised refugees' economic participation, transnational asylum relies on normative standards of protection contained in the Refugee Convention and relevant human rights law instruments.

While not a proposal for reform per se, Shachar's concept of decoupling protection and territory as a response to 'shifting border' policies equally inspired this book.[25] Shachar's vision employs the methods of the shifting border to unlock deterritorialised access to protection on the basis of approaches like pre-entry processing. Like Shachar, the transnational asylum framework draws on contemporary concepts of extraterritorial jurisdiction as alternatives to the current status quo so heavily reliant on territorial asylum.[26]

Finally, transnational asylum may offer some remedies to the substantial gaps in the GCR. The Compact is essentially silent on questions of access to territory, asylum procedures, safe third country arrangements and third country processing or protection. Indeed, the non-binding nature and generality of the GCR's objectives seem to have contributed to existing non-entrée, deterrence and externalisation approaches, substantially limiting the Compact's impact on policymaking in the Global North.[27] Transnational asylum goes some way to filling this gap, providing a set of guardrails to inform cooperation and providing concrete elements of fairer responsibility-sharing.

In sum, rather than offering a grand vision for reform of the refugee regime, transnational asylum offers pragmatic yet principled 'add-ons' that could form the basis of a protection framework. Given the parlous state of territorial asylum in the Global North, a transnational asylum approach built on a combination of pre-entry processing or binding obligations of resettlement, retained access to territorial asylum for some and limited third country processing would arguably represent a significant improvement to the status quo for refugees and the approaches presently on the table in many countries.

A final advantage of the transnational asylum approach over existing scholarly proposals is that it may prove easier to 'sell' to states as an incremental approach that adapts existing practices rather than calling for wholesale reform of the refugee regime. In the medium- to long-term, the transnational asylum approach may serve as a 'bridge' to more holistic reforms of the global protection regime if carefully tested and implemented across regions.

7.5 Final reflections

As states increasingly devise, propose and implement cooperative asylum approaches that go to the edge of – and in some cases breach – international obligations, taking states' putting forward alternative approaches is vital to the survival of the right to seek asylum in the Global North. This book has shown how cooperative asylum arrangements can provide minimum acceptable levels of protection for asylum seekers and refugees under international law and explored whether such arrangements have the potential to develop into a form of responsibility-sharing. While international refugee law does not forbid the transfer of a refugee between states, a primary object of the Refugee Convention is the provision of the greatest possible protection to refugees and this utilitarian intent should feature prominently in any transnational asylum arrangement.

Proposals and practice in this area are not going away anytime soon. A value of the transnational asylum framework thus lies in setting out for governments what is required for such cooperative arrangements to be rendered workable and internationally lawful. With respect to pre-entry processing, for example, destination states must be prepared to make substantial investments financially, operationally and legally to establish asylum procedures en route in line with their international obligations. With respect to third country processing and protection arrangements, transferring states retain responsibility for ensuring that key rights under the Refugee Convention are respected in law and practice, well beyond relatively narrow non-refoulement obligations.

Equally, transnational asylum arrangements cannot replace territorial asylum in destination states. While existing arrangements have been generally focused on shifting protection to third states, future transnational asylum arrangements must not preclude the possibility of seeking asylum in destination states for those in need of international protection. The catalogue of human rights and refugee law obligations owed to asylum seekers outlined in this book makes it clear that national asylum systems will remain in operation, even if some asylum seekers are subject to transfer without a full asylum procedure.

Finally, transnational asylum as a form of responsibility-sharing requires genuine international cooperation between destination and partner states, expressed through binding international agreements. Transnational asylum leverages the willingness of destination state governments to invest significant resources in developing the asylum systems of partner states. Transnational asylum arrangements have the potential to lead to the ratification of the Refugee Convention by partner states, the lifting of reservations, the establishment and strengthening of national asylum systems and the development of refugee integration programs. However, approaches undertaken in bad faith falling short of the international legal and policy standards outlined in this book are just more examples of deterrence, non-entrée and externalisation.

Ultimately, transnational asylum offers the building blocks of a protection framework. If implemented in good faith, based on principles of genuine international cooperation and respect for international human rights and refugee law obligations, the elements of pre-entry processing, territorial asylum, third country processing and binding resettlement obligations could combine to prevent loss of life on asylum-seeking routes, build asylum systems, provide safe access to protection to those who need it and share responsibility between states.

Notes

1 On this non-ideal model of refugee protection, see T Alexander Aleinikoff and David Owen, 'Refugee protection: "Here"or "there"?' (2022) 10 Migration Studies 464.

2 See UNHCR, Asylum Capacity Support Group (ACSG) Mechanism: Fact Sheet (June 2022) https://acsg-portal.org/wp-content/uploads/2022/06/ACSG-Fact-Sheet-June-2022-2.pdf accessed 23 December 2022.

3 James C Hathaway, 'The Global Cop-Out on Refugees' (2019) 30 International Journal of Refugee Law 591.

4 The EU considered in 2018 the use of 'disembarkation platforms' in third countries to filter irregular migrants intercepted in the Mediterranean between refugees

and economic migrants before reaching European soil. European Council, Conclusions – 28 June 2018, available at http://www.consilium.europa.eu/media/35936/28-euco-final-conclusions-en.pdf accessed 18 May 2021.

5 Tom de Boer and Marjoleine Zieck, 'The Legal Abyss of Discretion in the Resettlement of Refugees: Cherry-Picking and the Lack of Due Process in the EU' (2020) 32 International Journal of Refugee Law 54. See further Joanne Van Selm, 'The strategic use of resettlement: changing the face of protection?' (2004) 22 Refuge: Canada's Journal on Refugees 41 and Naoko Hashimoto, 'Refugee Resettlement as an Alternative to Asylum' (2018) 37 Refugee Survey Quarterly 162, 165. As Hashimoto explains, 'No state has a legal obligation proactively to admit refugees via resettlement who are still outside their jurisdiction; nor can a refugee claim a "right" to be resettled'.

6 As early as 2004, Van Selm noted: 'The emerging thought in Europe is that if a country resettles refugees, as opposed to seeing them arrive spontaneously, the authorities know who they are, the people enter legally, and the process can be managed'. Van Selm, 'The strategic use of resettlement: changing the face of protection?' 43.

7 Van Selm 47; Fiona H McKay, Samantha L Thomas and Susan Kneebone, 'It would be okay if they came through the proper channels': Community perceptions and attitudes toward asylum seekers in Australia' (2012) 25 Journal of Refugee Studies 113.

8 Refugee Law Initiative Declaration on Externalisation and Asylum (2022) 34 International Journal of Refugee Law 114 para 25.

9 UNHCR, *Expert Meeting on International Cooperation to Share Burdens and Responsibilities: Summary Conclusions* (2001) 4.

10 See, for example, Bachirou Ayouba Tinni and others, Asylum for Containment: EU arrangements with Niger, Serbia, Tunisia and Turkey (ASILE working paper, March 2023) https://www.asileproject.eu/asylum-for-containment accessed 9 May 2023.

11 For an account of small-scale and ad hoc pre-entry processing programs, see Pauline Endres de Oliveira and Nikolas Feith Tan, 'External Processing: A Tool to Expand Protection or Further Restrict Territorial Asylum?' (Migration Policy Institute, 2023).

12 1969 OAU Convention Governing the Specific Aspects of Refugee Problems in Africa (adopted 10 September 1969, entered into force 20 June 1974) 1001 UNTS 45 (OAU Convention). Article I(2) of the OAU Convention, however, goes on to extend the definition in the following terms:

> The term "refugee" shall also apply to *every person* who, owing to external aggression, occupation, foreign domination or *events seriously disturbing public order* in *either part or the whole* of his country of origin or nationality, is compelled to leave his place of habitual residence in order to seek refuge in another place outside his country of origin or nationality
>
> *(emphasis added).*

13 In addition to refugee status, the Qualification Directive includes subsidiary protection status, granted if the person would face a real risk of suffering serious harm upon return. Article 15 defines serious harm as the death penalty or execution; or torture or inhuman or degrading treatment or punishment in the country of origin; or 'serious and individual threat to a civilian's life or person by reason of indiscriminate violence in situations of international or internal armed conflict'.

14 Colloquium on the International Protection of Refugees in Central America, Mexico and Panama, *Cartagena Declaration on Refugees*, 22 November 1984. The Cartagena Declaration builds on the Refugee Convention definition to

include: 'persons who have fled their country because their lives, safety or freedom have been threatened by generalized violence, foreign aggression, internal conflicts, massive violation of human rights or other circumstances which have seriously disturbed public order'.

15 Martina Stevis, 'The EU at a Migration Crossroads: Speaking with Cecilia Malmström' *The Wall Street Journal* (26 June 2014). See further Pauline Endres de Oliveira and Nikolas Feith Tan, *External Processing: A Tool to Expand Protection or Further Restrict Territorial Asylum?* (Migration Policy Institute, 2023).

16 The European Union Agency for Asylum (EUAA) replaced the European Asylum Support Office (EASO) on 19 January 2022. Regulation (EU) 2021/2303 of the European Parliament and of the Council of 15 December 2021 on the European Union Agency for Asylum and repealing Regulation (EU) No 439/2010.

17 Guy S Goodwin-Gill, 'The Mediterranean Papers: Athens, Naples and Istanbul' (2016) 28 International Journal of Refugee Law 276, 285–88.

18 Regulation (EU) 2024/1348 of the European Parliament and of the Council of 14 May 2024 establishing a common procedure for international protection in the Union and repealing Directive 2013/32/EU, OJ L, 2024/1348, 22.5.2024.

19 European Commission, 'Proposal for a Regulation of the European Parliament and of the Council establishing a Union Resettlement Framework and amending Regulation (EU) No 516/2014 of the European Parliament and the Council' COM (2016) 468 final.

20 James C. Hathaway and R Alexander Neve, 'Making international refugee law relevant again: A proposal for collectivized and solution-oriented protection' (1997) 10 Harvard Human Rights Journal.

21 See, for example, Nikolas Feith Tan, 'The End of Protection: The Danish Paradigm Shift and the Law of Cessation' (2021) 90 Nordic Journal of International Law 60.

22 Hathaway, 'The Global Cop-Out on Refugees'.

23 Peter H Schuck, 'Refugee burden-sharing: A modest proposal' (1997) 22 Yale Journal of International Law 243.

24 Alexander Betts and Paul Collier, *Refuge: Transforming a broken refugee system* (Penguin UK 2017).

25 Ayelet Shachar, *The shifting border: Legal cartographies of migration and mobility* (Manchester University Press 2020) 5.

26 Shachar 74–88. See also Khalida Azhigulova, 'Bilateral Resettlement Agreements: Any Promising Future for Expanding Refugee Protection Space? A Case Study of the Guantanamo ex-Detainees Seeking Asylum in Central Asia' (Refugee Law Initative Working Paper No 19, 2016) 98. According to Azhigulova:

If used in a manner and with a due regard to human rights… bilateral resettlement agreements in general have a potential to become an efficient mechanism of inter-state cooperation in refugee protection not only within the same region but also between diverse geographic regions so long as such cooperation serves the self-interests of the participating states'.

27 A recent assessment of the GCR's impact in a number of states concludes that developed states tend to see the Compact as 'foreign policy, rather than a domestic responsibility'. Danish Refugee Council (DRC), the International Rescue Committee (IRC) and the Norwegian Refugee Council (NRC), 'The Global Compact on Refugees Three Years On: navigating barriers and maximising incentives in support of refugees and host countries' (2021).

BIBLIOGRAPHY

Achiume ET, 'Racial Borders' (2021) 110 *Georgetown Immigration Law Journal* 445.

Afeef KF, The Politics of Extraterritorial Processing: Offshore Asylum Policies in Europe and the Pacific (Refugee Studies Centre Working Paper No. 36, 2006).

Aleinikoff TA, 'The Unfinished Work of the Global Compact on Refugees' (2018) 30 *International Journal of Refugee Law* 611.

Aleinikoff TA and Zamore L, *The Arc of Protection: Reforming the International Refugee Regime* (Stanford University Press, 2019).

Altwicker T, 'Transnationalizing Rights: International Human Rights Law in Cross-Border Contexts' (2018) 29 *European Journal of International Law* 581.

Anker D, Fitzpatrick J and Shacknove A, 'Crisis and cure: A reply to Hathaway/Neve and Schuck' (1998) 11 *Harvard Human Rights Journal* 295.

Archbold LJ, 'Offshore Processing of Asylum Seekers–Is Australia Complying With Its International Legal Obligations' (2015) 15 *QUT Law Review* 137.

Aust HP, *Complicity and the Law of State Responsibility* (Cambridge University Press 2011).

Azhigulova K, 'Bilateral Resettlement Agreements: Any Promising Future for Expanding Refugee Protection Space? A Case Study of the Guantanamo ex-Detainees Seeking Asylum in Central Asia' (Refugee Law Initative Working Paper No 19, 2017).

Bar-Tuvia S, 'Australian and Israeli Agreements for the Permanent Transfer of Refugees: Stretching Further the (Il)legality and (Im)morality of Western Externalization Policies' (2018) 30 *International Journal of Refugee Law* 1.

Battjes H, *European Asylum Law and International Law* (Nijhoff 2006).

Besson S, 'The Extraterritoriality of the European Convention on Human Rights: Why Human Rights Depend on Jurisdiction and What Jurisdiction Amounts to' (2012) 25 *Leiden Journal of International Law* 857.

Betts A and Collier P, *Refuge: Transforming a Broken Refugee System* (Penguin UK, 2017) 234.

Betts A, Costello C and Zaun N, *A Fair Share: Refugees and Responsibility-sharing* (Delmi 2017).

Boed R, 'The State of the Right of Asylum in International Law' (1994) 5 *Duke Journal of Comparative and International Law* 1.

Boerefijn I, 'Establishing State Responsibility for Breaching Human Rights Treaty Obligations: Avenues under UN Human Rights Treaties' (2009) 56 *Netherlands International Law Review* 167.
Botero Á and Vedsted-Hansen J, 'Asylum Procedures' in Foster M, McAdam J and Costello C (eds), *The Oxford Handbook of International Refugee Law* (Oxford University Press 2021) 588–606.
Brownlie I, *Principles of Public International Law* (7th edn, Oxford University Press 2008).
Byrne R and Shacknove A, 'The Safe Country Notion in European Asylum Law' (1996) 9 *Harvard Human Rights Journal* 185.
Cantor D 'Fairness, Failure, and Future in the Refugee Regime' (2019) 30 *International Journal of Refugee Law* 627.
Cantor D and others, 'Externalisation, Access to Territorial Asylum, and International Law' (2022) 34 *International Journal of Refugee Law* 120.
Carrera S and others, 'Offshoring Asylum and Migration in Australia, Spain, Tunisia and the US: Lessons learned and feasibility for the EU' (CEPS Research Report, September 2018).
Carrera S and Guild E, *Offshore Processing of Asylum Applications Out of Sight, Out of Mind?* (CEPS, 2017).
Chimni B, 'Global Compact on Refugees: One Step Forward, Two Steps Back' (2019) 30 *International Journal of Refugee Law* 630.
Costello C 'The Asylum Procedures Directive and the Proliferation of Safe Country Practices: Deterrence, Deflection and the Dismantling of International Protection?' (2005) 7 *European Journal of Migration and Law* 35.
Costello C, 'Refugees and (Other) Migrants: Will the Global Compacts Ensure Safe Flight and Onward Mobility for Refugees?' (2019) 30 *International Journal of Refugee Law* 634.
Crawford J, *The International Law Commission's Articles on State Responsibility: Introduction, Text and Commentaries* (Cambridge University Press 2002).
Crawford J *State Responsibility: The General Part* (Cambridge University Press 2013).
Crisp J, 'A New Asylum Paradigm?: Globalization, Migration and the Uncertain Future of the International Refugee Regime' (2003) 1 *St Antony's International Review* 39.
Crisp J 'Finding Space for Protection: An Inside Account of the Evolution of UNHCR's Urban Refugee Policy' (2017) 33 *Refuge* 87.
Cruz A, *Shifting responsibility: carriers' liability in the member states of the European Union and North America* (Trentham Books and School of Oriental & African Studies 1995).
Da Costa K, *The Extraterritorial Application of Selected Human Rights Treaties* (Martinus Nijhoff 2012).
Dannenbaum T, 'Public Power and Preventive Responsibility: Attributing the Wrongs of International Joint Ventures' in Nollkaemper A and Jacobs D (eds), *Distribution of Responsibilities in International Law* (Cambridge University Press 2015).
Dastyari A, 'Detention of Australia's Asylum Seekers in Nauru: Is Deprivation of Liberty by Any Other Name Just as Unlawful?' (2015a) 38 *University of New South Wales Law Journal* 669.
Dastyari A *United States Migrant Interdiction and the Detention of Refugees in Guantánamo Bay* (Cambridge University Press 2015b).
Dastyari A and Ghezelbash D, 'Asylum at Sea: The Legality of Shipboard Refugee Status Determination Procedures' (2020) 32 *International Journal of Refugee Law* 1.
Dastyari A and O'Sullivan M, 'Not for Export: The Failure of Australia's Extraterritorial Processing Regime in Papua New Guinea and the Decision of the PNG Supreme Court in Namah' (2016) 42 *Monash University Law Review* 308.

Davies SE, *Legitimising Rejection: International Refugee Law in Southeast Asia* (Brill 2008).

de Boer T, 'Closing Legal Black Holes: The Role of Extraterritorial Jurisdiction in Refugee Rights Protection' (2014) 28 *Journal of Refugee Studies* 118.

de Boer T and Zieck M, 'The Legal Abyss of Discretion in the Resettlement of Refugees: Cherry-Picking and the Lack of Due Process in the EU' (2020) 32(1) *International Journal of Refugee Law* 54–85.

de Oliveira PE and Tan NF, *External Processing: A Tool to Expand Protection or Further Restrict Territorial Asylum?* (Migration Policy Institute, 2023).

den Heijer M 'Europe Beyond Its Borders: Refugee And Human Rights Protection In Extraterritorial Immigration Control' in Ryan B and Mitsilegas V (eds), *Extraterritorial Immigration Control: Legal Challenges* (Brill 2010) 193–94.

den Heijer M, *Europe and Extraterritorial Asylum* (Bloomsbury 2012).

den Heijer M 'Shared Responsibility Before the European Court of Human Rights' (2013) 60 *Netherlands International Law Review* 411.

den Heijer M 'The Practice of Shared Responsibility in Relation to Refoulement' (2016) in Nollkaemper A, Plakokefalos I and Schechinger J (eds), *The Practice of Shared Responsibility in International Law* (Cambridge University Press 2017).

den Heijer M and Lawson R, 'Extraterritorial Human Rights and the Concept of 'Jurisdiction'' in Langford M and others (eds), *Global Justice, State Duties: The Extraterritorial Scope of Economic, Social, and Cultural Rights in International Law* (Cambridge University Press 2013).

Dowd R and McAdam J, 'International Cooperation and Responsibility-Sharing to Protect Refugees: What, Why and How' (2017) 66 *International and Comparative Law Quarterly* 863.

Doyle M, 'The Model International Mobility Convention' (2017) 56 *Columbia Journal of Transnational Law* 219.

Edwards A, 'Human Rights, Refugees, and the Right 'to Enjoy' Asylum' (2005) 17 *International Journal of Refugee Law* 293.

Einarsen T, 'Mass Flight: The Case for International Asylum' (1995) 7 *International Journal of Refugee Law* 551.

Failla M, 'Outsourcing Obligations to Developing Nations: Australia's Refugee Resettlement Agreement with Cambodia' (2016) 42 *Monash University Law Review* 638.

FitzGerald DS, *Refuge Beyond Reach: How Rich Democracies Repel Asylum Seekers* (Oxford University Press 2019).

Foster M, 'Protection Elsewhere: The Legal Implications of Requiring Refugees to Seek Protection in Another State' (2006) 28 *Michigan Journal of International Law* 223.

Foster M 'Responsibility Sharing or Shifting? "Safe" Third Countries and International Law' (2008) 25 Refuge 64.

Foster M 'The Implications of the Failed 'Malaysian Solution': The Australian High Court and Refugee Responsibility Sharing at International Law' (2012) 13 *Melbourne Journal of International Law* 395.

Frances A, 'Bringing Protection Home: Healing the Schism between International Obligations and National Safeguards Created by Extraterritorial Processing' (2008) 20 *International Journal of Refugee Law* 273.

Frenzen N, 'The Practice of Shared Responsibility in relation to Extraterritorial Refugee Protection' in Nollkaemper A, Plakokefalos I and Schechinger J (eds), *The Practice of Shared Responsibility in International Law*, vol 3 (Cambridge University Press 2017) 506–26.

Gammeltoft-Hansen T 'The Extra territorialisation of Asylum and the Advent of Protection Lite' (DIIS working paper, 2007).

Gammeltoft-Hansen T, *Access to Asylum: International Refugee Law and the Globalisation of Migration Control* (Cambridge University Press 2011).
Gammeltoft-Hansen T 'International Cooperation on Migration Control: A Legal Research Agenda' (2018) 20(4) *European Journal of Migration and Law* 373.
Gammeltoft-Hansen T and Hathaway JC, 'Non-Refoulement in a World of Cooperative Deterrence' (2014) 53 *Columbia Journal of Transnational Law* 235.
Gammeltoft-Hansen T and Tan NF, 'The End of the Deterrence Paradigm? Future Directions for Global Refugee Policy' (2017) 5 *Journal on Migration and Human Security* 28.
Garlick M, 'The EU Discussions on Extraterritorial Processing: Solution or Conundrum?' (2006) 18 *International Journal of Refugee Law* 601.
Garlick M *The Potential and Pitfalls of Extraterritorial Processing of Asylum Claims* (Migration Policy Institute, 2015).
Garvey JI, 'The Future Legal Management of Mass Migration' (2018) 15 *International Lawyer* 121.
Ghezelbash D *Refuge Lost: Asylum Law in an Interdependent World* (Cambridge University Press 2018).
Ghezelbash D, 'Hyper-legalism and Obfuscation: How States Evade Their International Obligations Towards Refugees' (2020) 68 *American Journal of Comparative Law* 479.
Ghezelbash D and Tan NF, 'The End of the Right to Seek Asylum? COVID-19 and the Future of Refugee Protection' (2020) 32 *International Journal of Refugee Law* 668.
Giuffré M, 'State Responsibility Beyond Borders: What Legal Basis for Italy's Push-backs to Libya?' (2013) 24 *International Journal of Refugee Law* 692.
Glazebrook D, 'Papua New Guinea's refugee track record and its obligations under the 2013 Regional Resettlement Arrangement with Australia' (SSGM discussion paper, 2014).
Gleeson M, *Offshore: Behind the wire on Manus and Nauru* (NewSouth 2016).
Goodwin-Gill GS 'Safe Country? Says Who?' (1992) 4 *International Journal of Refugee Law* 248.
Goodwin-Gill GS *The Refugee in International Law* (2nd edn, Oxford University Press 1996).
Goodwin-Gill GS, 'The Extraterritorial Processing of Claims to Asylum or Protection: The Legal Responsibilities of States and International Organisations' (2007) 9 *UTS Law Review* 26.
Goodwin-Gill GS 'The International Law of Refugee Protection' in Fiddian-Qasmiyeh Elena and others (eds), *The Oxford Handbook of Refugee and Forced Migration Studies* (Oxford University Press 2014).
Goodwin-Gill GS 'The Mediterranean Papers: Athens, Naples, and Istanbul' (2016) 28 *International Journal of Refugee Law* 276.
Goodwin-Gill GS and McAdam J, *The Refugee in International Law* (3rd edn, Oxford University Press, 2007).
Goodwin-Gill GS and McAdam J, *The Refugee in International Law* (4th edn, Oxford University Press, 2021).
Hailbronner K, 'The Concept of 'Safe Country' and Expeditious Asylum Procedures: A Western European Perspective' (1993) 5 *International Journal of Refugee Law* 31.
Hashimoto N, 'Refugee Resettlement as an Alternative to Asylum' (2018) 37 *Refugee Survey Quarterly* 162.
Hathaway JC, 'The Emerging Politics of Non-entree' (1992) 91 *Refugees* 40.
Hathaway JC *The Rights of Refugees under International Law* (Cambridge University Press 2005).
Hathaway JC 'Why Refugee Law Still Matters' (2007) 8 *Melbourne Journal of International Law* 89.

Hathaway JC 'The Global Cop-Out on Refugees' (2019) 30 *International Journal of Refugee Law* 591.

Hathaway JC *The Rights of Refugees under International Law* (2 edn, Cambridge University Press 2021).

Hathaway JC and Foster M, *The Law of Refugee Status* (Cambridge University Press 2014).

Hathaway JC and Neve RA, 'Making International Refugee Law Relevant Again: A Proposal for Collectivized and Solution-oriented Protection' (1997) 10 *Harvard Human Rights Journal*.

Hathaway OA, 'Do Human Rights Treaties Make a Difference?' (2002) *Yale Law Journal* 1935.

Haus L, 'Migration and International Economic Institutions' in Zolberg A and Benda P (eds), *Global Migrants, Global Refugees: Problems and Solutions* (New York, Berghahn Books 2001).

Higgins C, 'In-country Programs: The Procedure and Politics of an Additional Pathway to Protection' in Juss SS (ed), *Research Handbook on International Refugee Law* (Edward Elgar 2019).

Hirsch AL and Bell N, 'The Right to Have Rights as a Right to Enter: Addressing a Lacuna in the International Refugee Protection Regime' (2017) 18 *Human Rights Review* 417.

Holly G, 'Transnational Tort and Access to Remedy under the UN Guiding Principles on Business and Human Rights: Kamasaee v Commonwealth' (2018) 19 *Melbourne Journal of International Law* 52.

Holly G 'Challenges to Australia's Offshore Detention Regime and the Limits of Strategic Tort Litigation' (2020) 21 *German Law Journal* 549.

Ineli-Ciger M, 'Protecting Syrians in Turkey: A Legal Analysis' (2017) 29 *International Journal of Refugee Law* 555.

Initiative RL 'Refugee Law Initiative Declaration on Externalisation and Asylum' (2022) 34(1) *International Journal of Refugee Law* 114.

Jackson M, *Complicity in International Law* (Oxford University Press 2015).

Jones M, 'Moving Beyond Protection Space: Developing a Law of Asylum in South-East Asia' in Kneebone S, Stevens D and Baldassar L (eds), *Refugee Protection and the Role of Law: Conflicting Identities* (Routledge 2014).

Kessing PV, 'Transnational Operations Carried Out from a State's Own Territory: Armed Drones and the Extraterritorial Effect of International Human Rights Conventions' in Gammeltoft-Hansen T and Vedsted-Hansen J (eds), *Human Rights and the Dark Side of Globalisation: Transnational law enforcement and migration control* (Routledge 2017) 81–98.

Kienast J, '"Crisis Rhetoric" and Derogations from the AFSJ: Is EU Asylum Policy Discriminatory or does its Implementation Reflect the Rule of Law?' (2022) 6 *Cuadernos Europeos de Deusto* 117.

Klein N, 'Assessing Australia's Push Bank the Boats Policy Under International Law: Legality and Accountability for Maritime Interceptions of Irregular Migrants' (2014) 15 *Melbourne Journal of International Law* 414.

Klug A and Howe T, 'The Concept Of State Jurisdiction And The Applicability Of The Non-Refoulement Principle To Extraterritorial Interception Measures' in Ryan B and Mitsilegas V (eds), *Extraterritorial Immigration Control* (Brill 2010).

Kneebone S, 'The Pacific Plan: The Provision of 'Effective Protection'?' (2006) 18 *International Journal of Refugee Law* 696.

Koh HH, 'America's Offshore Refugee Camps' (1994) 29 *University of Richmond Law Review* 139.

Lambert L "Who is Doing Asylum in Niger?." Anthropologie & Développement N° 51, 2020: Dossier–Perspectives Ouest-africaines Sur Les Politiques Migratoires Et Sécuritaires Européennes (2020) 85.

Lambert L, 'Extraterritorial Asylum Processing: The Libya-Niger Emergency Transit Mechanism' (2021) 68 *Forced Migration Review* 18.

Lanovoy V, 'Complicity in an Internationally Wrongful Act' in Nollkaemper A and Plakokefalos I (eds), *Principles of Shared Responsibility in International Law: An Appraisal of the State of the Art* (Cambridge University Press 2014) 134–68.

Lawson R, 'Life after Bankovic: On the Extraterritorial Application of the European Convention on Human Rights' in Coomans F and Kamminga MT (eds), *Extraterritorial Application of Human Rights Treaties* (Intersentia 2004) 83–123.

Legomsky SH, 'Secondary Refugee Movements and the Return of Asylum Seekers to Third Countries: The Meaning of Effective Protection' (2003) 15 *International Journal of Refugee Law* 567.

Lemberg-Pedersen M, 'Manufacturing Displacement. Externalization and Postcoloniality in European Migration Control' (2019) 5(3) *Global Affairs* 247.

Léonard S and Kaunert C, 'The Extra-territorial Processing of Asylum Claims' (2016) *Forced Migration Review* 48.

Liguori A, 'Some Observations on the Legal Responsibility of States and International Organizations in the Extraterritorial Processing of Asylum Claims' (2016) 25 *The Italian Yearbook of International Law* 135.

Linderfalk U, 'State Responsibility and the Primary-secondary Rules Terminology – The Role of Language for an Understanding of the International Legal System' (2009) 78 *Nordic Journal of International Law* 53.

Mann I, 'Maritime Legal Black Holes: Migration and Rightlessness in International Law' (2017) 29 *European Journal of International Law* 347.

Markard N, 'The Right to Leave by Sea: Legal Limits on EU Migration Control by Third Countries' (2016) 27 *European Journal of International Law* 591.

Mathew P, 'Australian Refugee Protection in the Wake of the Tampa' (2002) 96 *American Journal of International Law* 661.

Mathew P and Harley T, *Refugees, Regionalism and Responsibility* (Edward Elgar 2016).

McAdam J, *Complementary Protection in International Refugee Law* (Oxford University Press 2007).

McAdam J *Extraterritorial processing in Europe* (Kaldor Centre for International Refugee Law Policy Brief, 2015).

McAdam J 'The Enduring Relevance of the 1951 Refugee Convention' (2017) 29 *International Journal of Refugee Law* 1.

McConnachie K, 'Refugee Protection and the Art of the Deal' (2017) 9 *Journal of Human Rights Practice* 190.

McKay FH, Thomas SL and Kneebone S, "It Would Be Okay If They Came through the Proper Channels': Community Perceptions and Attitudes toward Asylum Seekers in Australia' (2012) 25 *Journal of Refugee Studies* 113.

Milanovic M 'From Compromise to Principle: Clarifying the Concept of State Jurisdiction in Human Rights Treaties' (2008) 8 *Human Rights Law Review* 411.

Milanovic M, 'Al-Skeini and Al-Jedda in Strasbourg' (2012) 23 *European Journal of International Law* 121.

Milanovic M 'Jurisdiction and Responsibility: Trends in the Jurisprudence of the Strasbourg Court' in Aaken Av and Motoc I (eds), *European Convention on Human Rights and General International Law* (Oxford University Press 2018).

Moodley R, Rethinking "Regional Processing": Could the Lessons Learned from the Comprehensive Plan of Action for Indochinese Refugees (CPA) Offer a Roadmap for International Cooperation in Response to 'Regional' Refugee Situations? (UNSW Law Research Paper, 2022).

Moodley R *Regional Processing by the European Union - A Bridge Over Troubled Water?* (UNSW, 2024).

Moreno-Lax V and Giuffré M, 'The Rise of Consensual Containment: From "Contactless Control" to "Contactless Responsibility" for Migratory Flows' in Juss S (ed), *Research Handbook on International Refugee Law* (Elgar Elgar, 2019).

Mussi F and Tan NF, 'Comparing Cooperation on Migration Control: Italy–Libya and Australia–Indonesia' in Mullally S (ed), *Irish Yearbook of International Law* (Hart-Bloomsbury 2017).

Netherlands Advisory Committee on Migration Affairs, External Processing: Conditions applying to the Processing of Asylum Applications outside the European Union (Advisory Report No 32, 2010).

Nethery A and Dastyari A, 'Refugee Externalisation Policies: What We Have Learnt and Where Are We Going?' in Azadeh Dastyari, Amy Nethery and Asher Hirsch (eds), *Refugee Externalisation Policies: Responsibility, Legitimacy and Accountability* (Routledge 2022) 209–18.

Nethery A and Holman R, 'Secrecy and Human Rights Abuse in Australia's Offshore Immigration Detention Centres' (2016) 20 *The International Journal of Human Rights*.

Noll G, *Negotiating Asylum: The EU Acquis, Extraterritorial Protection and the Common Market of Deflection* (Martinus Nijhoff 2000).

Noll G 'Risky Games? A Theoretical Approach to Burden-Sharing in the Asylum Field' (2003a) 16 *Journal of Refugee Studies* 236.

Noll G 'Visions of the Exceptional: Legal and Theoretical Issues Raised by Transit Processing Centres and Protection Zones' (2003b) 5 *European Journal of Migration and Law* 303.

Noll G and Vedsted-Hansen J, 'Non-Communitarians: Refugee and Asylum Policies' in Alston P, Bustelo M and Heenan J (eds), *The EU and Human Rights* (Oxford University Press 1999).

Nollkaemper A, 'Introduction' in Nollkaemper A and Plakokefalos I (eds), *Principles of Shared Responsibility in International Law: An Appraisal of the State of the Art* (Cambridge University Press 2014).

Nollkaemper A 'Shared Responsibility for Human Rights Violations: A Relational Account' in Gammeltoft-Hansen T and Vedsted-Hansen J (eds), *Human Rights and the Dark Side of Globalisation: Transnational law enforcement and migration control* (Routledge 2017).

Nollkaemper A and Jacobs D, 'Shared Responsibility in International Law: A Conceptual Framework' (2012) 34 *Michigan Journal of International Law* 359.

Nolte G and Aust HP, 'Equivocal Helpers—Complicit States, Mixed Messages and International Law' (2009) 58 *International and Comparative Law Quarterly* 1.

Noyes JE and Smith BD, 'State Responsibility and the Principle of Joint and Several Liability' (1988) 13 *Yale Journal of International Law* 225.

O'Sullivan M, 'The Ethics of Resettlement: Australia and the Asia–Pacific Region' (2015) 20 *The International Journal of Human Rights* 241.

Palchetti P, 'State Responsibility for Complicity in Genocide' in Paola Gaeta (ed), *The UN Genocide Convention: A Commentary* (Oxford University Press 2009).

Pickering S and Weber L, 'New Deterrence Scripts in Australia's Rejuvenated Offshore Detention Regime for Asylum Seekers' (2014) 39 *Law & Social Inquiry* 1006.

Popjoy JM, *The Child in International Refugee Law* (Cambridge University Press 2017).

Robinson WC, 'The Comprehensive Plan of Action for Indochinese Refugees, 1989–1997: Sharing the Burden and Passing the Buck' (2004) 17 *Journal of Refugee Studies* 319.

Ryngaert C, *Jurisdiction in International Law* (Oxford University Press 2008).
Salyer J, 'The Denial of Human Dignity in the Age of Human Rights under Australia's Operation Sovereign Borders' (2020) 32 *The Contemporary Pacific* 512.
Sari A, 'Untangling Extra-Territorial Jurisdiction from International Responsibility in Jaloud v. Netherlands: Old Problem, New Solutions?' (2015) 53 *Military Law and the Law of War Review* 287.
Sartori ME, 'The Cuban Migration Dilemma: An Examination of the United States' Policy of Temporary Protection in Offshore Safe Havens' (2000) 15 Georgetown Immigration Law Journal 319.
Schoenholtz AI, Ramji-Nogales J and Schrag PG, *The End of Asylum* (Georgetown University Press 2021).
Schuck PH, 'Refugee Burden-sharing: A Modest Proposal' (1997) 22 *Yale Journal of International Law* 243.
Schuck PH 'Refugee Burden-Sharing: A Modest Proposal Fifteen Years Later?' (John M. Olin Center for Studies in Law, Economics, and Public Policy, Research Paper No. 506, 2014).
Shachar A, *The Shifting Border: Legal Cartographies of Migration and Mobility* (Manchester University Press 2020).
Sharpe M, 'Mixed Up: International Law and the Meaning(s) of "Mixed Migration"' (2018) 37 *Refugee Survey Quarterly* 116.
Shaw M, *International Law* (Cambridge University Press 2008).
Shepson S, 'Jurisdiction in Complicity Cases: Rendition and Refoulement in Domestic and International Courts' (2014) 53 *Columbia Journal of Transnational Law* 701.
Spijkerboer T 'The Global Mobility Infrastructure: Reconceptualising the Externalisation of Migration Control' (2018) 20 *European Journal of Migration and Law* 452.
Spijkerboer T, 'Coloniality and Case Law on the Australian Asylum Offshoring Scheme' (2023) 7 *International Journal of Migration and Border Studies* 132.
Szablewska N and Ly R, 'Regional Collaborative Responses to the Global Migration Crisis: Refugee Law, Human Rights and Shared State Responsibility: The Australia-Cambodia Refugee Resettlement Agreement' (2017) 91 *Australian Law Journal* 186.
Tan NF 'State Responsibility and Migration Control: Australia's International Deterrence Model' in Gammeltoft-Hansen T and Vedsted-Hansen J (eds), *Human Rights and the Dark Side of Globalisation: Transnational law enforcement and migration control* (Routledge 2017).
Tan NF *International Cooperation on Refugees: Between Protection and Deterrence* (Aarhus University, 2018a).
Tan NF 'The Manus Island Regional Processing Centre: A legal taxonomy' (2018b) 20 *European Journal of Migration and Law* 427.
Tan NF, 'Conceptualising Externalisation: Still Fit for Purpose?' (2021) 68 *Forced Migration Review* 8.
Tan NF 'Visions of the Realistic? Denmark's Legal Basis for Extraterritorial Asylum' (2022) 91 *Nordic Journal of International Law* 172.
Tan NF and Gammeltoft-Hansen T, 'A Topographical Approach to Accountability for Human Rights Violations in Migration Control' (2020) 21 *German Law Journal* 335.
Tan NF and Kienast J 'The Michigan Guidelines on Protection Elsewhere' (2006) 28 *Michigan Journal of International Law.*
Tan NF and Kienast J, The Right of Asylum in Comparative Regional Perspectives: Access, Procedures and Protection (ASILE working paper, 2022).

Taylor S 'The Pacific Solution or a Pacific Nightmare: The Difference between Burden Shifting and Responsibility Sharing' (2005) 6 *Asian-Pacific Law & Policy Journal* 1.

Taylor S, 'Australian Funded Care and Maintenance of Asylum Seekers in Indonesia and PNG: All Care but No Responsibility?' (2010) 33 *University of New South Wales Law Journal* 337.

Thym D, 'Legal Framework for Entry and Border Controls' in Kay Hailbronner and Daniel Thym (eds), *EU Immigration and Asylum Law: Commentary* (2nd edn, C.H. Beck 2016).

Thym D and Hailbronner K, 'Legal Framework for EU Asylum Policy' in Hailbronner K and Thym D (eds), *EU Immigration and Asylum Law: Commentary* (2nd edn C.H. Beck 2016) 1023–53.

Towle R, 'Processes and Critiques of the Indo-Chinese Comprehensive Plan of Action: An Instrument of International Burden-Sharing?' (2006) 18 *International Journal of Refugee Law* 537.

Triggs GD and Wall PC, "The Makings of a Success': The Global Compact on Refugees and the Inaugural Global Refugee Forum' (2020) 32 *International Journal of Refugee Law* 283.

Türk V, 'The Promise and Potential of the Global Compact on Refugees' (2019) 30 *International Journal of Refugee Law* 575.

Türk V and Garlick M, 'From Burdens and Responsibilities to Opportunities: The Comprehensive Refugee Response Framework and a Global Compact on Refugees' (2016) 28 *International Journal of Refugee Law* 656.

Tzevelekos TP, 'Reconstructing the Effective Control Criterion in Extraterrestrial Human Rights Breaches: Direct attribution of Wrongfulness, Due Diligence, and Concurrent Responsibility' (2014) 36 *Michigan Journal of International Law* 129.

van Berlo P, 'The Protection of Asylum Seekers in Australian-Pacific Offshore Processing: The Legal Deficit of Human Rights in a Nodal Reality' (2017) 17 *Human Rights Law Review* 33.

van Selm J, 'The Strategic Use of Resettlement: Changing the Face of Protection?' (2004) 22 *Refuge* 39.

Vedsted-Hansen J 'Non-admission Policies and the Right to Protection: Refugees 'Choice Versus States' Exclusion' in Nicholson F and Twomey P (eds), *Refugee Rights and Realities: Evolving International Concepts and Regimes* (Cambridge University Press 1999).

Vedsted-Hansen J 'The Asylum Procedures and the Assessment of Asylum Requests' in Chetail V and Bauloz C (eds), *Research Handbook on International Law and Migration* (Edward Elgar 2014).

Vedsted-Hansen J, 'Asylum Procedures Directive 2013/32/EU' in Hailbronner K and Thym D (eds), *EU Immigration and Asylum Law* (Nomos 2016).

Wall P, 'A New Link in the Chain: Could a Framework Convention for Refugee Responsibility Sharing Fulfil the Promise of the 1967 Protocol?' (2017) 29 *International Journal of Refugee Law* 201.

Wilde R 'Triggering State Obligations Extraterritorially: The Spatial Test in Certain Human Rights Treaties' (2007) 40 *Israel Law Review* 503.

Wilde R, 'The Extraterritorial Application of International Human Rights Law on Civil and Political Rights' in Sheeran S and Rodley N (eds), *Routledge Handbook of International Human Rights Law* (Routledge 2013).

Wood T and McAdam J, 'Australian Asylum Policy all at Sea: An analysis of Plaintiff M70/2011 v Minister for Immigration and Citizenship and the Australia–Malaysia Arrangement' (2012) 61 *International and Comparative Law Quarterly* 274.

Wouters K, *International Legal Standards for the Protection from Refoulement* (Intersentia 2009).
Wouters K and Den Heijer M, 'The Marine I Case: a Comment' (2010) 22 *International Journal of Refugee Law* 1.
Zieck M, 'Refugees and the Right to Freedom of Movement: From Flight to Return' (2018) 39 *Michigan Journal of International Law* 19.
Ziegler R, 'No Asylum for 'Infiltrators': The Legal Predicament of Eritrean and Sudanese Nationals in Israel' (2015) 29 *Immigration, Asylum and Nationality Law* 172.

INDEX

Pages followed by "n" refer to notes.

Kolibri 360 GmbH
Ferdinand-Jühlke-Straße 7
99095 Erfurt, Deutschland
produktsicherheit@kolibri360.de